John Webster

John Webster

Citizen and Dramatist

M.C. Bradbrook

Columbia University Press
New York   1980

Library of Congress Cataloging in Publication Data

Bradbrook, Muriel Clara.
    John Webster, citizen and dramatist.

    Includes bibliographical references and index.
    1. Webster, John, 1580?–1625? 2. Theater – England –
London – History. 3. Dramatists, English – Early modern,
1500–1700 – Biography. I. Title.
PR3186.B7   822'.3 [B]   80-18274
ISBN 0-231-05162-X

Contents

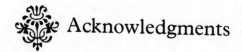 Acknowledgments

My thanks are due to the late Charles Frankel and the Trustees of the National Humanities Center, Research Triangle Park, North Carolina, for the opportunity to work in North America; to Mary Edmond for much valuable information, encouragement and for supplying the genealogical table; to Pat Rignold for help in preparing the manuscript; to Reavley Gair for new information about St Paul's Theatre; and to the staff of Weidenfeld and Nicolson for their help and forbearance, which make such a work truly collaborative. The remaining shortcomings are my own.

For Webster I have used the editions by John Russell Brown of the two tragedies, also making use of Lucas, the Scolar facsimiles and Gunby. Spelling has been modernized. For the other works I have used Lucas, Fredson Bowers' Dekker for early plays; I have read *The Valiant Scott* in Trinity College Library, but did not find it worth discussing. The quotation from Adams on p. 182 was given me by Guy Butler.

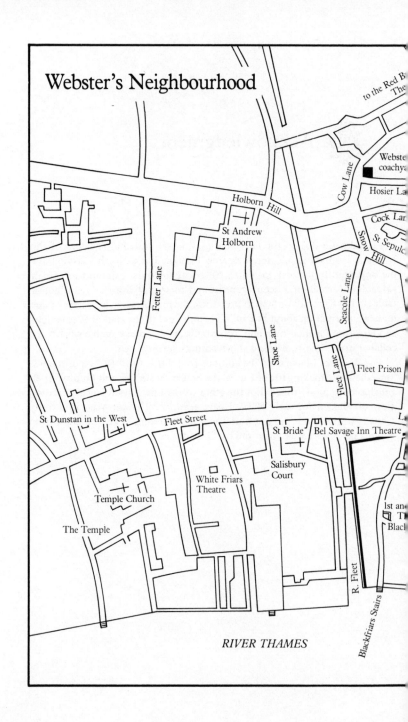

Webster's Neighbourhood

to the Red B
The

Webste
coachya

Hosier La

Cow Lane

Cock Lar

St Sepulc

Holborn Hill

St Andrew
Holborn

Snow

Hill

Fetter Lane

Shoe Lane

Seacole Lane

Fleet Lane

Fleet Prison

St Dunstan in the West

Fleet Street

St Bride

Bel Savage Inn Theatre

L.

Salisbury
Court

White Friars
Theatre

Temple Church

1st an
T
Black

The Temple

R. Fleet

Blackfriars Stairs

RIVER THAMES

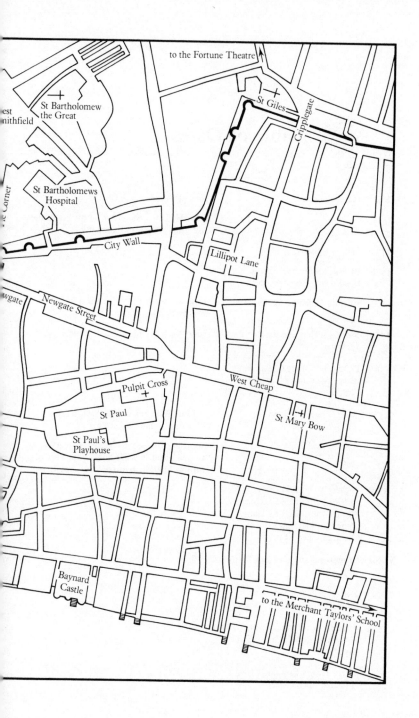

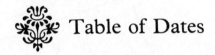 Table of Dates

1596	Pérez visits England (April–June)	
1597	Bacon's *Essays* published; Swan Theatre closed for plays; City inns closed for plays	John Webster admitted to the Middle Temple from New Inn (Oct.); Grand Christmas with Revels
1598	Stow's *Survey* of London published	John Davies expelled from the Middle Temple (Feb.)
1599	Globe Theatre opens; Paul's Theatre reopens	
1600	Blackfriars Theatre reopens; Fortune Theatre opens	
1601	Revolt and execution of Earl of Essex; Duke of Brachiano visits London	
1602	*Twelfth Night* given at Middle Temple (2 Feb.)	Webster writes *Caesar's Fall* or *Two Shapes* (lost) with Munday, Drayton, Middleton (May); *Lady Jane* with Chettle, Dekker, Heywood, Smith (Oct.); *Christmas comes but once a Year* (lost) with Chettle, Dekker, Heywood, for Philip Henslowe (Admiral's Men and Worcester's Men at Fortune and Boar's Head Theatres)
1603	Death of Queen Elizabeth I (24 March); accession of James I	
1604	Coronation of James I; peace with Spain; Pérez refused entry to England	Webster writes verses for Stephen Harrison's *Arches of Triumph* and the induction for the performance of *The Malcontent* by the King's Men
1605	Jonson and Chapman imprisoned for *Eastward Ho!*; Gunpowder Plot; Lady Penelope divorced (Nov.) and marries Charles Blount (26 Dec.); Red Bull Theatre opens	? John Webster marries Sara, daughter of Simon Peniall; *Westward Ho!*, by Dekker and Webster, entered in Stationers' Register (2 Mar.) and acted at Paul's Theatre; *Eastward Ho!*, by Marston, Chapman and Jonson, acted at Blackfriars Theatre; *Northward Ho!*, by Dekker and Webster, acted at Paul's Theatre. Simon Peniall Warden of Saddlers' Company
1606	Death of Charles Blount, Earl of Devonshire	John, son of John Webster, baptized at St Dunstan's in the West (8 May)
1607	Death of Lady Penelope	*Sir Thomas Wyatt, Westward Ho!* and *Northward Ho!* published

1608 Latest performance at Paul's
      Theatre (Feb.); King's Men
      open at Blackfriars Theatre

1611 Death of Pérez; Sir John
      Swinnerton, Merchant
      Taylor, Lord Mayor 1611–12

1612 First edition of Overbury's   *The White Devil* acted by the Red Bull
      Characters published; death   Company and published; *An Apology*
      of Henry, Prince of Wales (6   *for Actors* (Heywood, verses by
      Nov.)   Webster) published; *A Monumental
                                            Column* entered in Stationers' Register
                                            (26 Dec.); Edward Webster admitted to
                                            the Merchant Taylors Company (by
                                            serving his time), Feb.

1613 Marriage of Princess   *A Monumental Column* published;
      Elizabeth (14 Feb.), masques   *The Duchess of Malfi* acted by the
      in her honour; death of   King's Men at Blackfriars Theatre;
      Overbury (Sept.)   bequests to Webster, his wife and
                                            children by a neighbour

1614 Hope Theatre opens   Death of John Webster the elder
                                            (winter 1614–15)

1615   Webster admitted to Merchant Taylors
                                            Company (June); edits 3rd edition of
                                            Overbury's *Characters*, includes
                                            'Character of an Excellent Actor',
                                            attacking J. Cocke of Lincoln's Inn

1616 Ben Jonson's First Folio
      published; Earl and Countess
      of Somerset tried for
      Overbury's murder

1617 Cockpit Theatre opens   *The Devil's Law Case* acted; satirical
      (Feb.); damaged by riot;   attack on Webster by Henry Fitzjeffrey
      reopens June   of Lincoln's Inn

1621 Chapman, *Pro Vere*; Sir   Edward Webster marries Susan Walker
      Horace Vere surrenders at   (3 Oct.)
      Mannheim

1622   ? *Appius and Virginia* acted by boys

1623 Shakespeare's First Folio   *The Duchess of Malfi* and *The Devil's
      published   Law Case* published, recording lost
                                            play, *The Guise*

1624 Sir John Gore, Merchant   *Keep the Widow waking* (lost), by
      Taylor, Lord Mayor, 1624–5   Webster, Ford, Dekker, Rowley,
                                            licensed (Sept.); *Monuments of Honour*
                                            performed and published (Oct.); ? *A
                                            Cure for a Cuckold*, by Webster and
                                            Rowley, acted

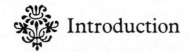 Introduction

The Citizen

John Webster, darkest of Jacobean tragic poets, remained himself in almost complete shadow until, in 1976, Mary Edmond identified him as the son of a wealthy coach-maker, living at the corner of Cow Lane and Hosier Lane, West Smithfield, in the parish of St Sepulchre-without-Newgate. John married Sara Peniall, youthful daughter of a saddler, raised a family and, on his father's death, was admitted by patrimony to the powerful Merchant Taylors Company, as his only brother Edward had previously been through apprenticeship.

Although no baptismal record survives, it may be assumed, if he were the elder son, that he was born in 1579 or 1580. The Merchant Taylors' School provided enlightened literary training, the Middle Temple supplied literary friends.

Webster's whole life was rooted in the parish where he lived and the surrounding ones of the Ward of Farringdon Without the Walls; in this area lay the Middle Temple, the Fortune and the Red Bull Theatres were close by, and the new Cockpit or Phoenix Theatre, where his later plays were given, not far away. His greatest triumph came however with the performance of his *The Duchess of Malfi* by the King's Men at Blackfriars.

The Websters' coach-yard, leased from St Bartholomew's Hospital, adjoined the home of a great lady, famed for learning, beauty and wit, whose love story ended in disaster. Penelope Rich, Sidney's Stella, defied ill fame; though her husband and later her sons were among the leaders of the Puritans, she was the acknowledged mistress of the renowned soldier, Charles Blount. Some of the most stormy events of her life took place near Webster's home, demonstrating that all the passions of Renaissance Italy were to be found on his doorstep. Fellow dramatists had known the grim fortress of Newgate jail, built in the gatehouse of the City. Here in 1598 Ben Jonson had faced a charge of murder, and in 1608 Webster's friend John Marston had been imprisoned; possibly, too, Chapman and Jonson (once more!) had been imprisoned here for the play *Eastward Ho!*, written in reply to one by Webster.

The first martyr of Queen Mary's reign was John Rogers, Vicar of St Sepulchre; on 4 February 1555 he had been burnt at the stake in Smithfield before the eyes of his wife and eleven children. Webster's first play was on the theme of another of the martyrs commemorated in Foxe's *Acts and Monuments*, Lady Jane Grey. Yet in the very year that Webster's *The Duchess of Malfi* marked the climax of his tragic power, Ben Jonson's *Bartholomew Fair*, most genial of his comedies, presented the other side of life in this corner of the City, where fortune-tellers lurked in Cow Lane.

In Part One of this book, in attempting to give a context for the citizen-poet whose life is known in outline, whose lesser works are set in London but his greater ones in Italy, I have adopted the display method of taking four representative figures and telling their stories at some length. All four left their stamp on the places where Webster lived, and all four have themselves left their own literary record behind – except Penelope Rich, for whom records remain in the work of Philip Sidney and lesser poets. This method Webster would have understood.

The double qualification of locality and literary record allows me to present a context for Webster that is specific. It is neither theoretical nor descriptive but demonstrative. Richard Mulcaster, of Merchant Taylors' School, John Davies, poet of the Middle Temple, Penelope Rich and her follower, Antonio Pérez the Spanish spy, have been chosen as Monuments for a Temple of Fame (good and ill), a Masque of Notables, or London Pageant. Especially the two last, tragical victims of Fortune's fickleness, provide for the modern reader a re-entry into Webster's world, not by reconstruction but by reconstitution.

Mulcaster left Merchant Taylors' School just before Webster would have entered, but the founding headmaster had put a lasting stamp upon it. John Davies was expelled from the Middle Temple in Webster's second term, but in circumstances that a newcomer would not forget. Penelope Rich became a legend in her lifetime. I do not claim that she supplied the Horatian precepts, evoked cryptically, in note taker's shorthand, on the title page of *The Duchess of Malfi*; stage ghosts had been dissolved to mourners' fancies; her memory, if retained, for us as for him, is but 'the ghost of a rose'.

As the context, not the content of his tragedies, her legend was part of the soil in which his imagination was nourished. Such legends sometimes circulated in ballad form or as 'winter's tales' for the fireside, and later found their way into popular plays – Simon Eyre the Lord Mayor, Jane Shore the goldsmith's wife were celebrated by Webster's friends, Dekker and Heywood. Webster himself wrote a comedy on a local scandal. But the term 'Monument', used for two of his more serious works, and in his own motto ('Non norunt haec monumenta mori', 'These monuments do not know how to die') points to the speech he himself put into the mouth of Sir Philip Sidney,[1] asserting on behalf of poetry how great literary achievement turns the life of the City into something that will live into the future. The greater the work, the less it can be reduced to any one 'source'. It is not really relevant to point out that Penelope's guardian, the Earl of Huntingdon, was a customer of John Webster and Sons, or that *Love's Labour's Lost*, where Pérez may have been depicted as Armado, was printed by William White, the Websters' next-door neighbour. It is perhaps more relevant that all four of my characters were already living in print. For a satirist, Henry Fitzjeffrey (see Chapter 8, page 169), implied that Webster's relations were with books rather than with people. A close reader and 'critic', a slow writer, in literature he was a radical conservative, who preserved older conventions whilst turning them into something different; he also turned the matter he remembered from his reading into something very different. The man who could work the maxims of dull contemporaries into high tragedy was not able to make a legend out of the late Prince of Wales; but what went into his memorial poem was reworked a year later into the fabric of *The Duchess of Malfi*.

In setting women and servants at the centre of great plays, Webster was something of an innovator. These figures include Bosola, the spy who dominates *The Duchess of Malfi* and whose name heads its cast. Antonio Pérez, the fourth of my figures, is the first international spy to have left an autobiography and a mass of letters. Intelligence networks, a political novelty, evolved as part of the new diplomacy necessitated by the rise of the modern sovereign nation-states of Western Europe. When he first arrived in 1593 Pérez was also the first Spaniard to have been seen in London for many years.

The writings of Pérez reveal an extraordinary tissue of sexual and political violence. As he assiduously courted Lady Rich, the sister of his patron Essex, his story becomes part of the Devereux legend. He was also involved in the unmasking of the Lopez conspiracy in 1594; Lopez himself resided in St Bartholomew's Hospital. At the time of the conspiracy, Webster would have been fourteen. At the time of the rebellion and execution of Essex, he would have been about twenty-one. Next year, in 1602, we meet him as a playwright for the first time. Pérez died in 1611, and the next year his story was revived by Edward Grimeston (a cousin of George Chapman) in his *General History of Spain*. Like that of Lady Rich, it is of great interest for itself.

The Dramatist

Part Two of this book records the progress of Webster's intermittent dramatic career. It would appear, as G. E. Bentley pointed out, that he was not a fully professional playwright.[2] Although the first records show him, with collaborators, pushing out plays in a couple of weeks, his own tally of four collaborations, four independent works and four lost dramas would hardly, over a quarter of a century, supply the kind of affluence needed for him to be admitted to his father's company. The actor 'John Webster' turns out to be a ghost. Webster is ignored by Ben Jonson, when in his *Conversations* (1619) he castigates dramatists from Shakespeare to Sharpham.

Neighbourhood links connected him with the group of actors who lived in Clerkenwell, for whom Heywood was resident dramatist and fellow-sharer, but the satirist Fitzjeffrey terms Webster 'the playwright-cartwright'. It seems to me most probable that his father sent his elder son to the Middle Temple to qualify him for helping with large mercantile ventures, and for dealing with distinguished customers. In this way James Burbage, at the Shoreditch Theatre, sent his elder son to train with a scrivener, and Cuthbert Burbage served on the office side, whilst the younger Richard Burbage became an actor. If John Webster the younger was in what would now be investment and accounts, while his brother Edward ran the works department as a qualified coachbuilder, John Webster the elder had provided fairly for both. (*A*

Speedy Post, by J.W. *Gent.*, 1624, a book of model letters, has been claimed for Webster by one scholar.

Local records and repertories are increasingly the subject of theatrical history. The publications of the Malone Society, the Records of Early English Drama from Toronto University Press and the new Revels Series from Manchester are matched by histories of the Shoreditch Theatre, the Rose Theatre and the Second Theatre at St Paul's. Webster's apprenticeship began with the group under Philip Henslowe, who had built up a theatrical 'empire'; he wrote both for the Admiral's Men at the new Fortune playhouse, and for Worcester's Men at the Boar's Head. After an intermission caused by plague, he reappears with his friend Dekker, writing witty comedy for the choristers of St Paul's, who performed at a small theatre in the cloisters. By 1605 they were experienced, and some of them were no longer boys, but they were kept on to act, and their master exploited them ruthlessly:[3] here Webster presented farcical city comedy, from rather a gentlemanly point of view; whilst his earlier tragedy was a citizens' play. More important for the development of his thought was the collaboration in 1604 with Marston, for the King's Men, when *The Malcontent* was adapted from the choristers' repertory.

Both at his school and at his lawyers' Inn Webster's dramatic experience would have been with indoor theatre, the Theatre of the Hall; and this was evidently what he preferred. After Paul's closed in 1608, he remained off stage till 1612, when *The White Devil* was put on at the Red Bull in Clerkenwell, his nearest theatre. It did not succeed, though Dekker had written a kind of advertisement of its 'Brave triumphs of poesy and elaborate industry'[4] and wished his 'worthy friend' good fortune. Success was to come later, when it was played indoors, but meanwhile Webster published the text, with a warm tribute to the leading actor and a defiance to the many-headed monster, the crowd. His *The Duchess of Malfi*, played by the King's Men indoors at their Blackfriars Theatre, succeeded from the first.

When Queen Anne's Men moved from the Red Bull to their own indoor theatre Webster wrote a bravura part for their leading man as the villain hero of *The Devil's Law Case*. This could have been the opening play; as I suggest in Chapter 8, Webster had already taken the company's side in the controversy with Lincoln's Inn that preceded the opening of the Cockpit. Webster seems to have written later plays to help this acting troupe in their difficulties; one was a collaboration with its leading comedian, William Rowley.

The Lord Mayor's Pageant which Webster wrote and directed for the installation of Sir John Gore in October 1624 is the culmination of his theatrical ventures: a politically daring climax providing his final judgment upon the government of the day.

Seen in theatrical context, Webster's plays invite new approaches. In the preface to *The White Devil* he praises Chapman and Jonson in the same breath as his old friends Dekker and Heywood; no one else would have linked these dramatists together. He did not thank Marston, from whom he learned most; for Marston by now had left the scene and taken holy orders.

Whilst Webster's tragedies are unique in the burnish of their phrasing, the transformation of other men's phrases into something rich and strange, they also rely on the art of performance in its full complexity to bring out the shifting perspectives of his art. The great emblematic set-pieces at the death of Brachiano, Vittoria, Flamineo and the Duchess of Malfi leave at the centre of tragic action a deeper mystery, a heavier darkness, beyond the words. The art of the actor is essential for characterization, and it binds together the staccato movement of the plot.

A generation younger than Richard Burbage, the star of the Queen's Men, Richard Perkins excelled in diversified parts. If Burbage interpreted Hamlet's antic disposition, and the double personality of the Malcontent, Perkins had trained on the quick-change tactics of the Jew of Malta. To hold together a character divided within itself, playing a double game like Flamineo or Bosola, the actor requires the intimacy and concentration of an indoor theatre, so that gradually, through many contradictions and inner divisions, by the finer touches of modelling, 'integrity of life' can emerge.

This development by gradual revelation, within the character itself, closely resembles the actual scenic development of the masque under Inigo Jones. It was on New Year's Day, 1611, a year before *The White Devil*, that in *The Masque of Oberon* the English stage saw Jones's introduction of sliding shutters, which, by moving back and forth, enabled the scene to be changed. Opening with a prospect of a barren rock, the masque next showed within the rock, when it opened, a fairy palace. Another set of shutters slid back to open the palace doors, revealing the fairy realm; finally the fairies divided, to reveal Oberon himself – the Prince

of Wales. The unfolding of character, and the disjunctive movement of his plots – seen by many critics as one of Webster's weak-
nesses – gives the actor the equivalent of Inigo Jones's 'carpentry',
as Jonson was later scornfully to term it.[5] Perhaps the coach-
maker's son had some sympathy with carpentry. He had written
verses to praise the triumphal arches erected by Stephen Harrison
for the coronation procession of James I.

About ten years ago it was fashionable to illustrate Jacobean
tragedy by comparisons with Italian mannerist or baroque painting.[6] Webster would not have known these paintings and he certainly could not have relied on any mutual appreciation to establish
their conventions with his audience. Indeed, his verses to Harrison
are distinctly provincial in their judgments. It was the baroque
art of Inigo Jones, the movement and perspective of his masques,
that Londoners knew.

Thanks to the work of Roy Strong, his writings and his exhibi-
tions of Jacobean painting, today we are better informed both
about the nature of English Jacobean painting and the art of Inigo
Jones.[7] The last was displayed in the Banqueting House that he
built in Whitehall – the only Jacobean theatre to survive (built
in 1622; in 1637 a painted ceiling was installed by Charles I). It
is now possible to envisage the earlier theatre designed by Jones:
the little Cockpit, first of its line in Drury Lane, revealed in detail
through the plans in the Jones drawing at Worcester College,
Oxford. This was the theatre of Perkins and of Webster; it was
the prototype of later theatres too.

Webster could himself have taken part in Jones's *Masque of the
Middle Temple and Lincoln's Inn*, presented at Court for the marriage of the Princess Elizabeth in February 1613, and written by
his friend Chapman. For it had a cast of several hundred – attendants, halberdiers, baboons etc.

The last of the Middle Temple masques before the Civil War,
given after Webster's death for Princess Elizabeth's sons, was
Davenant's *Triumphs of the Prince D'Amour* (1635), which had no
less than ten changes of scene. It was attended by the Queen, disguised as a citizen's wife; she sat with the audience, accompanied
by Penelope Rich's son, also disguised as a citizen.[8] (Such an
exchange of roles between royalty and mock-royalty would have
been unthinkable earlier, but the Queen had become an actress
herself.)

In his own final theatrical event, *Monuments of Honour* (1624), of which he was clearly so proud, Webster became poet, designer and supervisor, as well as appearing as an actor by reason of his membership of the Merchant Taylors, the presiding Livery Company. Here at last the author was united with the Citizen and Freeman of London.

Attempting to work out Webster's dramatic career, I have had to limit myself in several ways. One is in respect of the repertories and audiences of his various theatres. Some of these are being investigated, and how much such close investigation is needed my own deficiencies will show. Another is in respect of Webster's borrowings; they need closer study both in terms of Jacobean rhetoric and of structural-linguistic apparatus of the present time. A third is the precise relation of his tragedies to the masques of Jonson, Chapman and Beaumont, in terms of their scenic production as well as their poetry. Each of these matters calls for a full-length study.

The social background of late Elizabethan and early Jacobean drama, and the development of its leading forms during the period 1603–13, were the subject of Volume VI of my *History of Elizabethan Drama, The Living Monument*, 1976. Jonsonian comedy and Shakespearean tragedy and romance were considered in terms of actor–audience relations, and the evolving theatres with their various specialities (including the Court masque). Since *The Living Monument* overlaps with Webster's apprentice years, it may serve as introduction to the greater works of his maturity. The present study follows naturally upon the explorations there begun.

Too late for consideration, I learn that a bibliographical analysis of the work of Nicholas Okes, Webster's printer, by Peter Blayney, is forthcoming from Cambridge, which should transform the study of the text, for no such close examination of the work of any printer of this period has been attempted before. Okes, who printed the 1608 Quarto of *King Lear*, specialized in playbooks. Born in 1580, apprenticed at Christmas 1595 to Richard Field, he married Elizabeth Beswick on 8 December 1603, and in 1606 set up in business at the sign of the Hand near Holborn Bridge, with one press, a scanty supply of type and two assistants. He was Webster's contemporary as well as his neighbour.

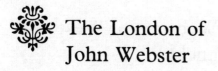

PART ONE

The London of
John Webster

CHAPTER ONE

The Websters of West Smithfield

'Less is known of the life of John Webster than of those of the great Greek dramatists.' Such was the opinion of F.L. Lucas, when in 1958 he reissued some part of his great edition of the *Works*.

Thanks to the research of Mary Edmond (see the Bibliography), much more is now known. On the basis of the facts which she extracted from the records of the City of London, parochial and probate, from those of the livery companies, and the further material towards which these direct us, it is now possible to establish an outline for Webster's life. This can be filled out by our general knowledge of the City of London and its people in Elizabethan and Jacobean times. If a man can be placed within an exact spot in the City, if his trade and his connections are fixed, consequences may reasonably be inferred, for we know a great deal about London. It was described by letter-writers, dramatists, writers of sermons and writers of pamphlets; it was pictured and it was celebrated; it was denounced, and it was legislated for; its separate institutions are separately chronicled, for (as the headquarters of the government and the law courts, the military centre, the centre of trade and of finance) its churches and schools, its Guildhall and its Exchange offered models of intellectual and institutional innovation. London led the kingdom. The Londoners were self-conscious and intensely organized.

Born into this city of perhaps 150,000 inhabitants (it had grown to 250,000 by 1605 and was much greater by the time Charles I came to the throne), until he is located, John Webster remains as unremarkable as his very plain English name. Afterwards it is possible to see what kind of life he would lead, and in turn to apply this knowledge to a consideration of his work. As Shakespeare's successor in Jacobean tragedy, Webster transformed the life he met around him, for tragedy implies transformation; he was also rooted in it, for tragedy implies engagement.

The trivialities of that life are directly reflected in his minor works. He could be a dutiful chronicler of local triumphs and local scandals, a patriotic citizen who deplored Court vice, and a genial caricaturist of social types. How could the author of *The White Devil* and *The Duchess of Malfi*, after those masterpieces, perpetrate *A Cure for a Cuckold*? How could this strong individualist, whose flavour is as distinctive as cinnamon or aloe, become not only anonymous but indistinguishable from the surrounding brethren of the craft with whom he readily collaborated?

The most important fact about Webster's origins might have been deduced from his being admitted by patrimony to the freedom of the Company of Merchant Taylors on 19 June 1615. This meant that he belonged to that wealthy and stable group of citizens who formed the body of the twelve Great Companies, by which the City was governed. No man of insufficient substance could have claimed membership of the Merchant Taylors. The details which have been discovered by Miss Edmond fill out the picture.

John Webster the elder, the dramatist's father, grew up to serve his apprenticeship in West Smithfield, and was made free of the company on 20 December 1571, being presented by Anne Sylver, widow of Antony Sylver, who lived in Chick Lane, West Smithfield, and in the parish of St Sepulchre's. He engaged in the new and profitable business of building, selling and hiring coaches. Hence the location of his work near West Smithfield, London's chief horse market. As John Webster the elder in turn presented many apprentices to the company, his coach-yard must have been a large and flourishing one. It stood at the corner of Cow Lane and Hosier Lane in Smithfield's north-west quarter.

This new and rapidly growing industry had been introduced only in 1555, when Walter Rippon built the first English coach for the Earl of Rutland; waggons, litters and carts were the traditional means of transportation. By 1564 the Queen had a coachman. But as there was no Company of Coachmakers in London until late in the seventeenth century, the builders became attached to other companies, for without such membership it was forbidden to trade in the City (Rippon was freeman of the Leathersellers, doubtless because of the need for straps and harness). The Worshipful Company of Taylors and Linen Armourers of the

Fraternity of St John the Baptist in the City of London, incorporated under Edward I, had formerly made the padded harness for knights and their horses, and had supplied pavilions and funeral palls. The sumptuous linings of coaches, the furnishings of the escutcheons and horses' trappings, footcloths and cushions, linked them in trade to the Merchant Taylors.

By the end of the sixteenth century, the number of coaches was causing difficulties in the crowded streets of London. In 1601 an attempt was made to limit their number, but in 1603, because of plague, 'there was not a good horse in Smithfield or a coach to be set eyes on'.[1] In 1613 a maximum of 430 was suggested. In 1618 the Venetian Ambassador protested that carts were not giving way to noblemen's coaches. These 'Hackney hell carts' had a rank at the Maypole in the Strand after 1634; next year it was ordered that they must not be hired for less than three miles, and no one who did not keep four horses could own a coach. The Thames watermen soon protested at this competition from coaching; in 1622 Taylor the Water Poet lamented that

> Carroches, coaches, jades and Flanders mares
> Do rob us of our shares, our wares, our fares;
> Against the ground we stand and knock our heels,
> Whilst all our profit runs away on wheels.
> [*The World runs on Wheels*, 1622

Later he inveighed not against coaches of the nobility but against the 'caterpillar swarm of hirelings. They have ruined my poor trade ... carry five hundred and sixty fares daily from us.'

Four-wheeled waggons for country passengers were drawn by seven or eight horses in file, 'one behind the other, with plumes and bells, embroidered cloth coverings'. A lackey ran before a nobleman's coach to clear the way, while liveried footmen marched behind (see *The Puritan*, IV. i. 30–33). Some of these would add to the congestion in London. A dialogue, *Coach and Sedan, pleasantly disputing for precedence, the Brewer's Cart being Moderator*, appeared in 1636. The traffic problems of the Blackfriars Theatre were among the most acute; in 1613 the first recorded traffic jam occurred in its neighbourhood through the throngs of coaches. A coach became the status symbol of the gentry. At the centre of its satire on City pretensions, the scandalous success of 1605, *Eastward Ho!* by Marston, Jonson and Chapman, emphasized the great desire of Gertrude, the goldsmith's daughter, to ride down to her hus-

band's country place in a coach. She mounts the coach, to
family acclamation, but it turns out to be a hired one; when
the post-horses are taken out of it she is left stranded with her
maid. This sort of episode would be familiar to hirers of
coaches like Webster. In *Northward Ho!*, the play's sequel, the
whore Doll on the road is pursued in another coach and pair
by her Welsh lover. Coaches were associated with the wicked
aspects of Court life,[2] with rides to the suburban centres of sin,
and with assignations. Middleton's Lady Kix takes her 'physic'
in a coach (*A Chaste Maid in Cheapside*, 3, iii. 176).

The coach trade, a growing luxury business, was not however
the only trade served by the elder Webster's yards. He was described as 'waggon-maker'; he provided carts for the condemned
to be taken from Newgate jail to the place of execution at Tyburn,
or to be used for whipping malefactors 'at the cart's tail' through
the City, for carting bawds and for the trades of Smithfield market.
He provided also the floats or pageants for City shows and the
hearses for great public funerals; the masquers' elegant chariots
for Court performances might also have been fashioned in his yard.

Like most City men, he tried profitable side-lines. During the
dangerous plague years of 1592–3 John Webster the elder was sued
for building houses in Holborn Fields and Chick Lane, contrary
to the Queen's proclamation.[3] The land belonged to James White.
Webster was associated in several bonds and recognizances
with the Coates family of St Giles, Cripplegate, where on 4
November 1577 he had married Elizabeth Coates.

The parish of St Sepulchre in the Ward of Farringdon Without,
the most westerly ward of the City, was not a fashionable quarter.
'The most corrupt is St Powker's parish, by reason of many
fruiterers, poor people and stinking lanes, as Tanner Lane, and
Seacoal Lane and other such places', observed Stow; Stinking
Lane was so named from the offal flung there from slaughtered
sheep and cattle. When Samuel Pepys accidentally knocked a joint
of meat off a stall he had to pay for it, for it became inedible. The
squalor was increased by the dung and stench from the horse market, which was not even paved till 1615 (this prevented cheaters
from selling lame horses, by obliging them to pace on level
ground).

Jousts and tournaments had in earlier times been held in the
market of Smithfield; here the boy king, Richard II, had challenged Wat Tyler, who was then killed on the spot by the Lord

Mayor, Walworth. Here religious martyrs had been burnt in
Queen Mary's time. Of the elms of Smithfield, where the secular
criminals had formerly been hung, by Elizabeth I's reign not one
remained. Traitors were now drawn upon hurdles from Newgate,
down Holborn, past St Giles (where they were offered a last drink)
to Tyburn. Newgate jail, in the City gatehouse, which was adorned
with sculptured figures, had fetid dungeons beneath and crowded
arches above for prisoners. Behind a grating a prisoner was sta-
tioned, to beg from passers-by. It was among the most dreaded
of prisons, for its mortality rate was appalling; the dead were taken
to St Sepulchre's.

The large parish of St Sepulchre and the priory of St Bartholomew shared other last duties towards these poor wretches. When,
in 1605, Robert Dove, a member of the Merchant Taylors Company, gave fifty pounds for the tolling of the great bell of St
Sepulchre's on nights before executions, and also for the parish
clerk to go at midnight with twelve solemn rolls of his handbell
and an exhortation to repent, the benefaction was witnessed by his
fellow Liveryman, John Webster the elder, who was a Common
Councilman of the Vestry.

His son was to remember that benefaction in the scene of the
Duchess of Malfi's death:

> I am the common bellman
> That usually is sent to condemned persons,
> The night before they suffer.

Shakespeare's Lady Macbeth also speaks of 'the fatal bellman'.

Newgate, Smithfield and St Bartholomew's were at the western
end of the great ward of Farringdon Without, once known as 'a
garden without a wall'. The ward included the great houses in
Holborn and Fleet Street, the liberties of St Bartholomew the
Great and the Less, Whitefriars, and the Savoy, two Inns of Court
(the Inner and Middle Temples), the old palace of Bridewell, and
many parishes. It housed many distinguished foreigners, refugee
traders and impecunious gentlemen taking advantage of the 'hospital' of the Savoy, or of the many inns along the roads leading
westward, where the Temple and Holborn Bars marked the limits
of the Lord Mayor's jurisdiction. In 1595 the records reported
twenty-eight gentlemen resident in the ward,[4] but it was not an
area favoured by the really powerful City families, who clustered
in one or two wards within the walls. New inmates within the City

were forbidden, which explains why the foreign refugees (such as those who arrived after the Spanish sack of Antwerp in 1576) settled outside.

The government of the City was confined to a few families. The most recent historian of its evolution (Frank Freeman Foster; see the Bibliography) found that fifteen families stood out from the rest. However, young men who came up to the capital intermarried into the livery-company where they had been admitted. The citizens were constantly replenished from the country, which enabled London to grow, in spite of its high mortality rates. So, although the population was a close-knit group, leadership was open to talent and ability.

The Crown did not interfere in City affairs; indeed, it was said by Pollard that 'Tudor despotism consisted largely in London's dominion over the rest of England'. A more agreeable way of putting the facts is that a third of all Tudor charitable foundations came from Londoners, who in many cases made provision for the country regions from which they came.

Not all these great men were native English; the greatest of the denizens, with a house in Bishopsgate and a country estate at Babraham, was Sir Horatio Palavicino, of a noble Genoese family, who succeeded Sir Thomas Gresham as chief financial advisor to the Crown, and from 1580 to 1592 guided Burghley on finance and Walsingham on intelligence. He became an energetic speculator in all sorts of commodities, from alum to Spanish prisoners-of-war. His chief assistant was named Justiniano, a name to be used by Dekker and Webster in their comedy of London life, *Westward Ho!*

Sir Horatio operated on an international scale and did not concern himself with the City administration. But the Florentines and Flemings built triumphal arches for the coronation entries of monarchs. Moreover, the old trade guilds, which took over the government during Mountford's rebellion in 1263, and after 330 years had grown to thirty or more, were now largely composed of merchants and bankers with international connections. Such a comedy as Dekker's *The Shoemakers' Holiday*, though it romantically includes the 'gentle craft' at work, makes its hero a trader in foreign enterprises. Collectors of customs and 'undertakers' for northern mines or for the great overseas markets, the Russian (1555), Levant (1581) or East India (1611) Companies, if they had not Palavicino's command of foreign languages, his interest in the fine arts, or his international family ties, yet ranged widely. By the bond of their livery-company they might also be joined with more modest citizens in a fraternity which cut across barriers. The Freemasons, who claim to be descendants of a guild, perhaps represent its social structure more adequately than the City Companies which still, today, elect the government of the City of London, still hold their great dinners, still maintain the medieval rites of the Loving Cup and Tudor habiliments. (Their London headquarters, as it happens, stands almost exactly on the site of the Cockpit Theatre, where Webster's later plays were given.)

By the 1590s, smaller fry among the guildsmen were speculating in theatrical enterprise. The career of Francis Langley – builder of the Swan Theatre – which has been recently investigated, shows how the nephew of a Lord Mayor and a Draper (in Langley's case, largely a euphemism for money-lending) might struggle, by getting the Manor of Paris Garden, to become a member of the gentry. He engaged in the shadiest transactions concerning the captured Portuguese Carrack, brought into Plymouth in 1592. While the great Palavicino was engaged in bidding for the captured cargo of pepper (he let it go to a London syndicate for £50,000), Langley was concealing a 'great diamond', looted by a common sailor, after the mariner had met some goldsmiths at the Theatre. Cecil was much concerned with recovering this jewel, reputedly of twenty-six carat. Eventually it came to the Queen's hands, but concealment of looted treasure ruined Langley and his brother-in-law, the Clerk of the Privy Council, Sir Antony Ashley.

If the link between such affairs and the life of the theatre is direct, the link between the great trader and the little man was ensured by the groupings that remained from a much simpler medieval city. The guilds, through their leading members, exercised control over London at the highest level of government by the Mayor and Aldermen, but at the grass-roots level they delegated to parish officers. Although the Reformation reduced the power of the Church, it did not really interfere with the very useful local offices of scavenger, constable and third borough (petty constable) or the power of the vestry. It was the parishes, for instance, that made plague returns. The Parish Clerk was a minor officer of some significance and the Parish Clerks had their own guild or fraternity. They had given plays at Clerkenwell in King Edward IV's time. All these men were Freemen of the City.

To this level of the social hierarchy John Webster the elder evidently belonged, and the tradition that late in the seventeenth century placed his son as Parish Clerk of St Andrews, Holborn, was not unreasonable, although there is no verification. That the Websters were well thought of in their neighbourhood is attested by the bequests of various citizens – substantial men – not only to the father but also to the son and to his family. In 1597–8 John Webster the elder was assessed very heavily for taxes in his parish: at £12, one of the highest figures.

Unfortunately the parish records of St Sepulchre, Holborn, were lost in the Great Fire of London, which reached its westernmost limit at Pye Corner in Smithfield. Thus, the story of John Webster, dramatist, cannot be reconstructed in the way that Shakespeare's main dates can be found in the register of Holy Trinity, Stratford. The record of his son's baptism is kept elsewhere. John, the son of John Webster of St Pulcher's, was baptized as dwelling in the house of Simon Peniall, saddler in the parish of St Dunstan's in the West, on 8 May 1606. Simon and Sara Peniall (*née* Coxe) had been married at the same church in 1584;[5] but their children were baptized at St Bride's, Fleet Street. Sara, the eldest girl, baptized 20 April 1589, would have been seventeen years and one month when this child was born in the house of his maternal grandparents. John Webster had married a girl of sixteen – identified as 'Sara', for in 1614 a neighbour, Thomas Andrew, left £10 to John Webster the elder and £5 each to John Webster the younger and to Sara his wife; another neighbour, who died in 1617, left twenty shillings each to Webster's daughters Sara and Elizabeth, twenty shillings to his son John, and forty shillings to 'the rest of the Websters' children'. So clearly the dramatist had rather a large family and was of good standing in the neighbourhood. When his son was baptized in 1606, Webster was living in Nag's Head Alley, near Cow Lane.

Simon Peniall, Warden of the Saddlers' Company in 1605, and a parish officer at St Dunstan's, had evidently moved between the baptism of his daughter and of his grandson, to the more aristocratic quarter of St Dunstan's, although some of his family remained in St Bride's parish. Grandfathers were often godfathers; though his company was a minor one, Peniall was evidently a big fish in a little pool.

John Webster's brother Edward stood his senior in the guild, having been admitted late in the lifetime of their father, in 1612.

After the elder John Webster's death, it was Edward who renewed the lease of the coach-yard, held of the Priory of St Bartholomew. Later Edward became Constable of the ward; he married a widow (Susan Llewelyn, *née* Walker) whose parents lived almost opposite the premises in Cow Lane, and whose mother, Mrs Walker, when she died, left Susan £100, five shillings to each servant in their household and forty shillings'-worth of bread for the poor, to be distributed by Edward. As has been mentioned (see above, page 4), in 1617 John Webster, the head of the family, was satirized by a lawyer as 'the playwright-cartwright', and the whole group appears close-knit and prosperous. Webster was well rooted at the level of family and neighbourhood.

His printer, Nicholas Okes, son of John Okes, Horner, was of the parish of St Sepulchre. His was a different position from that of the players who aspired to make their companies into something like a livery-company, with the same control and monopoly rights. After 1597, adult players were banished to the suburbs by a City decree – to the sprawling, ill-regulated areas which the Crown sometimes tried to get the City to control. The City steadily declined to assume such onerous details. Whilst condemning strongly the sinfulness of Southwark and Moorfields, the City Fathers only occasionally extended their interest to these regions. A benevolent private attempt by two Lord Mayors, Leate and Halliday, to turn Moorfields into a public recreation ground took eleven years (1605–16); and in spite of all the problems, attempts to build new roads or more bridges were always prohibited. Every inch of ground was used: Bow Church's old grave-yard in Hosier Lane now had houses on it; St Paul's Cathedral had become filled with little sheds and stalls and private dwellings. The closeness of City life, 'in populous city pent,' meant that everyone knew each other in one parish, and the lesser characters would learn all about the affairs of their greater neighbours, whose servants would pass the time of day and indulge in gossip, and whose officials might come with some request that was almost a command. London is still largely a collection of villages, and the identity of Chelsea or Clapham, the parts of Kensington around St Mary Abbott's, or the tight-clinging street communities of the East End, provide intensely local circles of concern to this day.

Smithfield offered not only a great horse fair but also a field for public events; for ten days, from 24 August, it was the site of St Bartholomew's Fair, the greatest of the London fairs. This was opened by the Lord Mayor and Aldermen in their robes; all other fairs were prohibited at that season. Originally a cloth fair, it had become a general occasion for trade and entertainment. Cockney zest at its most outrageous was displayed in Ben Jonson's comedy of the scene. Its own judicial court was at a tavern in Giltspur Street at the corner of Cock Lane.[6]

This invasion by all sorts of tricksters, mountebanks and idlers had originated by the terms of the endowment of the ancient foundation of St Bartholomew's Hospital by Rahere the Monk, dating from 1133 in the reign of Henry I. When the priory was dissolved by Henry VIII, the principal beneficiary was Robert Rich,[7] but the citizens succeeded in 1544 in regaining possession of part of the buildings for the continuance of the Hospital, and part of the church also remained standing. Within the liberty of St Bartholomew's, Lyly the poet resided, and later the head of St Bartholomew's Hospital, the Portuguese physician Roderigo Lopez, was to be the centre of a spectacular trial. On 7 June 1594, after a commission at Guildhall, which included Lord Rich, had found him guilty on charges of attempting to poison the Queen, the unfortunate old man was executed with all the gruesome barbarity of a traitor's death. Webster would at this time have been about fourteen years of age.

A little further along the road from St Bartholomew's had stood the Charterhouse, whose monks Henry had executed sixty years before. That building had become a school; Greyfriars had become an orphanage (Christ's Hospital). Through the intervention of the great City patron, Sir Thomas Gresham, a thousand marks from the City and an equal sum from the King restored the Hospital. The old religious centres in many cases simply disappeared, but, among the institutions that superseded them,[8] schools and orphanages were prominent.

It was the duty of the livery-companies to be charitable; the Merchant Taylors built two sets of almshouses (one set near the Tower in Hog Street, one in Threadneedle Street), but in addition they provided a new kind of fraternal bonding by the foundation of the Merchant Taylors' School. This must have had the effect of working the young pupils more firmly into the mesh of the social group to which their families were attached.

Given the structure of London society at that time, it does not really seem open to any question that Webster would have

attended the school founded by his father's company, the school
for which his father provided pageant waggons. It would have
been an act not merely of eccentricity but of ostracism for a
member of the company to send his child anywhere else. This particular school, however, was more than a new innovatory bond;
it bore the impress of one of England's greatest educationalists,
whose voice sounds quite articulately across the years from his
time to the present day. In 1561 the Merchant Taylors' School
had been founded for 250 boys; it was almost twice the size of
Colet's school at St Paul's, whose statutes (1549) were adopted
for the new foundation. The manor of the Rose in the ward of
St Lawrence Poultry, which belonged to the last Duke of Buckingham, was purchased for a schoolhouse, where a High Master,
Under Master and two ushers were to teach the boys from seven
in the morning until five in the evening, with a mid-day break
and one half-holiday a week. Prayers were said three times a day,
kneeling. Richard Hilles, who put down most of the purchase
money (£500), had been, as a young man of eighteen, bold enough
to write a commentary on St James, for which he had to go
into exile at Strasbourg. Schools were in fact a sure way of implanting the reformed faith, and whilst the children might
be of any nationality, they all had to learn the national forms
of prayer and catechism. No doubt Hilles was in touch with
the merchants among whom he had spent his exile during the
1540s.[9]

The High Master chosen in 1561 was Richard Mulcaster, son
of a Cumberland squire whose family had been there since the
days of William Rufus. A scholar of Eton and King's (where he
was taught by the Provost, Sir John Cheke), and later a student
of Christ Church, he was already teaching in London, being indeed the most remarkable young teacher of his time, and at this
date only thirty. The school hoped to attract endowment, but at
the beginning it was a venture of faith, sustained from the revenues
of the Merchant Taylors Company. Each of the four teachers received a yearly salary of £10; Mulcaster hesitated to accept, but
Hilles supplied an additional £10 from his own purse, which only
brought the stipend up to that enjoyed by the Head Master of
the Free Grammar School of Stratford-upon-Avon.

Mulcaster's twenty-five years as High Master assured the school
such a reputation that boys were sent there from all parts.[10] At
first a connection was built with Pembroke Hall in Cambridge,

to which Edmund Spenser and Lancelot Andrewes both proceeded from the school, but when Sir Thomas White, another Merchant Taylor, established St John's College at Oxford he tied a number of awards to the school, which the Fellows were persuaded to implement (with some pressure, for they were a poor foundation and Catholic, as was White himself). Jenkins, the master who taught Shakespeare, was a graduate of St John's, son of a poor servant of Sir Thomas White, and therefore most probably also a scholar of Mulcaster. (The lists up to 1611 are incomplete.[11] Spenser, for instance, can only be identified as a Merchant Taylors' boy because of a grant from another charity towards his university expenses. Hence, the absence of Webster's name from the surviving lists does not exclude him.)

After some disputes about pay, Mulcaster eventually resigned in 1586, and Henry Wilkinson, who had been the second master, was appointed. He had been a Fellow of Trinity College, Cambridge, where Cartwright, the noted Calvinist, had been Master. A further proof of the Merchant Taylors' religious views is the struggle to keep Catholic interference from St John's College, Oxford, out of the school. The Merchant Taylors' School produced a stream of bishops, from Lancelot Andrewes to Matthew Wren.

As boys could enter at about nine years of age, Webster most probably arrived just as Mulcaster left, but the tradition had by then been firmly set. Places in the school were assigned by the Master and Wardens of the Company, 150 being free places, and the remainder carrying fees of varied sums.

Mulcaster's views on education were by no means merely academic. He believed in music and plays to teach his boys 'good behaviour and audacity'.[12] In the early 1570s Mr Mulcaster's boys had been the leading group and at least two of them became dramatists. One was Thomas Lodge, son of a Lord Mayor. The other was Thomas Kyd, whose father belonged to the parish of St Mary Woolnoth and was a scrivener; he was entered on 6 November 1568 and would have been among the senior boys in the school when, at a performance in March 1574, given at Merchant Taylors' Hall, the Livery were unable to find places because 'at our common plays and such like exercises which be commonly exposed to be seen for money, every lewd person thinks himself (for his penny) worthy of the chief and most commodious place'. Moreover, these gatherings 'bringeth the youth to such an impudent familiarity with their betters that of times great contempt of masters, parents and magistrates followeth there from'.

No more plays were to be presented in the Common Hall. The group had given *Timoclea at the Siege of Thebes before Alexander* at Hampton Court, some time between 11 January and 5 February 1574; of course, the City would pay to see the show as played before the Queen. There had also been prepared a masque of the six Virtues (ladies with lights), but 'for the tediousness of the play' it was not called for. The boys needed special cotton-lined hose (two pairs) and two dozen pairs of gloves, for which last item two shillings and sixpence had been disbursed. This and other elegant plays, such as *Perseus and Anthromisus*, given on Shrove Tuesday, sound very like the sort of classical plays with which the Choristers' Theatre was in 1575 established by John Lyly at St Paul's. They were gentlemanly and courtly exercises in wit, and Webster, who was remarkably tenacious in his adherence to memory, may, towards the end of his career, in his *Appius and Virginia*, have been recalling the old play of that name (first given in 1565), for his drama becomes more explicable if seen as written for boys (see pp. 178–9). It also had possibly a second and admonitory meaning: many of these early plays, under guise of a fable, sought to warn or persuade.

It was not an easy duty to play at Court. When, on Shrove Tuesday 1574, nine boys from Merchant Taylors' were sent to play, they had first to rehearse their play at the Revels Office, and then were carried from St Paul's wharf in two tilt wherries, with their tutor and their dresser, and their properties towed behind them in a barge. For one night they lay at Court, for another at 'Mother Sparro's at Kingston', with their wherries waiting day and night to take them whenever the Queen should please to command their play. They returned to London on Ash Wednesday, many of them 'cold and sick and hungry', and were landed at the Blackfriars to be warmed and fed. Each child received a shilling; Newdigate, their trainer, had forty shillings, and the Revels Office paid for transportation and lodging.

However, when the men's Theatre opened in 1576, the children were soon displaced in royal favour; but they were still much in demand for speeches at City pageants and civic occasions, such as the great thanksgiving celebrations for the defeat of the Armada in 1588, when Webster might be expected to be among the junior boys in the school. In time of plague, the school was closed, and the great outbreak of 1592–4 would have coincided with Webster's years at the top of the school, so that his career as a scholar must have been badly interrupted.

Webster's education would have followed the regular pattern of the institutions he attended, and this is now familiar enough. The basis of schooling was the teaching of languages; the aim, skill in communication and the ancient culture, secular requisites for good government. But the very individualistic views of Mulcaster gave a rather different turn to the regular curriculum.

The craft of writing and the craft of pleading had themselves their basic books of rules, which can be followed in these years fairly closely. Mulcaster's modernism, given the special authority of print, acquired by this the force of a manifesto – the first of its kind. The rapid development of the arts of language during the reign of Elizabeth I, and more particularly the second half of it, has not been equalled before or since.

'I am servant to my country,' wrote Mulcaster (*Elementary*, page 267). It was a form of service to the nation to improve the language, for it was 'bearing the joyful title of our liberty and freedom'. 'I love Rome, but London better, I favour Italy, but England more, I honour the Latin but I worship the English' (page 269). The asseveration coming from a notable linguist who taught Hebrew (which was not taught at St Paul's), carries more weight as he proceeds to mark the objections against the use of English, answering them one by one: 'Our English tongue doth need no such pruning, it is of small reach, it stretcheth no further than this island of ours, nair [nor] not there over all. What though? Yet it reigneth there, and it serves us there, and it would be clean brusht for the wearing there. Though it go not beyond the sea, yet it will serve on this side' (page 271). Indeed, he foresees a growth in trade and influence overseas which will spread English even further, and 'for fine translating in pithy terms, either peer to or passing the foreign quickness, I find it wonderful pliable, and ready to discharge a quick conceit, in very few words' (page 286).

The linking of language skills with patriotism, especially among the merchant group of Londoners, who had been among the first to import the forbidden Bible in English, was well established; the man who taught on Hilles' foundation would find such sentiments very readily understood.

Mulcaster's two works on education, *Positions* (1581) and *The First Part of the Elementary* (1582), give a statement of the views which are likeliest to have shaped his school teaching. For Mulcaster, education includes the whole nurture of the child, 'divided into two parts, the one whereof is knowledge to increase understanding, the other is behaviour to enlarge virtue'. He is speaking from experience and it is to experience that he appeals. He argues passionately that bright young children should not be overtaxed; they will overwork, and either grow up weakly or not grow up at all: 'Good things grow on hardly at their first planting.' Parents and schoolmasters must consult each other about the proper age at which to begin education and the special needs and aptitudes of any one child. The first thing to be taught is reading, and it should be taught in English, for this is in fact a more difficult language than Latin, and the child will need it all the time. Reading must be taught slowly and very thoroughly; then writing. Drawing and even painting should start early. Music should be taught early too. Holding back the child is to his mental advantage; otherwise he grows doctrinaire and inflexible:

I do see many toward wits, of reasonable good reading, and of excellent utterance ... marvellously overshoot themselves ... they see all circumstances, and some small assurance, that all the authors they read do soothe all that they say: they will push out in public certain resolute opinions, before either their wits be settled or their reading ripe ... mastering of the circumstance is the only rule that wise men live by ... the only odds between folly and wit.

                                                        [*Positions*, pages 8–9]

At Merchant Taylors' therefore Webster would have had the chance to practise 'pithy terms' in his native tongue, to use English for his serious readings, and to respect it as equal to the classics. He would not have been handicapped by his own slow methods of composition, which he himself described in later life, since Mulcaster believed in moving slowly; and he would have acquired facility in drama, have been expected to act, and been given some training.

Mulcaster believed in bodily exercise; few public schoolmasters of modern times could compare with his thorough programme of exercise and training, which occupies twenty-nine chapters in *Positions*. These range from speaking aloud to football, of which game, as a North countryman, Mulcaster heartily approved, though in the City it was considered barbarous.[13] He also approved of wrestling, of the 'top and scourge', and gave directions for walking, riding, hunting, shooting, swimming, dancing; how vigorously and persistently they are to be undertaken depends on the learner's constitution, and the schoolmaster is to be 'trainer',

for while the body is committed to one, and the soul commended to another, it falleth out most times that the poor body is miserably neglected, while nothing is cared for but only the soul, as it proveth true in very zealous divines ... and that in this conflict the diligent scholar, in great strength of soul bears most-what about him but a feeble, weake and sickish body. [page 126].

Mulcaster is plainly aiming at a complete man, after the model of Philip Sidney, rather than a learned man; he is following the humanist ideal of *l'uomo universale*, for he recognizes the need of shaping his programme to the individual; 'Art' would prescribe certain rules and conditions, but the 'artificer' must modify them to fit circumstances:

Art will not relent, she cannot make curtsey, her knees be grown stiff and her joints fast knit, yet curtsey there must be ... The rule is, no noysome savour near the newly exercised; how shall the poor boy do, that is to go home through stinking streets and filthy lanes? The rule is, change apparel after sweat; what if he have none other? or not there where he sweateth? [page 131].

As was proper in a book dedicated to the Queen, he includes a whole section on the education of girls, which he seems to restrict to reading, writing, languages and music. Girls may be taught with boys, and their education should continue until about fourteen. He distinguishes between education for the gentleman and for the commoner, deploring the habit of claiming gentry through riches: 'For the most part it is miserably scraped to the murthering of many a poor maggot, while lively cheese is lusty cheer, to spare expenses, that Jack may be a gentleman.... For to become a gentleman is to bear the cognisaunce of virtue, whereunto honour is companion' (page 194). Yet though he wishes gentlemen's training to be better than the common, 'that cannot be. For the common, well appointed, is simply the best, and even fitted for them.' Later he asks, 'For how can education be private? it abuseth the name, as it abuseth the thing.' He abides always by the custom of the country, since the end of education is social profit in the education of individuals, whose faults are more seen, and therefore sooner corrected, in public studies. Whilst 'to write and to read well which may be jointly gotten is a pretty stock for a poor boy to begin the world withal' (page 34).

Mulcaster wrote with the natural authority of great experience, as one who knows his tools, who thinks for himself and flexibly, but whose principles are evident. His very prejudices are (at a distance!) endearing evidence of a strong personality, who emerges as a mixture of Dr Johnson and William Cobbett.

By contrast with *Positions*, the *Elementary*, dealing with the writing of the English tongue, is a set-piece of apologetic, aimed at justifying the nobility of English, remarking on its conformity with custom and reason (though not with the kind of rules that prevailed in the learned tongues), and even arguing for its organic development. Prerogative is

a private thing in itself, and the very life blood, which preserveth tongues in their natural best from the first time they grew to account, till they come to decay and a new period grown, different from the old, though excellent in the altered kind and yet itself to depart, and make room for another, when the circular turn shall have ripened alteration [page 78].

He goes on boldly to declare, 'I take this present period of our English tongue to be the very height thereof.' He has earlier advanced such unexpected reasons for making a tongue of account as 'all kinds of trade and all sorts of traffic':

If the spreading sea, and the spacious land could use any speech, they would both show you where, and in how many strange places, they have seen our people, and also give you to wit, that they shall deal in as much and with as great variety of matter as any other people do, whether at home or abroad. Which is the reason why our tongue doth serve so many uses, because it is conversant with so many people, and so well acquainted with so many matters, in so sundry kinds of dealing. ... For he that is so practised, will utter that which he practiseth in his natural tongue and ... rather than he will stick in his utterence, will use the foreign term, by way of premunition, that the country people do call it so, and by that means make a foreign word, an English Denizen [pages 90–91].

Nevertheless, Mulcaster's verbal tools appear curiously primitive: the use of abbreviations, and a glossary of common words, from 'abaie', 'abandon', 'abase' and 'abash' to 'zealous', 'zeal' and 'zealousness', including such curiosities as 'ketler', 'kidgell', 'nosethrill', 'yalp' and 'yex'. The whole is under eight thousand words. Compared with the insights and sweep of *Positions*, the second work shows primitive difficulties in the actual training for the use of written English, which suggests that the best work would be oratorical rather than orthographical. Details of spelling and pronunciation, a little allegory about Reason, Custom and Sound, alternate sharply; bold claims for classic status are marked with technical details such as might train a musician in fingering.

The chief recreation of the City was in sermons, delivered at St Paul's Cross, within St Paul's, or within the Temple Church. Here Hooker had preached out of the substance that was to produce *The Laws of Ecclesiastical Polity*, to be opposed by his deputy, a strong Calvinist, in counter-sermons. At Westminster Hall, a great man might plead for his life, a Last Dying Speech could become a Testament. The arts of the theatre were part of this stream of oratory, which was itself the cultural life of the capital. A book might be no more than a frozen oration.

The schoolboy would grow up in this atmosphere of the spoken word, and Webster, having absorbed the material benefits of the Merchant Taylors' School, would find such proclivities strengthened as he proceeded to the next step of his education.

CHAPTER TWO

The Middle Temple: a Literary Centre

Although the evidence that John Webster was entered at the Middle Temple is not as firm as the assumption that he would have attended the Merchant Taylors' School, it does not depend solely on the entry of a John Webster of London from the New Inn – an Inn of Chancery – on 1 August 1598, as noted in the records: 'Primo die Augusti anno 1598, Magister Johannes Webster nuper de Novo Hospitio generosus filius et heres apparens Johannis Webster de London generosi admissus est in Societatem Medii Templi.' Webster the dramatist's association with the Inn is shewn by his continuation of the *Characters* of Sir Thomas Overbury, who was also a member of the Inn, and his dramatic association with Marston and Ford, both Templarians. He collaborated with Marston on *The Malcontent*: Ford supplied a poem of praise on publication of *The Duchess of Malfi*, and an elegy (now lost) on Overbury. Marston's general dramatic style deeply influenced Webster, as Webster in turn influenced Ford. The three dramatists – Marston, Webster, Ford – are closely linked in a way which illuminates the great plays, and their significant works follow from common membership of a Society where literature was diligently cultivated. The only other major Jacobean dramatist with a legal training was Beaumont, from the Inner Temple.

Webster's preoccupation with trial scenes is continuous. The first play he is known to have written, *Sir Thomas Wyatt*, contains one; another forms the climax of the first part of *The White Devil*; in *The Devil's Law Case* and *Appius and Virginia* such scenes are again climactic. *The Devil's Law Case* resembles a legal investigation, the course of action depending on a labyrinthine pursuit of the facts and of the true identities of the leading figures. The lighter plays, *Westward Ho!* and *Northward Ho!* survey the citizens from that lofty point of vantage cultivated in the lawyers' theatre at St Paul's. Entering the Inns meant for Webster immediately entering a closed circle of privilege, a step towards acquaintance with still higher circles of privilege. Whatever their origins, the 'young Masters of the Inns of Court' were all gentlemen.

The Inns of Court were great households, as well as centres of learning. John Marston's father built his own set of chambers, which he shared with his peccant son and heir. There were in residence at the Middle Temple about two hundred Inner Barristers (corresponding to undergraduates at a university), ruled by Utter Barristers, of whom the most distinguished were elected Benchers and formed the governing 'Parliament' of the Inn. Distinguished sojourners might be admitted on nomination by the Benchers to this Liberty, which, though technically and geographically within the ward of Farringdon Without, was not subject to the City government. To oblige the Earl of Essex, his secretary, Sir Henry Wotton, might be accommodated; Sir Walter Ralegh also resided, though with no intention of studying the law. If studious and independent, the Inns were also open to be used by the parliamentary committees who sometimes met in the Hall, already thronged by clients coming to the chambers, whilst young lawyers frequented all the City's haunts of pleasure, as their own satirists did not fail to record.

Many a citizen sent his son and heir to the Inns,[1] although efforts were made to restrict the membership to those who produced at least three generations of lineage: tradesmen were less partial to the universities.[2] The third university of the kingdom (as Sir George Buc was later to term the Inns of Court) had greatly expanded with the increase of litigation. Law, as the most esteemed and profitable of all professions, replaced the Church as the *carrière ouverte aux talents*, for the area of canon law had shrunk considerably at the Reformation. Country gentlemen also began sending their sons to the Inns to qualify for the new office of Justice of the Peace; great officers of the law and serious students who would succeed them cohabited with relatively wealthy young men, who came to live on the fringes of the royal Court. One and all aspired to some connection with Whitehall, that great magnet which lay a little to the westward of the Inns, as well as with the ancient seat of justice at

Westminster Hall, where special seats in 'le cribbe' were reserved for students.

Although the Inns had so greatly expanded, among two hundred it was still possible to maintain some family structure. At the Revels of Gray's Inn in 1594, 'the family and followers' formed a group in one of the processions, which might include all members of the Inn not otherwise assigned a special role; as a satirist observed, 'they use Revels more than other men'.

The Benchers ruled the Inns like the Fellows of a college. At Candlemas, with many ceremonious exchanges of hippocras, they indulged in a slow and stately dance round the fire that still, in medieval fashion, was set in the centre of the Hall; but the 'young fry' – aged seventeen and upwards – were noted for wild behaviour and often hoped for a wilder reputation than they earned. Shakespeare's Justice Shallow boasted that as a member of Clement's Inn (an Inn of Chancery attached to the Inner Temple) he knew where the *bona robas* were, and fought with Sampson Stockfish, a fruiterer, behind Gray's Inn: 'I think they will talk of mad Shallow yet' (*2 Henry IV*, III.ii.14–15). John Davies, of the Middle Temple, satirized a country gentleman among the vulgar pleasures of Bankside, in the earliest group of fashionable *Epigrams* (1590):

> Publius, student at the common law,
> Oft leaves his books and for his recreation,
> To Paris Garden doth himself withdraw,
> Where he is ravished with such delectation
> As down among the dogs and bears he goes
> Where while he skipping cries, To head, to head,[3]
> His satin doublet and his velvet hose
> Are all with spittle from above bespread.
> Then is he like his father's country hall,
> Stinking with dogs and muted all with hawks,
> And rightly too on him this filth doth fall,
> Who for such filthy sports his books forsakes,
> Leaving old Plowden, Dyar and Brooks alone
> To see old Harry Hunks and Sackerson.

John Davies, *Poems*, ed. R. Krueger, 1975, pp. 184–9[4]

In the fifteenth century, the great lawyer Fortescue had advised the study of singing, music and dancing, and 'such other accomplishments and diversions (which are called Revels) as are suitable to their quality and such as are usually practised at Court'[5] In such sports, which lasted from supper to breakfast, the Lord of Misrule reigned from Christmas Eve till Twelfth Night or perhaps till Candlemas (2 February). Under the Tudors the Christ-mas Prince arrived to continue the education of the young by setting up a model of the royal Household. Such a Grand Christ-mas, as these Revels were called, happened at the Inns only from time to time, for it could become extremely costly. But music, dancing, poetry, spectacle, and wooing games were permitted. The competitive element was by no means absent from such occasions.

A comparison with the universities shews how relatively remote, unpretentious and limited were such festivities there. At St John's College, Cambridge, the statutes obliged the Fellows to act as 'Lord' in turn, and keep the three chests of clothing that were used for Christmas sport. The University Wits, who provided the first generation of dramatists, included sons of a country saddler, a shoemaker and a poor parson (Greene, Marlowe, Nashe), who went up on special charitable grants and could not possibly have afforded the Inns of Court. Thomas Lodge was an exception, but he was the son of a Lord Mayor of London.

The good will of the Inns was useful even to the greatest. The Earl of Leicester did not disdain to cultivate it at the Inner Temple; for him, in 1561, that Society produced the politically significant play of *Gorboduc*. A translation of Seneca's *Thyestes* had already hailed lawyers, 'Minerva's men', as 'the finest wits', taught how to write by the Muse herself. The first wave of English dramatic poetry to ripple the surface of mid-Tudor writing came from the Inns. When the professional players set up in London, the lawyers continued their courtly revels, the most extensive script to survive being the *Gesta Grayorum*, recording the reign of the Christmas Prince at Gray's Inn (the largest and wealthiest of the four Inns of Court) in 1594, when they performed plays of their own and also hired Shakespeare's company to perform *The Comedy of Errors*.

The Grayans in 1594 may have been celebrating the resumption of normal life in London, after two years of plague which had prorogued the Law Terms and shut down all festivity. There had been no such grandeur for many years. In mock royal style, the great of the land were invited to contribute: Lord Burghley sub-scribed £30. Household officers were elected; the Most Noble Order of the Helmet was established. Much depended on gorgeous costumes, for these helped rôle-playing. The show was spectacular and ceremonial, though the actual proceedings of the law were

absurdly parodied; orations and proclamations were interspersed
with plays, feasts and dancing. Thirty-three-year-old Francis
Bacon was among the wits who composed the scenario. In the latter part of the celebrations, the company moved out of the Inn,
visited the Lord Mayor, received a royal salute from the Gunners
at the Tower, and presented a masque at Court, *Proteus and the
Adamantine Rocks*, which so pleased the Queen that she invited
the Christmas Prince to take part in the jousting next day. This
was an exercise in public relations which at the same time, in private, allowed for a good deal of scurrility and horse-play.

The compliment to the Queen, 'true adamant of hearts', was
graceful, and yet in their plays the Inns had established a tradition
of discussing dangerous subjects, such as the succession, that
could never have been treated directly on the public stages. Here
however the Queen's policy might be criticized. (The Succession
Treatise of the great Plowden, advocating the Stuart claim for the
succession, had been written at the Middle Temple in 1566.)[6] In
the Halls of the Inns were the true private stages, where the young
men dramatized those topics that they had discussed at their 'bolt-
ings': disputes between Inner and Utter Barristers, held every
night in the year and combined with private amities and hatreds.
Hints could be picked up from the Revels to form the basis of
further disputings; private jokes would intensify their exclusive-
ness. There were notable Revels in 1597, the year Webster joined
as a freshman or 'puisne'; but the tone differed from those at
Gray's Inn only three years before, registering a change from
security and parody of accepted institutions to insecurity and
much more destructive infringements of order.

At the Middle Temple Revels of 1597–8 was reflected something of the split between the artificial cult of Astraea, the Virgin
Queen,[7] and the mortifying depth of bitterness, frustration and
cynicism that now surrounded a wrinkled, splenetic but powerful
old autocrat whose life stood between all and a dangerous, uncertain succession. The Court hyperbole by the players in an epilogue of 1599 wished that the children of her present Counsellors
of State might be 'grave and aged seen' at a Council Board where
she still presided. (See *The Riverside Shakespeare*, Appendix IV,
p. 1851, where it is tentatively attributed to Shakespeare himself.)
Elizabeth's state was known to her maids of honour, who had to
be dragooned into taking their turn of service; it was known to
young Essex, who flared into declaration that her mind was as

crooked as her carcase; it was known to all the inner circle. Her physical image had been fixed for the public by Hilliard. She herself would not use a mirror; she remained still Diana, Oriana, Pandora, publicly idolized, covertly judged.

The chief guest of honour at these special Revels, or Grand Christmas, of the Middle Temple, was the Earl of Essex himself, who, although the Queen's chief favourite, could sometimes bring disgrace upon himself by intemperate moodiness. The coachmaker's son, among the youngest members of the Inn, would see the great earl dining at the Benchers' Table, and get his first taste of an imitation of Court ceremony. For the Revels were intended to teach the young men the proper behaviour at a royal Court; the mock ritual was intended to be carried out with mock gravity. This had happened at Gray's Inn in 1594; but such decorum was not maintained on the later occasion.

The troubles at the Middle Temple in 1597–8 centred on John Davies, a twenty-nine-year-old Utter Barrister, whose satiric epigram has been quoted. He was one of a group from Winchester School that included the future Sir Henry Wotton and John Hoskyns, a talented writer who, however, had been expelled from New College six years previously for the extreme scurrility of the speech he made at Commencement as the Fool (*terrae filius*). Hoskyns was the son of a yeoman, Davies of a wealthy tanner from Wiltshire; all three were later to become famous, but they were now at the earliest, most competitive stage of their careers.

John Davies had already written and published his fantastic poem *Orchestra* (1596), in which the old idea of the cosmic dance was shewn by Love to 'fair Penelope, Ulysses' Queen'. Davies claimed to have written it in a fortnight, and his latest editor takes it as a parody of, or jest against, learning, a 'mock encomium, the genre that by praising the insignificant or contemptible prepares the rhetorician to argue on all sides of the question. Any Elizabethan who had ploughed through *De natura deorum* must have laughed heartily...' (Robert Krueger, Introduction to John Davies's *Poems*, 1975, p. lxiv.) If so, the final version of her Court dancing before Elizabeth – 'Our glorious English court's divine image, As it should be in this our golden age' – must surely be taken as the ambitious young man's true, ultimate objective.

Davies wished to present himself as a skilful, eloquent leader of the Revels. He ends with praise of other poets, beginning with

Chaucer and ending with 'the Swallow', the young recipient of
the dedication, 'his very friend, Richard Martin':

> To whom shall I this dauncing poem send
> This suddaine, rash, half-capriole of my wit?
> To you, first mover and sole cause of it,
> Mine own-selves better half, my dearest friend.

At court, dancing was the climax of the Revels, and it was prominent at the Inns; but for the ambitious young wits, the chance
to catch the eye of great nobles, and dance into favour (as some
did), prompted all they did. John Davies could never have hoped
to dance well himself; he was to be unflatteringly described by
John Manningham, of the Middle Temple, in his diary thus: 'John
Davies goes wadling with his arse out behind as though he were
about to make everyone he meets a wall to piss against . . . he never
walks but he carries a clokebag behind him, his arse sticks out
so far.' He was also pockmarked, whereas Martin was apparently
'of a cheerful and gracious countenance . . . tall bodied and well
proportioned; of a sweet and fair conversation'.[8]

No wonder then that Richard Martin, who earlier had riotously
played as Lord of Misrule, was elected as Prince d'Amour, whilst
Davies, who as the senior had collected £30 from the Earl of
Shrewsbury, was elected as his Fool and given the name of Stradilax. When everyone was playing the Fool in any case, and when
the tradition at the Middle Temple was mainly one of noise and
disorder, this was an invitation to broad farce, as well as exposing
Davies to being the butt of others. He bought for the occasion
some wildly expensive garments of marmalade-coloured tufftaffeta.

Among the nobles attending was the Earl of Northumberland,
a member of the Middle Temple, famous for his learning,[9] and
a friend of Ralegh; his wife was a sister of the Earl of Essex.
Sir Charles Blount was also a member of the Inn, which he had
entered in 1579 and from whence he first gained, as Sir Christopher Hatton had before him, the favourable notice of the
Queen;[10] he was the acknowledged lover of Lady Penelope Rich,
Essex's elder sister. Her attendance at the Revels can be established from the dedication to her during the next year of the *Diana*
of Montemayor, translated by Bartholomew Young, a member of
the Society who mentioned playing French orator at these Revels.
Lord Rich, who had accompanied the Earl of Shrewsbury on
the Embassy to Paris, would therefore also have been present;

indeed, the Embassy may have provided the special occasion of these Revels and induced their particularly bawdy tone. Davies, as Fool, took upon him the further name of Erophilus, or Exophilus, 'in saucy imitation' of the Earl of Essex – a jest that, except in the Earl's presence, would have lost its point. The young men may have limited themselves to the 'low style', as being easier for amateurs, although as much earlier as 1591 the precocious Davies had written an oration for an entertainment for Lord Burghley and provided an epithalamium for the marriage of Lord Burghley's grand-daughter to the Earl of Derby in January 1595.

He was in fact making his way upward by his skill in providing entertainments, but on this occasion he seems to have been piqued by the rôle assigned to him. The excitement of the Revels generated intense feelings. As usual, they contained mock orations and such regular paradoxes as a speech in favour of woman's inconstancy.[11] The mood for love poetry was itself satiric, in the tone of the fashionable poems of young John Donne, late of Lincoln's Inn and at this time Secretary to the Lord Keeper, Egerton.

The first events of the 1597–8 Revels were held within the Inn, as was customary, but afterwards moved out to City and Court. On 27 December Stradilax was satirized and on New Year's Eve he made three 'confessions'. On 8 January he recited an obscene 'comparison of pork', which offended the noble ladies present – the Christmas Prince was dining with 'a royal gentleman'. Afterwards the ceremonies renewed the league of amity with Lincoln's Inn, and on Candlemas night the Prince resigned, after hearing advice from his Counsellors: 'One advised him to follow the Sea; another to Land travel; a third to marry a rich widow; and a fourth to study the Common Law. He chose the last and refused not the third if she stood in his way.' Stradilax's appearance was mocked by the Orator, a young poet whom Davies had honoured in the conclusion of *Orchestra*, and the oration was applauded in John Hoskyns's 'Fustian Answer' to this 'Tufftaffeta Oration', made extempore in old-fashioned language at the petition of Sir Walter Ralegh; it is largely a parody of Wilson's *Art of Rhetoric*. To the Orator Hoskyns declared:

Alas what am I whose ears have been purgited with tenacity of your speeches and whose nose[12] hath been perfumed with the aromicity of your Sentences that I should answer your oration both voluminous and tropical with a replication coarse and curtal for you are able in troops of tropes and centuries of Sentences to muster your meaning nay you have such

woodpiles of words that unto you a Cooper is but a Carpenter and Rider
himself deserves no Reader.

He goes on to utter the nonsense that 'Even as the snow advanced
upon the points of cacuminous mountains dissolveth and coagu-
leth itself into humourous liquidity even so' the Prince is disposed
to resign. It may be imagined what covert jests at the expense of
the ever-young royal virgin of sixty-five might have been perpe-
trated, under the forms of compliment; what general scurrility
ensued in Court as the Orator was condemned, as discontented
lover, to prison in the Fort of Fancy, and legal proceedings were
inaugurated under the Prince's laws: 'If any man swear his foul
Mistress fair, his old Mistress young, or his crooked Mistress
straight ... he shall be condemned as a foresworn Sorcerer for
the one and a false seducer of the innocent in the other', or 'If
any subject naturally born, for want of Wit court his Mistress with
the fruits of silence ... he shall be imprisoned in the Isle of Idiocy
and censured by the Bishop of St Asses.'

In the 'New Year's Honours', Stradilax created himself a lord;
but epigrams against him were posted up throughout the City at
Queen Hithe, Newgate, the Stocks, Pillory, Piss Conduit and 'but
that the Provost Marshall was his inward friend, it should not have
missed Bridewell'. Exactly a week after the Revels ended, the Fool
made a mad assault on the Prince. On 9 February 1598, as the
Minutes were to record, he entered

with his hat on his head and armed with a dagger and attended by two
persons armed with swords; and going up to the Barristers' table, where
Richard Martin was sitting quietly at dinner, he pulled out from under
his gown a cudgel, commonly called a bastinado (subito sub toga detrahens
baculum quem vulgariter vocant *a bastinado*) and struck him over the head
repeatedly with such violence that the bastinado was shivered into many
pieces. Then returning to the bottom of the Hall, he drew one of the swords
belonging to his attendants, and flourished it repeatedly over his head, turning his face towards Martin, and then hurrying down the water steps of
the Temple, threw himself into a boat.

He was disbarred, expelled from the Society, 'never to return',
and also sent to jail.

This tragic-farcical end of a promising youthful career was as
close as the Revels of the Inns of Court ever approached to that
very common stage situation in which government was over-
turned, or wrongs were avenged, by a set of masquers. The pre-
carious relation between jest and earnest, the disruptive breaking

of rituals which were designed to contain violence, became central in the plays of both Marston and Webster.

Davies retired to Oxford. He vigorously pursued his writing, in a lofty strain, and sought the advocacy of his friends for reinstatement. *Nosce Teipsum* (1599) was, on the advice of Charles Blount, dedicated to the Queen; the Earl of Northumberland also stood Davies's friend, as another specially dedicated copy witnessed. More Court entertainments were written for Burghley's son, Robert Cecil (himself a hunchback), who, with the Lord Chief Justice Popham and the Lord Keeper Egerton, succeeded finally, after Davies had suffered three years' penance, in gaining readmission for him. On 31 October 1601 Davies made his humble apology. Before long, Charles Blount's influence in Ireland obtained for him the position of Irish Attorney-General, and he spent nearly all his working life there, later becoming Solicitor-General.

His series of acrostic verses on the Queen, *Astraea*, which was entered in the Stationers' Register on Accession Day 1599, represents the smoothest pastoral vision of a nymph enjoying eternal spring – an enamelled image to match Hilliard's portraits. In her very latest entertainment, in summer 1602, Davies shewed Time standing still in her presence – a necessary fiction, a heroic absurdity, an Arcadian dream, but a game played with a true queen, not a mock prince.

Rough badinage and a contest of wits might be no indication of personal hostility, for, from their childhood, disputes were practised by schoolboys; Paul's churchyard rang to the contests between them. But in the bitterness of his exclusion, in *Nosce Teipsum* Davies recognized that 'the desire to know first made men Fools' – and the wages of Folly might be death:

> Like him that knew not poison's power to kill
> Until (by tasting it) himself was slain.

The Law ('Minerva') could not teach him what now he knows too well:

> I know my life's a pain and but a span,
> I know my sense is mock'd with everything;
> And to conclude, I know myself a *Man*
> Which is a proud and yet a wretched thing.

Davies was not alone in the disastrous freedom with which he reacted to what appears to have been a baiting from Martin, his 'dearest friend'; and for much slighter uses of such freedom, though in a more public manner, Wotton and Hoskyns were both to be disgraced by James I. Wotton's career was cut short in about 1611. Hoskyns spent a whole year as close prisoner in the Tower, in rooms from which the light of day was barred.[13] Aubrey reports that in his youth he had fought a duel with his friend Benjamin Rudyard, the narrator of the Revels; in his middle age Hoskyns wrote to his wife, 'I cannot be persuaded that any man that hath wit of his own is afraid of another's wit, as no good soldier that hath a sword fears another man's sword, and for my part I had rather die with wit than live without it.'

Hoskyns's book *Directions for Speech and Style* (?1599), written for the guidance of a young fellow Templar with whose family he was acquainted, restores decorum to the Inn: the author of the 'Fustian Answer' puts forward brevity, perspicuity, 'as Ladyes use in their attire, a kind of diligent negligence', and, lastly, 'respect', as principles to help in discerning what is fitting. In illustrating the terms of rhetoric, Hoskyns makes use of his 'Fustian Answer' to show their misuse. Correct usages are drawn from one work alone – Sidney's *Arcadia*, first published in 1590. Hoskyns held this up as the model of how a gentleman should write and speak in English. Although it uses rhetorical terms, his treatise is practical and succinct, designed to improve the young lawyer's own case and discredit his opponent's.

Brevity, clarity, simplicity and 'life, which is the very strength and sinew, as it were of your writing' should be combined with 'respect', or a sense of the tactful words to use on any occasion. He advises comparing of contraries, as 'He that prefers wealthy ignorance before chargeable study, prefers contempt before honour, darkness before light, and earth before heaven' (page 21).[14] He also, like Sidney, favours irony: 'He was no notorious malefactor, but he had been twice on the pillory and once burned in the hand for trifling oversights' (page 26). Although a book of synonyms is useful, he scorns them, as they are 'foamed out by schoolmasters', and he also scorns sententious formulae: 'It is very true that a sentence is a pearl in discourse, but is it a good discourse that is all pearl?' (page 39).[15] The ease and confidence of Hoskyns's *Directions* shew the distance that lay between himself and such mid-Tudor works as Wilson's *Art of Rhetoric* (1561), which he parodies, or even Mulcaster's writings of 1581 and 1582. Rhetoric is his servant, not his discipline. He takes what he wants as an advocate and a tutor. If Mulcaster could have talked –

rather impatiently, perhaps – with Shakespeare's schoolmaster Holofernes, Hoskyns would have joined with the courtiers to mock him.

Sidney himself had thought the wit of 'small learned courtiers' preferable to that of schoolmasters. He would have admired the heroic pastoral blandness of Davies's *Astraea*, the 'half-capriole' of *Orchestra* – a poem which Hoskyns condemns as being like 'the German magnificence, that serves all the good meat in one dish' (pages 22–3). Hoskyns's little treatise was used by Ben Jonson and copied by many later writers, for it was well calculated to strengthen a thinking use of the 'figures'.

For the purpose of the Revels, Sidney's love poetry also provided a model. He had mocked 'poor Petrarch's long deceased woes' and had mocked himself with his much admired *ironia*, for which his friend Fulke Greville (also a member of the Middle Temple) had so praised him. He knew how to practise gentlemanly negligence, *sprezzatura*:

> Fly, fly, my friends, I have my death's wound, fly:
> See there that boy, that murdering boy, I say,
> Who, like a thief, hid in dark bush doth lie,
> Till bloody bullet get him wrongful prey.
> [*Astrophel and Stella*, sonnet xx

Yet Astrophel, shot through with a white wench's black eye, found the evil in his world grotesquely ridiculous. In the Realm of the Young Knight – bright and youthful, alert and intelligent – even dragons, however horrid, were only dragons.

The generations of Davies, Hoskyns and Martin, and of Marston and Webster, had lost Sidney. In Davies, or Hoskyns, the protest and code-breaking is at first lightly done; it is part of a game. The 'Gulling Sonnet', which makes light of Davies's own tragedy, is a mock confession of great courage (or bravado):

> Into the Middle Temple of my heart
> The wanton Cupid did himself admit,
> And gave for pledge your eagle sighted witt
> That he would play no rude uncivil part
> Long time he cloaked his nature with his art,
> And sad and grave and sober he did sitt;
> But at last he gan to revel it,
> To break good rules and order to pervert.
> Then love and his young pledge were both convented
> Before sad Reason, that old Bencher grave,
> Who this sad sentence unto him presented

By diligence, that sly and secret knave:
That love and wit for ever should depart
Out of the Middle Temple of my heart.

Indeed, Davies was reckless enough to jeopardize his reinstatement by yet another jest. He was said to have written, whilst in prison,

Now Davis for a bird is in
But yet it is but for a Martin.

Sixteen years' banishment in Ireland were to make a good lawyer out of Davies; his series of *Reports* were most respectfully dedicated to Lord Chancellor Ellesmere, who had been his good friend during his distress. He returned to England in 1619.

Davies died of apoplexy the day before he was admitted as Lord Chief Justice; his enemy Martin expired of a surfeit a month after being made Recorder of London. Hoskyns, having made a rich marriage, and having also secured his two step-daughters' portions by marriages to his younger brother and a nephew (his matrimonial career sounds like a blueprint for a comedy), died as Sergeant Hoskyns. All three lawyers remained but amateurs of the pen. In the writings of John Marston, the younger member of the Inn whose work was to be publicly burned, along with Davies's scurrilous epigrams, in 1599, the mood of the Revels passed into theatrical currency. Their effect on John Webster, the obscure freshman from the City, was not to be revealed for a decade.

John Marston came from Warwickshire, where his father was Recorder of the severely Protestant town of Coventry, with a house in the market-place. His mother, *née* Maria Guarsi, was the daughter of an Italian physician, and through her he was a cousin to Everard Guilpin, who made something of a name for himself at Gray's Inn, rivalling Davies as an epigrammatist. The epigram, which anatomized London society, was a medium in which the brilliant, alienated youth of the day could assert themselves against the world: it was classical, therefore confident; it was authoritative, and therefore offered an appearance of conviction; but the world depicted was insecure, a world of knaves and fools. The epigrammatist, or the satirist, drew recognizable portraits whilst protesting that he was depicting only vice in general.

Marston's father, who had been Lent Reader at the Middle Temple in 1592, by this means secured a special entry for his son at the age of sixteen, with exemption from the customary residence requirements; the young John Marston thus began as a very privileged student, possibly in 1595. Eroticism and satire, both fashionable, were his scandalous choice for poetry of an ambivalent, yet pointed, wit, and at the same time he achieved a personal tone which is unmistakable and which sets him apart from the common conventions of Davies, Guilpin or Hoskyns. It was wickedly and accurately parodied by Ben Jonson:

> Ramp up my Phlegon Muse, be not afraid
> But boldly nominate a spade a spade
> ... for now we list
> Of strenuous vengeance to clutch the fist.

The Malcontent, his masterpiece, however, is written in a totally different style.

The élement of parody in Marston's drama for the Choristers' Theatre has been the subject of a critical debate.[16] He exploits his own scepticism by a new version of the old Revenge convention – a large example of code-breaking.

Meanwhile, in the year of the disastrous Revels, Marston had satirized John Davies as Ruscus. Ruscus was one who dropped letters of commendation (written to himself) for others to read; who clutched at some distinguished figure, holding on 'with nods and legs and odd superfluous talk'.[17] Marston's own method of commendation was different: 'He that thinks worse of my rhymes than myself, I scorn him, for he cannot: he that thinks better, is a fool.'

That Marston himself was influenced by the Revels of the Inn may be seen in one of his last comedies, *The Fawn*, where he ends with a Parliament of Cupid, to try offenders, closely modelled on the judicial court of the Prince d'Amour.

Marston considered himself an expert on City vice, even in matters where the coach-maker's son might have had better information:

> Shall Lucea scorn her husband's lukewarm bed?
> Because her pleasure being hurried
> In jolting Coach with glassy instrument
> Doth far exceed the Paphian blandishment.[18]
> [*The Scourge of Villainy*, II, ll. 121–4

But Marston's achievement was to put this into English verse – really to extend the boundaries of what it was not only possible but fashionable to say.

His invitation to his readers is itself an insult:

> I'll keep open hall,
> A common and a sumptuous festival;
> Welcome all eyes, all ears, all tongues to me,
> Gnaw, peasants, on my scraps of poesy.
>   [*The Scourge of Villainy*, I, ll. 27–30

Having written a pornographic *Metamorphosis of Pygmalion's Image* to melt his stony, and probably imaginary, mistress, he now claims it as a satire on erotic poetry and disclaims all Petrarchists or brothellists

> Using enchantments, exorcisms, charms,
> The oil of sonnets, wanton blandishment,
> The force of tears and seeming languishment
> Unto the picture of a painted lass.
>   [*The Scourge of Villainy*, VIII, ll. 89–92

His first play, written for the next Christmas sports, satirizes the common players in a sketch built on an old moral framework. Marston's poetry can never be accepted wholeheartedly, for everything is open to repudiation or substitution. In 1599 his father died, mournfully testifying to his 'wilful disobedient son's' disregard of the law, adding: 'God bless him and give him true knowledge of himself and to forgo his delight in plays, vain studies and fooleries.'

Instead, Marston took to writing for the newly re-opened Choristers' Theatre at St Paul's. The treacherous Revels which were played by children were more murderous than those at the court of a Christmas Prince, yet, as presented by these children, even further from reality. Marston always hoped the true 'sons of Maia' would support him, but when he was put to scorn on the stage in Jonson's *Poetaster*, it was Richard Martin, as Jonson was later to testify in a grateful dedication, who ensured the appearance of *The Poetaster*, which could not have been considered other than an unfriendly act to his fellow Templarian.

Dramatic prose adds ferocity to the attack on women:

I was wont ... call her whore; but now that antiquity leaves her as an old piece of plastic t'work by I only ask her how her rotten teeth fare every morning and so leave her. She was the first that ever invented perfumed smocks for the gentlewomen and woollen shoes, for fear of creaking, for the visitant. She were an excellent lady, but that her face peeleth like Muscovy glass.

> [*The Malcontent*. I, viii. 35–42

Ben Jonson had first introduced this style to the private theatres; its transmission to Webster may be seen in his character of an old lady:

Bosola. To behold thee not painted inclines somewhat near a miracle; these in thy face here were deep ruts and foul sloughs in the last progress; there was a lady in France that having had the small pox, flayed the skin off her face to make it more level and whereas before she looked like a nutmeg grater, after she resembled an abortive hedgehog....
Old Lady. Do you call this painting?
Bosola. No, no but you call it careening of an old morphew'd lady, to make her disembogue again. There's rough cast phrase to your plastique.
[*The Duchess of Malfi*, II. i. 26–36

Using familiar and noble sentiments in new and shocking contexts, Marston attacks the follies of London itself (the pride of ambassadors, a contemporary issue in 1604), and its religious hypocrisies. This, the gravest undertone in the whole piece, makes it not inconceivable that the author of such virulent satire should himself within five years renounce the theatre for the pulpit and take holy orders. This was not before, in August 1608, he had expiated the scandal of his plays by a spell in Newgate jail. When finally, many years later, he was buried in the Temple Church beside his father, his tombstone bore the inscription 'Oblivioni sacrum'.

In his Malcontent, the figure of the Prince and the figure of the Fool become one and the same. The curiously close relation of King and Fool was traditional, but not to have one man play both parts. As a means of returning from banishment, the Malcontent plays the fool at the usurper's court, where he triumphs in the disguise of the Revels. The traditional rôles assigned to Martin and Davies also are fused. A masked dance is made the occasion of the usurper's overthrow.

A younger writer at the Middle Temple assiduously imitated Marston in two plays, *The Fleire* and *Cupid's Whirligig*, which in their own day enjoyed success at the Blackfriars and the Whitefriars Theatres. Edward Sharpham, a gentleman of a Devonshire family, was entered at Michaelmas 1594 as a pupil of Sir John Davies, to whom as 'my beloved Master' he offered a congratulatory sonnet for his *Humours in Heaven on Earth* (1605). The lines of Davies's former poems are 'dark', but these, he says, are 'most familiar' and will spread his fame widely.

Sharpham is not 'dark' so much as 'subdued to what he works

in': the idiom of drama peculiar to the Inns. It is almost as if he were writing in one of those private languages that evolve in schools, the fighting services, the sports arena. But his units are not slang words; they are dramatic conventions. The story of *The Fleire* is a parody of *The Malcontent, The Fawn* and *The Dutch Courtesan*, with echoes of Marlowe and Shakespeare, and of the plays that Dekker and Webster had written for the Children of Paul's. The Duke, here named Antifront, in exile in London, serves as pander to his two daughters under the disguise of the Fleire (or flouter). They have set up as courtesans but make themselves so common that they are called whores. They subsequently try to engage in a little light-hearted poisoning, are detected and prevented, and eventually married off to members of foreign and English nobility!

The text reads as if it were a collection of after-dinner stories which had supplied Sharpham with a libretto. Only in the context of about half-a-dozen other plays does *The Fleire* acquire any meaning at all; deprived in the course of time of its particular context, his verbal wit is in itself as flat as stale beer. The frigidity of the bawdry, resembling the worst of John Ford's,[19] derives from a callow group of young men. Some of the emphasis is now on their poverty. In the opening scene a young gentleman is seeking employment as gentleman usher; and to the query of Lady Florida, 'Are you a gentleman?' he replies, 'Yes, sure, madam, for I was both born and begotten in an Inns a Court.' To which a waiting gentlewoman responds, 'Sure, madam, then he's a gentleman, for he that's but admitted to the house is a gentleman, much more he that's begotten in the house' (I. 137–43). Elsewhere the Inns of Court 'puny' (freshman) is said to slander gentlewomen and claim the favours of citizens' daughters, but to lie with his laundress. One Inns of Court man is found in hell, damned for having money in his purse.

When Sharpham died in April 1608, at Westminster, he made William Gayton of Westminster, a Merchant Taylor, his residuary legatee. Gayton had only pitiful bequests to dispose of ('To my cousin William Langworthy my pale carnation silk stockings'). Francis Beaumont, of the Inner Temple, son of a Judge of the Common Pleas, was reputedly poor enough when with John Fletcher, son of a former bishop, he took to working for the common players, the King's Men. It appears that the Inns were attracting young men to seek their fortune on the fringes of the extravagant Stuart court. Webster was saved from this kind of insecurity; but, as his father's coachyard was close at hand, he may have suffered some insolence from the gentry which Davies, the tanner's son from Wiltshire, or Hoskyns, the yeoman's son, escaped. (This Inn had however special connections with the West Country and all the Western men knew their own region. (Webster made use of two witticisms from Sharpham's second play, *Cupid's Whirligig*, for Flamineo in *The White Devil*, and Sharpham referred respectfully to the plays *Westward Ho!* and *Northward Ho!* in which Webster collaborated; see page 113.)

Both the practice of their skill and the manner of their life disposed the lawyers to enjoy, and to create, plays. Their own revelling was seasonal, whereas by the end of the sixteenth century the theatre was a permanent institution. In dedicating his second play to the 'noblest nurseries of liberty and humanity in the kingdom', the Inns of Court, Ben Jonson recommended it for reading only when 'the cap and gown is off and the lord of liberty reigns'.

The lawyer's habit of mind requires him to become expert in all the facts of a case, and then to forget it in favour of his next case. This develops a memory like that of an actor, who must similarly immerse himself in his part and then discard it. It is natural for a lawyer to think in terms of alternative points of view; it is also essential for him to controvert his opponent by turning his words against himself, making his plea his undoing. This too is the art of dramatic irony. The practice of the law, involving an art of performance, is fenced and safeguarded by ritual and ceremony.

It was a lawyer's training that produced the new style of the essayist. Bacon's first collection appeared in the same year that John Webster appeared at the Middle Temple. Worldly wisdom constructed an idiom which lent itself to the theatre, whose language is so much more complex than words on a page, being sharpened to define what lies below the surface of life. Bacon's essay 'On Revenge' ('Revenge is a kind of wild justice . . .') is the best brief statement of the ethics behind the Revenge Play of his time.

What Webster had learnt from his school education was a respect for English authorities as well as for the classics, so that, although he praised classic models, he followed English ones. What he acquired from the Inns was a taste for pageantry, a preference for indoor staging, a knowledge of the value of trial scenes, practice in verbal satire and perhaps some insight into the psychology of violence. Above all, he acquired a friend and mentor in the person of John Marston, whose style was to shape his own greatest works.

CHAPTER THREE

The Lady of St Bartholomew's: a London Legend

It has already appeared that whilst the satiric bitterness of the theatre to which Marston's first Jacobean writings belonged represented a corrupt court, a dark place of the spirit, the style which was recommended to the young lawyers by Hoskyns was based on Sidney's *Arcadia*. This work continued to go through edition after edition, to be translated into French, Italian, German and Dutch, and to keep its popularity throughout the seventeenth century. It offered the ideal of humanist nobility – an English model, for Sidney's social concerns had always distinguished him from the Italian courtly model of Castiglione, although he carried Castiglione in his pocket. Sidney himself was an ideal who was not forgotten. In 1624 Webster's latest work revived him as one of the chief inhabitants of the Temple of Honour (see page 181).

The funeral of Sidney, an event of Webster's childhood, a great and pompous display of national mourning, must have engaged the Webster family professionally – the hearses, the palls, the mourning cloaks and plumes must have taxed the united tradesmen of London to provide them. Chivalry was dead. The dark world of the satirist is the obverse of the bright world of the pastoralist, and the two figures – satyr and shepherd – are sometimes opposed in pediments, in frontispieces or in masques.[1] The ornate and artificial fashioning of Sidney's gallery of 'speaking pictures' in *Arcadia* displays the main characters in varying moods and situations but always unremittingly heroic, always on the top note. Young Prince Pyrocles is introduced in a shipwreck:

Upon this mast they saw a young man – at least, if he were a man – bearing the show of about eighteen years, who sat as on horseback, having nothing upon him but his shirt, which being wrought with blue silk and gold had a kind of resemblance to the sea, on which the sun, then near his western

home, did shoot some of his beams . . . holding his head up, full of unmoved
majesty, he held a sword aloft with his fair arm, which often he waved
about his crown, as though he would threaten the world in that extremity.

[*Arcadia*, Bk 1, ed. Feuillerat, 1965, p. 10

Pyrocles appears like a god of the sea, though later his disguise
as an Amazon produces an ambiguity of another kind. The king
falls in love with him, and the queen, who has penetrated his disguise, does the same, whilst his beauty and valour combined
enable him to overcome an armed mob storming the king's retreat.
These characters are presented in a much more realistic way; they
appear rather like a group of modern workmen, under Sidney's
keen but not unfriendly observation:

the town dwellers demanding putting down of imposts; the country fellows
laying out of commons . . . for the artisans, they would have corn and wine
set at a lower price and bound to be kept so still; the ploughmen, vine
labourers and farmers would none of that. The countrymen demanded that
every man might be free in the chief towns; that could not the burgesses
like of. The peasants would have all gentlemen destroyed; the citizens,
especially such as cooks, barbers and those others that lived most on gentlemen, would but have them reformed. . . .

[*Arcadia*, Bk 2, ed. cit., p. 315.

Sidney could range freely between the high style and the low; the
low style was kept for the wicked. The ambiguities of his golden
world of heroics are accentuated by the revision of the early version
and by its more moral design; in the first version, the Amazon
was discovered in bed with the heroine Philoclea, whilst the other
hero, Musedorus, attempted to rape the Princess Pamela.

Webster's ambiguities were of a different kind from Sidney's;
but they arose from the need to reconcile the golden world of Sidney and the brazen world of Marston. The splendour of his Italy
is the splendour of Arcadian beauty and chivalry mixed with
another, an incompatible, element. The result is explosive.

Sidney's presence is represented directly in Webster's tragedy
in two ways. He makes wide use of the classical tragic writing of
William Alexander, Earl of Stirling, whose 'Monarchical Tragedies', monuments of unactable dullness, were written for Sidney's sister, the Countess of Pembroke, and her circle according
to the classic recipe. Webster hankered after this style, as he confessed in the preface to *The White Devil*, but he hankered equally
after the live stage. He took Alexander's choric maxims and put
them into his dialogue, sharpened and improved by his mordant

wit. (Alexander later completed the unfinished *Arcadia*, at the Countess of Pembroke's request.)

At the climax of his masterpiece, *The Duchess of Malfi*, Webster directly quotes for the first time from that part of *Arcadia*, Book II, which describes the imprisonment of the two heroines, Pamela and Philoclea, by the evil Cecropia, who 'with eyes cast like a horse that would strike at the stirrup', is cowed by the captive Pamela's 'fair majesty of unconquered virture', in which 'Captivity might seem to have authority over tyranny'. Pamela shed 'a light more than human, which gave lustre to her perfection', as the Duchess of Malfi's dead face dazzled the eyes of her brother: 'Cover her face: mine eyes dazzle: she died young.'

Though his tragic scene is so different, yet Webster's heightened style is the equivalent of Sidney's. The Duchess's banter of her husband (III. ii. 61–2),

> You have cause to love me, I enter'd you into my heart
> Before you would vouchsafe to call for the keys,

no less than her stateliness in prison (IV. i. 5–8),

> a behaviour so noble
> As gives a majesty to adversity:
> You may discern the shape of loveliness
> More perfect in her tears than in her smiles,

are taken directly from *Arcadia*. The waxwork shows of her dead husband and children with which the Duchess is tormented are also copied from *Arcadia*, where each of the Princesses is shewn the 'execution' of the other. Prince Pyrocles, who also sees the supposed death of Philoclea, cries to a servant who wishes him long life, 'And I soon death to you, for the horrible curse you have given me.' The Duchess is given this cry of despair (IV. i. 93–4). Later, when she asks her waiting maid, 'What do I look like now?' the reply, once more reshaped from *Arcadia*, defines the emblematic and eternalized image or icon which is grief incarnate:

> Like to your picture in the gallery,
> A deal of life in show, but none in practice.
> [IV. ii. 31–2

As a miniaturist will sparingly touch in pure gold, so Webster kept for the strongest moments the pure gold-on-black of Philip Sidney. Sidney himself (and the images he created) became sacred icons. The supreme example of this use was the later adaptation, in *Eikon Basilike*, of the captive Pamela's prayer for the captive King Charles I.

Webster belonged to the group of 'citizens that lived most on gentlemen', and his reliance on models is as plain as his skill in adapting them. He used the old model of Revenge tragedy, built by his former schoolfellow Kyd, for a totally different purpose. He used Alexander's tragedy (and the pirated *Tragedy of Mustapha* of Sidney's closest friend, Fulke Greville) but modified them also. For a received tradition, he offered a personal variant. But every writer in the high style needed a heroic lady for service – even if, like the lady of that last tragic exemplar of chivalry, Don Quixote, she were largely a figment of his imagination. Webster had within the priory of St Bartholomew the great lady who had adorned the Revels of the Middle Temple in 1597–8 – the beloved of Sidney, Essex's sister – but he knew her also in poetry so powerful that Gabriel Harvey thought it could be substituted for that of Homer or Virgil. Penelope was identified with Philoclea, the younger heroine of *Arcadia*, although Sidney had probably begun the romance before he met and fell in love with her. The elder heroine was identified with the Countess of Pembroke. With the waning of the cult of Astraea, as practised by Davies, the image of Essex's sister, acknowledged queen of his little court, would have attracted all those who could feel her closeness to – and her remoteness from – themselves.

Sidney's sonnets are the most dramatic of all sequences, except Shakespeare's; and his *Arcadia* was the basis for many plays; one of the most successful, Beaumont and Fletcher's *Philaster*, is close in time to Webster's great plays. But the generation that had lost Sidney discovered the dramatic possibilities of the bad woman: the great lady insolent in her power, like Marston's Duchess Aurelia in *The Malcontent;* the bawds like Macquerelle; vindictive whores like the Dutch Courtesan. These plays were the productions of the children's theatre at St Paul's and Blackfriars, patronized by the lawyers, where Webster also made his contribution in his two City comedies. In the great tragedies however he blends what he has learnt from this work with the deep intensity, the high relief that is found in Sidney's heroic figures. In this he approaches somewhere near the supreme example of the heroic and the naturalistic in fusion – Shakespeare's Cleopatra.

The plays contain details that link them with London, as in a great painting some little feature may introduce a familiar note.

For example, *The White Devil* contains, in the midst of its Italian splendours, odd references to Irish customs (I. ii. 30–2; IV. i. 73; IV. ii. 95–7) which would link up with Penelope's later life, as well as with the Tower of London, with Wales, with 'the art of Wolner in England'. (He swallowed glass, iron etcetera as a trickster at inns and fairs.)

As *Arcadia* itself was a model for noble imitation, and anticipated in some ways the function of a Court masque, presenting an enlarged and purer version of the self for its courtly performers, so Webster, like Marston before him, presented the deep ambiguities, the beauty and deformity, the misery and splendour of the great, but with a new kind of bitter intimacy. The noblest courage feeds and fuels the blindest egoism; the Duchess of Malfi, dismissing any threat to her wishes, reveals to the spectators her dangerous over-security. 'But for your brothers?' brings from her

> Do not think of them...
> Yet should they know it, time will easily
> Scatter the tempest.
>   [I. i. 468–72

Webster succeeded more powerfully than Marston in bringing his Evil Place, his Italian court, into focus; its characters were seen as flesh and blood, not as puppets. It may be that he needed his adult actors – whose praise he carefully set out (see pp. 119–20) – to animate the 'speaking pictures'. The technique by which memories of his young manhood were worked into his tragedy cannot be formally analysed as the constituents of some chemical compound can be analysed, and a formula supplied. He was not even writing for a patron, as Shakespeare apparently was in his sonnets. He had worked at his craft with others and proved his skill; in his two great plays he wrote for himself ('Non inferiora secutus' is the motto on the title-page of *The White Devil*) and for the ages.

If there can and should be no crude and direct identification here, of the kind which invites decoding, the story of the Lady of St Bartholomew's demonstates that the paradoxes of those tragedies could be matched from the tragedian's own neighbourhood. It is presented as part of Webster's London.

When, after a lifetime's devotion, the Earl of Devonshire, Charles Blount, married the woman who had borne his five sons, King

James told him that he had married 'a fair woman with a black soul'. Before this, Penelope Devereux had for twenty-four years been the unwilling wife of Robert, third Baron Rich, whose inheritance included the Priory of St Bartholomew, which had been her London home. For Smithfield, the Great House dominated the neighbourhood, as would a manor in the country.

Penelope gained power as the sister of the Earl of Essex, whose fall and execution in February 1601 led to her own imprisonment. When finally she shared the triumph of her faithful lover Charles Blount, the most successful soldier of the age, conqueror of Ireland, who had repelled the Spaniards at Kinsale and subdued Tyrone, their attempt to legitimize their union came to shipwreck and neither long survived the disappointment.

Many poets acclaimed Sidney's Stella – Spenser, Daniel, Constable, Matthew Gwynne, John Davies of Hereford and young John Ford. Daniel implicitly and Ford explicitly celebrated her in their elegies for the Earl of Devonshire, Ford prefixing to his a very lame acrostic on her title, defying those who would deny it to her, and ending, 'I strive to please not many'.

Fame, even identity, came to women through the tributes of men. 'He was a sun and she a moon,' sang one of those celebrating the dead Sidney. Matthew Roydon declared that Sidney had improved her natural beauty:

> Although thy beauty do exceed
> In common sight of every eye;
> Yet in his poesies we read,
> It is apparent more thereby.
> He that hath love and judgment too
> Sees more than any others do.
> (*Elegy or Friend's Passion for his Astrophel*)

Spenser presented her as the inspiration of Sidney's great deeds; she was the 'siren' of Campion's epigram:

> Penelope, Astrophili quae vultu incendit amores
> Olim, et voce ducem dulci incantabit Hibernicum

('Penelope, whose beauty lit the fire of love in Astrophil in former days, and who with her sweet voice enchanted the Irish general').

No portrait of Penelope, if any survive, has been identified; but her beautiful mother, Lettice Knollys, transmitted the striking black eyes and golden hair, an inheritance of the Boleyns which they shared with the Queen. Mary Boleyn, grandmother of

Lettice, sister to Queen Anne Boleyn and, some said, her prede-
cessor in the favour of Henry VIII.

With her beauty, Lettice transmitted also independence, vehe-
mence and courage; Penelope seems to have escaped the moodiness that clogged her brother's vitality. Indeed, Lettice Knollys,
thrice widowed, was to live till 1640; and even at ninety years of
age she was to walk briskly at her country home at Chartley, in
Stafford, where she had brought up her four children while her
first husband, Walter, Earl of Essex, was campaigning in Ireland.
He had made some move to betroth his eldest child, Penelope,
to the heir of his trusted second-in-command, Sir Henry Sidney,
before, in 1576, he collapsed and died at the age of thirty-six from
that scourge of armies, dysentery.

When two years later his widow married the great Earl of
Leicester, it was rumoured that her first husband had been poisoned
by his successor. He did not foster the Essex children; they had
been committed to the devout Earl of Huntingdon, President of
the Council of the North – whose wife however was Leicester's
sister Catherine. Children of the nobility seldom lived at home,
but were placed to their advantage – or their parents'.

Family networks produced political units and economic fighting
groups. At court, anyone of eminence would be related in a variety
of ways to the rest of their circle.

In the sixteenth century, kin groupings remained powerful in politics,
but slowly gave way to religious conviction and personal ambition as the
state strengthened its grip on society and began to attract loyalties to itself.
Even so, much of the political in-fighting of the century revolved round
certain kinship rivalries, in particular that between the Howards and the
Dudleys. ... It has been shown conclusively that clientage was a primary
cement of faction in the Elizabethan period....[2]

Marriage was an economic treaty between two families, and the
individuals might not even meet until their parents or guardians
had settled the matter. Fluctuations in family groups might be
compared to modern market quotations; the marriage market was
rigorously organized in money terms. Intermarriage as a way of
social bonding led to early betrothals, and to remarriage of the
widowed.

Penelope was thirteen, Philip Sidney twenty-two when the first
moves were made by her father towards betrothal. But Sir Henry
was not entirely devoted to Essex; moreover, Philip as heir
presumptive to his childless uncles, the Earls of Leicester and

Warwick, was worth keeping in the market – he was indeed being sought in marriage for a Princess of Orange, but the Queen forbade the alliance.

When Penelope was brought to Court, a match was planned, through Lord Burghley, with the wealthy and orphaned Lord Rich.[3] Young Essex, a fellow-Ward in Chancery and a fellow undergraduate at Cambridge, professed himself pleased. Penelope – unwillingly, it was afterwards said – was married on 1 November 1581. Sidney almost immediately fell in love with her. This left him indignant with himself, as he records in Sonnets ii and xxxiii of *Astrophel and Stella*; and when 'known worth did in mine of time succeed' left him also with a wound 'that while I live will bleed'.

Sonneting was not a method of transcribing experience: it was part of a social image created by the poet. Sidney's quite personal irony and pain, his quarrels with himself, lead to a violent attack on Stella's husband, by a use of a pun on his name which threatens to become tedious, and, in the best rhetorical convention, to an attack on Stella herself as thief, murderess, tyrant, traitor, witch and even devil – 'though cloth'd in Angel's shining'. She tempted him to leave Heaven for her:

> You Witch, you devil (alas) you still of me beloved,
> You see what I can say.
>
> [Fifth Song

Yet all this was not mere rhetoric, for even on his deathbed Sidney confessed, 'There came to my remembrance a Vanity wherein I had taken delight – whereof I had not rid myself. It was my Lady Rich', whom he piously renounced. By then he had been for three years married to the nineteen year old Frances Walsingham, daughter of his old friend Sir Francis, who paid his debts and who, after his death at Arnhem in October 1586, was to pay for his funeral. In literary terms, Penelope was widowed also.

Some of Sidney's verses were suppressed by his sister as too intimate, and though we hear of dozens of kisses, the attempt to possess Stella ends in 'most rude despair' (*Astrophel and Stella*, Sonnet cviii).

> Astrophel, she said, my love,
> Cease in these effects to move....
> Trust me, while I thee deny,
> In myself the smart I try;

Tyrant honour thus doth use thee,
Stella's self might not refuse thee....
                    [Eighth Song

After the deaths of Sidney and, in 1588, of Leicester, the young
Essex rose to leadership of his stepfather's party, in opposition
to Burghley and the pacifists; in 1587 at twenty-one, he became
the Queen's Master of the Horse, a key post that had been Leicester's. His youthful entourage modelled themselves on Sidney,
who in the final codicil of his will had left Essex 'his best sword'.
Robert Sidney, Philip's younger brother, was naturally an intimate, and in 1590, to the fury of the Queen, Essex married Philip's
youthful widow.

Before this happened, Charles Blount, who as soldier and
scholar was the true heir, had won Sidney's Stella. (One story
asserted there had been an early precontract between them, but
this is hardly likely, for Blount was but the younger son of an
impoverished house.) At the Accession Day Tilting of 1590 he
is identified as her knight by the inevitable pun,

> Comes Sir Charles Blount, in or and azure dight:
> Rich in his colours, richer in his thoughts,
> Rich in his fortunes, honour, arms and art.
>   [George Peele, *Polyhymnia*, II

The colours, it will be noted, are those of Pyrocles, lover of Princess Philoclea, at his first appearance in *Arcadia*.

At Arnhem Blount, like Sidney, sustained a wound in the thigh,
from which he suffered all his life. But it did not prevent his tilting,
and also challenging the Earl of Essex to a duel over a favour
bestowed on him by the Queen, for his tilting success. They met in
Marylebone fields and Essex was worsted, after which friendship
grew between them.

By this date, 1590, Penelope had borne the first of Blount's
children, and her mother, twice widowed, had married a young
kinsman of his, one Christopher Blount, who was seven years older
than Penelope.

As the young Lady Essex still resided with her widowed mother,
Lady Walsingham, his clients at Court would turn to Essex's
sister. Penelope had her lodging at Essex House in the Strand,
and her power now became directly political.

The relation of brother and sister was the most disinterested
in the family network, since they were not as a rule involved in

the marriage bargaining that might alienate parents and children, or in the envy that younger brothers felt for the heir.[4] (Webster however was to show an exception to this rule in *The Devil's Law Case*.) Penelope became the intermediary in a secret correspondence with James of Scotland, the most favoured heir to the throne; letters went through a young Douglas in Edinburgh. Penelope devised a code wherein the jealous Queen was 'Juno', old Burghley 'Aeolus', James 'Victor', and herself 'Ryalta' – the Exchange. Her picture was sent to James through Henry Constable, the poet, and the King commended 'the fineness of her wit, the invention and well writing' she shewed. The language of courtship was an obvious way to transmit diplomatic information – love tokens also played a part. Lord Rich's letters here and there betray that he was in the secret; in the autumn of 1595 Penelope at Chartley had received some letters from Essex destined 'for the other party'. Rich makes some heavy jokes about secret correspondence, and about Essex's immunity as a counsellor, to his brother-in-law. Chartley would have been a convenient staging-post for Scotland.

Eighteen months later Rich himself conveyed some secret letter to his wife, who was recovering from smallpox, and told Essex she would meet her brother in the fields. 'If you dare meet her, I beseech you preach patience to her, which is my only theme of exhortation.'

In the postscript of one of her own letters to Essex, Penelope saucily adds, 'You imagine my lord Rich hath no employment for a language secretary except he hath gotten a mistress in France' – where he had been on an embassy.

By December 1595, when they stood godparents to Robert Sidney's heir, Penelope and Blount were able to answer for one another's whereabouts. He had now succeeded to the family honours as 8th Lord Mountjoy, maintained a house in Holborn, and, to gratify his military tastes without allowing him to go to war, had been made Governor of Portsmouth.

The Queen forbade service overseas. 'You will never leave it,' she said, 'until you are knocked on the head as that inconsiderate fellow Sidney was. You shall go when I send you. In the meantime see that you lodge in the court, where you may follow your books, read and discourse of the wars.'

Charles bought from Essex a country house at Wanstead, where Sidney had once devised an entertainment for the Queen, and where Leicester had secretly married Penelope's mother. Here the lovers met discreetly. In 1597 the Queen allowed Blount to go on the Islands Voyage as second-in-command to Essex; this brought him the Garter.

The lovers went together to plays at the Middle Temple and Essex House, where on one occasion the party was kept up by two plays until 'one o'clock after midnight'. At Wanstead Charles built up a good library, including playbooks for recreation.

There were a surprising number of Catholics in the family; until the year before he married, Christopher Blount had been one, and Dorothy, Penelope's younger sister, after a runaway marriage with Sir Thomas Perrott, was now, after being newly widowed, married to the Earl of Northumberland, a staunch Catholic and a vigorous opponent of King James's claims for the succession. Their quarrels were so violent that the husband turned his wife out of doors, saying he would rather James were buried than crowned, and that he and his friends would die rather than see it. To which his wife replied that she was ready to eat their hearts with salt in the market-place and pay for her sin on the gallows, rather than any other king should reign.

On one occasion Blount rescued Penelope from an attempt to convert her to Catholicism; he was well read in theology. The Jesuit Gerard, who was staying in Essex with the Huddleston family, was summoned by her, and he arranged to come and hear confession. But she wrote to Charles, 'intending perhaps to break with him', and

At once he rushed down to see her and began to talk her out of her resolve for all he was able. He was a Protestant and well read, and cleverly persuaded her to ask her 'guide' the answers to certain doubts he himself had about the faith. He assured her that if he was convinced he too would become a Catholic. Meanwhile he begged her to take no irrevocable step – unless she wanted him to commit suicide. . . .

He succeeded first in persuading her to postpone her reconciliation, then to drop the idea altogether (*John Gerard*, tr. Caraman, 1951, pp. 34–5).

This skilful piece of diplomacy must have happened in about 1592.[5] There is ample testimony to Charles's personal magnetism; when, as an impoverished young student at the Middle Temple, he won the Queen's favour he never followed the rashnesses of Essex and Southampton; indeed, after that early duel with Essex, the Queen had praised him: 'By God's death, it was fit that some one or other should take him [Essex] down and teach him better manners, otherwise there would be no rule with him.'

In midsummer 1598 a storm blew up. Robert Sidney was defeated in a contest for office in which Essex had backed him; the Earl turned his back on the Queen, she boxed his ears, and he clapped his hand on his sword. As a result of this, not unnaturally, he kept away from Court. Early in 1599 he was opposing Charles Blount's appointment as leader of the forces which were destined for Ireland, and succeeded in getting the position for himself, with the fatal consequences that are part of history. The Queen had wished to appoint Blount and so had Essex's cousin Knollys. The Irish campaign would be very different from the raid on Cadiz – wearing, reductive tactics against guerrillas relying on foreign aid. 'I have beaten Knollys and Mountjoy in the Council, and by God, I will beat Tyrone in the field,' was Essex's boast before he rode out of London on 27 March 1599 to frenzied, general acclaim, with Southampton, Christopher Blount, Lord Rich and others of his circle. At Michaelmas, broken by the guerrillas in the country that had broken his father, and in defiance of very clear orders, he made his desperate dash into the Queen's presence, bursting into her room before she was dressed, his face and clothes spattered with mud. On 1 October he was put under arrest in York House, under the Lord Keeper.

His little court was at once plunged into mourning and confusion, as the weakness of his position was exposed. Elizabeth swore once again, 'By God's son, I am no queen. That man is above me. Who gave him command to come here so soon? I did send him on other business.' When it came to a showdown, there had been no doubt where real power lay. Essex fell ill, as all disgraced favourites did; indeed, his life was despaired of. Penelope and Dorothy appeared at Court, reproachfully clad in deep mourning, poor Lady Essex in mean black, not worth £5. They were commanded home, and then, when they attracted too many visitors, retreated into the country.

Rich (who had left Ireland at the first chance) and Mountjoy stood by Essex; as a token of solidarity, the Earl of Southampton and the Countess of Rutland – Sidney's daughter – stood godparents to Essex's daughter, christened 'without much ceremony'. Southampton and Rutland passed their time in going to plays. The Queen now firmly appointed her own candidate, Charles Blount, to the Irish command. With some reluctance, on 7 February 1600 he rode quietly out of London to the long job of campaigning. But in the meantime he had been in touch with James of Scotland.

As deputy-elect, he had been approached by the sick Essex, and according to a later confession by Sir Charles Danvers, a follower of Southampton, Blount had agreed to an earlier proposal of Essex, that Irish troops should be brought in to overthrow the men in power (Burghley was now dead, and his son in control) and get the succession fixed on James. If this were so, it was of course treasonable: but James, if indeed approached, did not respond. When, a little later, Southampton was sent over by Essex to urge Blount on this course again, Blount had changed his mind, and refused to follow the dangerous proposal (Falls, pp. 114, 135). Instead, he turned towards Cecil. Southampton returned and joined in the fatal progress of the Essex faction, which was strongly supported by Penelope.

In February 1600, shortly after her lover had departed for Ireland, Penelope wrote an impassioned letter to the Queen in defence of her brother. He was due to appear before the Privy Council, and in the midst of extremest flattery she dropped dark hints that his enemies would not give him a fair hearing. She herself was summoned at once to the Privy Council to explain this letter ('insolent, saucy, malapert ... an aggravation of the offence') and was kept under surveillance in her own house – which of course meant St Bartholomew's. On making humble submission, she soon gained leave to steal away to the country. Later in the year Lord Rich was trying to use her to make representation about his lands (as she had been used by Essex to make representations for Sir Robert Sidney). She had still some power, and still some sense of duty towards Rich, for when he fell ill in September 1600, she went to him at Leighs, in Essex, and nursed him with devoted care.

Charles was campaigning in Ireland with great success, raising the morale of his troops and moving speedily. The year wore on with plots and counterplots. Some meetings were held by the group in Blount's house in Holborn, some at Drury House nearby, where Sir Charles Danvers lived with the Southamptons. A year and a day from Charles's riding out of the City, Essex staged his desperate attempt at armed revolt. There was a supper at Essex House the night before, at which Penelope was present, and where also, it would appear, an agent of the Queen was present too. The plan to raise the City reached Westminster, and the Queen took action overnight. So did Penelope, who sent into the City, summoned a friend, Sir Harry Bromley, asking his aid, and, as soon as the party of Essex, having received the Queen's messengers and locked them into Essex House, had proceeded on their crazed way through Ludgate, Penelope took coach and went to seek further aid outside the City from the Earl of Bedford. He shook her off and took his men to Court. A barricade of coaches was set up across the road to Westminster; Essex, having totally failed to move the citizens, and seen Christopher Blount wounded and captured by the city bands, returned from the City by water to Essex House in the Strand. His closest friends were now defending the Queen and preparing to reduce him to submission. The Lord Admiral, the Earl of Nottingham, arrived with a storming party, Anthony and Francis Bacon were there; but it was Robert Sidney, no other, who gave the ultimatum – one hour for Lady Rich and Lady Southampton to leave, after which the attack would begin.

Essex had assembled about three hundred gentlemen, his personal 'following'. He and Southampton taunted the attackers at first, but after burning compromising documents, including some letters from James, which he wore in a little bag round his neck, he surrendered and with Rutland, Southampton and Sir Charles Danvers was sent to the Tower. The Lord Admiral committed Penelope to the custody of the keeper of the Privy Purse, Henry Sackford, from whose custody she demanded, through the Council, her male cook, bedding and hangings for her chamber, to be supplied by Lord Rich – who complied.

Lord Rich was also present to answer to his name when Essex was tried before his peers; Penelope was examined privately by Robert Cecil and the Lord Admiral, who reported that she was humble and penitent. She was released into the custody of her husband and would therefore have been in residence at St Bartholomew's when Essex and Southampton were found guilty of treason and condemned to death. For an act of armed rebellion the *general* treatment was merciful. Southampton was reprieved, on account of his youth (he was actually twenty-seven), but on 25 February Essex was executed, having in his last days fallen into abjectly confessional and penitent melancholy. He did not hesitate to implicate his sister, and even, as the Lord Admiral was later to reveal to Charles Blount, to mention their liaison.

With Essex, Christopher Blount suffered death; Lettice lost both a son and a husband. Sir Charles Danvers faced death bravely ('Only his cheeks quivered a little'); Gilly Meyrick and Essex's secretary, Cuffe, were hanged, drawn and quartered at Tyburn (the servants, as usual, suffered the most severely).[6]

Blount had been campaigning in Westmeath, in spite of the earliness of the season, when the dreadful news reached him on 22 February, three days before the execution. He knew, of course, that if Southampton or Essex or Charles Danvers had implicated him in the correspondence with James and the proposal to bring in troops, he would himself be facing a charge of treason. He sat down and wrote with his own hand to Cecil a very careful letter 'from the camp at Donore in MacGeoghan's country this 24 February', confessing that while 'my long and inward familiarity with the principal actors of this miserable tragedy' might rouse suspicion, yet he was confident in his own conscience and in Elizabeth's justice. There was no 'infection' of this in his army, and he promised to hold down the Irish 'if there hath been any seeds of this sedition sown'. He begs Cecil to make his petition to Her Majesty 'that it will please her to believe that nothing on earth, neither an angel from heaven, shall make me deceive the trust she hath reposed in me and when she doth think otherwise it shall be no punishment, but a benefit, for me to die' (Falls, pp. 151–3, from SP. Ireland, CCVIII, part I, 54).

The Queen sent back an equally masterly letter, in which she assured him of her confidence, adding that any who had been involved, if they repented, would be pardoned. The confessions of Essex, Southampton and Danvers (who had been sent over on a final mission by Essex, and had received a final negative) implicated but at the same time cleared Blount. This part of the evidence was simply suppressed. The Irish campaign was at a critical stage, an invasion from Spain was expected, and seven months later Don Juan de Aguila was indeed to land at Kinsale, from which well-entrenched position he was to proclaim that he was holding it first for Christ and second for the King of Spain and would maintain it against all foes.

Elizabeth and Cecil knew that Blount was too valuable to be removed; so, whilst being denied his request to come over and report, he was left probably unaware how much had been testified about his Scottish connections. Some two months after the execution, the Lord Admiral sent a jestingly reassuring letter with news of Penelope, but containing the very words used by Essex in his confession of *this* aspect of affairs:

And now, said he, I must accuse one who is most nearest to me, my sister, who did continually urge me on with telling me how all my friends and followers thought me a coward and that I had lost my valour; and then thus 'that she must be looked unto, for she hath a proud spirit'; and spared not to say something of her affection unto you. Would your lordship have thought this weakness and this unnaturalness in that man?

[Falls, pp. 153–4]

He enclosed a letter which Penelope had written to himself, hoping that 'when you consider what a youth I am' this correspondence would not make Blount 'afraid' (the Admiral was sixty-five). This letter is in Penelope's most generous spirit towards Blount; but it shows that she felt it necessary to disengage herself from her brother with counter-charges of undue influence:

For my deserts towards him that is gone, it is known that I have been more like a slave than a sister, which proceeded out of my exceeding love to him rather than his authority. ... Your lordship's noble disposition forceth me to deliver my griefs unto you, hearing a report that some of those malicious tongues have sought to wrong a worthy friend of yours. I know that most of them did hate him for his zealous following the service of Her Majesty, and beseech you to pardon my presuming thus much, though I hope his enemies can have no power to harm him.

[Falls, 156

As to Blount's request to be relieved, the Lord Admiral wrote gaily, 'I think Her Majesty could be most glad to see you and look upon your black eyes here, so she were sure you would not look with too much respect of other black eyes. ... But for that, if the Lord Admiral were but thirty years old, I think he would not differ in opinion from the Lord Mountjoy.'

Blount did what he could to protect the remnant of the group who were with him in Ireland; he sent over Sir Charles Danvers's brother, Sir Henry, with the news of the capture of Kinsale, and himself soldiered on to reduce the rebel Tyrone. This he succeeded in doing just as Elizabeth died; the news of her death was suppressed by him, lest it should lead the rebels to hold back and treat for better conditions from James.

This was two years later; the accession of James in March 1603 revived the fortunes of the Essex party, whilst two leaders of the opposition, Cobham and Ralegh, now found themselves arrested and charged with treason. Penelope was one of those summoned to the Border to greet Queen Anne and the heir, Prince Henry;

Southampton, liberated from the Tower, rushed up the Great North Road as far as Huntingdon to greet the King. Blount arrived home in June and was created Earl of Devonshire. Penelope was made Lady of the Bedchamber and given the precedence of the ancient Bouchier Earls of Essex, fifth in precedence in the kingdom. Cecil, who had been approached by Blount, and who had become a faithful ally, stood a good friend to both. Penelope was now openly living with Blount, though her office would give her rooms in Queen Anne's establishment. On Twelfth Night, 1604, she appeared with the Queen as one of the lady masquers in Samuel Daniel's *Vision of the Twelve Goddesses*; appropriately cast in the rôle of Venus, she wore a mantle of dove-coloured silver, embroidered in doves, and presented at the shrine of Peace a rainbow-coloured scarf:

> The lovely Venus, in bright Majesty
> Appears in mild aspect, in dove-like hue
> With th'all-combining scarf of amity
> To ingird strange nations with affections true.

Queen Anne enjoyed her vivacity; her fine dresses outshone those of the older ladies who expected preferment. Next year Penelope appeared in the first of Ben Jonson's masques (she would already have seen the shows he had written for Queen Anne's southward progress). Among the Daughters of the Niger, lady masquers who in the *Masque of Blackness* floated in on a great scallop shell, Penelope was Ocyte. They were all richly dressed, but their apparel was 'light and courtesan like' and their hands and faces were black. They descended two by two, Penelope with the Countess of Suffolk, who had been the wife of Richard, Lord Rich, and was therefore her mother-in-law![7] Their emblem was two naked feet in a river.

Penelope's nephew, the young Earl of Essex, was being brought up with the royal children; his mother, Lady Essex, twice widowed, was found a match in one of Blount's Irish captains, Richard de Burgh, Earl of Clanrickarde, who was President of Connaught and, though loyal, a Catholic. With him she went over to Athlone. Blount was now one of the most trusted counsellors; as victor over the invading Spaniards he sat at the Council table with Cecil and Northampton when at long last peace with Spain was concluded. Perhaps Penelope's knowledge of the tongue may have proved of service in the entertainment of the Constable of

Castille and his train. Among those deputed to wait on them, King James had sent his players, in their scarlet liveries. Penelope later invited the Florentine Ambassador to sup in her chambers at Court with the King.

Suddenly the Wheel of Fortune turned again. In November 1605 Lord Rich was granted a divorce in the Consistory Court of the Bishop of London on Penelope's own confession of her adultery with a person unnamed. The Archbishop of Canterbury chid the husband and commended the wife – why, it is hard to see – and bade him 'go among his Puritans', who were plentiful enough round Leighs.

At Wanstead, on St Stephen's Day, 1605, Charles and Penelope were married in the secrecy of so many other weddings, by his chaplain, a young Fellow of St John's College, Cambridge, who afterwards was to become one of the rulers in Church and State – William Laud. This act was in direct defiance of the canons of 1604, which had crystallized the position on divorce, and in defiance also of the injunctions and promises given a month before.[8]

This had been a judicial separation; remarriage was totally unacceptable to the Church and particularly to King James, who forbade them both the Court. Except through the channels of the University, Laud found his promotion blocked and ever thereafter observed St Stephen's Day as a day of special penance. His biographers subsequently alleged that he thought the two had had a precontract – if this had been the case, it would, of course, have nullified the marriage to Rich and would have afforded a much better basis for proceeding.

Whilst the actual conditions by which marriage could be contracted were very uncertain, because it was both an ecclesiastical ceremony and a secular contract, the conditions for divorce were purely ecclesiastical; adultery was not a *civil* offence. Yet the contract *per verba de praesenti*, made by the parties before witnesses, constituted a legal though irregular marriage, and, whilst the Church and State condemned it, they also recognized it. Marriage need not be clerical; divorce had to be. The only way of escape was by a decree of nullity – such as Henry VIII sought from Catherine of Aragon, who had been married to his elder brother.

The question of inheritance and descent was the difficult one. Charles Blount was now wealthy and had titles which he wished to leave to his heir. Penelope was also the mother of five children by Rich, including a boy, whose advantageous marriage to the heiress Frances Hatton she had recently planned (it took place on 26 February 1605). But she was pregnant again by Blount; her eldest son by him, Mountjoy, was now of an age to be put on the marriage market also.

There is no record that Penelope and Blount had ever been unfaithful to each other, though he had charmed the Irish ladies and, being officially free, had been mentioned as a possible husband for Ormonde's heiress, as well as for the Lady Arbella Stuart.

Being well read, Blount compiled a treatise in justification of his action, which he submitted to the King.[9] With copious illustrations from the Fathers, he sought to prove that judicial separation was an error, and that true divorce permitted remarriage, thus enabling him to reclaim this 'poor lost sheep', Penelope. She had pleaded in the Consistory Court under fear of her husband, who had cruelly misused her and turned her out to 'stipend'. The King remained unconvinced, but Blount continued to perform all his usual functions as one of the great officers of the Crown; as Master of Ordnance he appeared on a committee to consider an Act of Attainder for various offenders in 'the late most detestable and damnable treason', the Gunpowder Plot. Among those imprisoned was Penelope's brother-in-law, the Earl of Northumberland, whose second cousin had been one of the conspirators. He spent the rest of his life in the Tower, though his alienated wife Dorothy made an appeal on behalf of their children. He himself composed a treatise, praising the life of learning rather than the courtship of women,[10] which was seized and preserved with his other papers.

Charles Blount's defence of his marriage is an anticipation of the argument which John Milton was to put forward nearly half a century later: the case for a personal and close relationship as the only basis of marriage. Milton could appeal to some extreme reformers, Blount, whilst marshalling the Church Fathers, could only appeal to the personal sympathy and charity of the King. A few years earlier, before the canon laws had been clarified, he might have had a case. No doubt he consulted friends at the Middle Temple, and the story could not but be widely known. It was the future of their children under the law which concerned the two lovers. Bastards were penalized in various ways; Webster later wrote plays upon this theme (*The Devil's Law Case* and *A Cure for a Cuckold*).

The tension did not last long, for in a few months the Earl sickened and died of pneumonia at his new Palace of the Savoy. His will, signed the day before his death, disposed of his great wealth to his 'very dear and loving wife' and to their children, who are all named – even a child in the womb is provided for. A vivid picture remains of Penelope's grief; she threw herself on the ground in a corner of the chamber, refusing all nourishment: 'Noctu, interdiu in thalami sui angulo, humi jacens.'[11]

At the grand funeral in Westminster Abbey, the heralds refused to impale the Devereux coat of arms with the arms of Blount; the chief mourner was the Earl of Southampton, who had also witnessed the will, along with the chaplain, William Laud. All the great of the land came to condole with Penelope, however, and Cecil as ever proved a faithful friend. To him, she wrote six months later, on returning from a visit to her mother, to describe the frolics of her young nephew, the Earl of Essex, and Cecil's schoolboy son, the young Lord Cranborne – how they would not be parted, how 'desperately' they rode. 'My mother, I think, will grow young with their company.'

Penelope was not long to outlive her Charles. She died on 7 July 1607, and about her death there are conflicting reports. So notable and so brilliant a sinner must be expected to provide lessons at her departure; the lessons were claimed both by the Church of England and by the Church of Rome. According to the first, 'The Lady Rich fell sick, sent for Doctor Layfield, disclaimed her last marriage, sent for her first husband to ask forgiveness, and died penitently.'[12] But the Jesuit, Father Gerard, who had hoped to convert her, gives a dreadful end to Charles and a pious death-bed reconciliation to Penelope:

Incapable of shaking himself free from his infatuation, he died of a broken heart. With his last breath he invoked not God but his goddess, his 'angel' as he called her, and left her his sole heir. ... Frequently she would talk about me to one of her maids of honour who was a Catholic. ... I was in fact composing a letter, when I got word that she had died of fever. Happily she had been reconciled to the Church on her death-bed by one of our Fathers.[13]

There was indeed a certain Mistress Deacon in Brussels who had attended on the Lady Rich, and the man who took Laud as his chaplain cannot have been averse from ceremonies. But the mysterious end of Penelope did not receive the public celebration that had been accorded to Blount by his poets. Samuel Daniel implicitly mentions her:

> Summon Detraction to object the worst
> That may be told and utter all it can;
> It cannot find a blemish to be enforced
> Against him, other than that he was man
> And built of flesh and blood, and did live here
> Within the regions of infirmity
> Where all perfections never did appear...

but at his end

> The action of our death especially
> Shows all a man.

John Ford, of the Middle Temple, dedicating the poem, *Fame's Memorial*, to Penelope as Countess of Devonshire – a title even the unfriendly were prepared to give – was but twenty-one years old (and twenty-three years younger than Daniel). His attitude is one of justification, not for the marriage but for the love story:

> Linked in the graceful bands of dearest life
> Unjustly termed disgraceful, he enjoyed
> Content's abundance; happiness was rife,
> Pleasure secure; no troubled thought annoyed
> His comfort sweet; toil was in toil destroyed.
> > Maugre the tongue of malice, spite of strife,
> > He lived united to his heart's delight.

Ford attacks the 'chaff' of his own day; and indeed, the wedding masque (*Hymenei*) of Penelope's young nephew, from which she had been excluded, revealed in Frances Howard the truer White Devil. This child (the daughter of that same Countess of Suffolk who had companioned Penelope the previous year) had been married at the age of thirteen to young Essex by a plan on which James plumed himself. Nine years later she was to seek her freedom in order to marry the King's new favourite, the Earl of Somerset, to which end she brought a suit of nullity, and by way of revenge murdered an opponent of the union, Sir Thomas Overbury. She was to be the centre of the most infamous scandal that even the Court of James produced, and in 1619 her mother, the Countess of Suffolk, was to be tried in the Star Chamber, along with her husband, for embezzling Treasury funds. Francis Bacon, in prosecuting, compared her to an Exchange woman who kept her shop whilst her creature, Sir J. Bingley, cried, 'What do you lack?'

Penelope had been generous, eager, seeking to advance the unpopular cause. She pleaded for a poor Irishman, 'the best disposition that I found in any of his nation'. She encouraged young Catholics like Henry Constable or Bartholomew Young.[14] Her last and third rôle, as the irregularly wedded wife of Charles Blount, Earl of Devonshire, was probably the most heroic, though it can hardly have been said to have earned the praise that Ford offered to 'A saint divine, a beauty fairly wise'.

Both Charles and Penelope patronized the arts: among the first signals of her revived fortune had been the dedication by John Florio of his translation of the *Essays of Montaigne* (1603) to 'one of those whose magnanimity and magnificent frank nature have so bedewed my earth when it was sunburnt, so gently thawed it when it was frost bound, that I was more senseless than the earth if I returned not some fruit in good measure'.

This magnanimity, this greatness of spirit, led her to rebel against what was in general acceptance as a necessary evil: marriage with an uncongenial partner, who may indeed have sometimes indulged in downright brutality. One of Sidney's sonnets rather suggests this (*Astrophel and Stella*, xciii) where her vexation, 'harms' and 'hurts' bring 'sighs' and 'tears' from her.

Rich lived to purchase the Earldom of Warwick, and an experienced wealthy widow, to rename his mansion at St Bartholomew's, Warwick House, and to be named himself by unkind rhymesters 'Cornu Copia'. Of Stella's brood no less than three became earls and fought on different sides in the Civil War. She has been identified, rather improbably, with Ford's pathetic Penthea in *The Broken Heart*, but there seems in her far more of Webster's Duchess, or of Ford's more heroic Calantha.

CHAPTER FOUR

Antonio Pérez, the Spanish Spy: a London Legend

In the early 1590s Antonio Pérez, 'Spanish traitor' and spy, regained throughout Western Europe a shadow of the power that for ten years he had enjoyed as the Italian secretary of Philip II of Spain.[1]

Pérez, born in 1540, was certainly of illegitimate and probably unimportant origin. Gonzalo Pérez, his putative father, a minor cleric and earlier secretary to Charles V and Philip II, had once won a ring of Queen Mary for his prowess at tilting; but rumour fathered Antonio on Pérez' master, the Prince of Eboli, one of the great princes of Spain and also a most trusted counsellor of Philip. Antonio, educated at Italian, Flemish and Spanish universities, established links abroad which he retained throughout his life – his last protector was an Italian. Promoted by his 'father' and by Eboli, he won the coveted secretarial position at twenty-eight. His extraordinary flair gave him an instinct for 'the next move' in the political game, enabling him to deploy all the arts of the possible. He was brilliant at dispatches, but more important was the temperament – nervously alert, gay or melancholy, mercurial – that held so many to him, above all his devoted wife (by twenty-eight he had seduced and married Juana di Coello).

The phrasing of letters and of speeches could provoke or prevent war; since the days of Petrarch, the Italians had relied on eloquent speeches for very practical results. Later, Antonio was to be known as *paedagogus oratorum*, which in modern terms might be translated as a first-class public relations man.

That he controlled the best intelligence service in Europe proved the downfall of Pérez. The King jealously sought through Pérez intelligence about his brilliant, ambitious half-brother Don John of Austria – a Sidney on a European scale – victor of Lepanto

(1571), saviour of Europe from the Turk, the darling of the courts and camps, who had been sent in April 1576 to govern the Netherlands.[2] Don John's own secretary, Juan de Escovedo, a young man from Santander in northern Spain, trained and nominated by Pérez, but transformed by his lord's charm into a devoted servant, became a menace to the intelligence system when the relations of the brothers grew strained. Antonio consulted the King, who counselled that Juan de Escovedo, now in Madrid, should be given 'a titbit' – that is to say, poisoned. Consequently a poor Moorish servant girl, who was quite innocent, was hanged after an unsuccessful attempt; but on 31 March 1578 Escovedo was run through with a sword in the street, so neatly that he died at once. This could not have pleased Philip, who always preferred that his victims should have time to make confession. The assassins made good their escape;[3] but the murdered man, in a horoscope cast by a friar, had been warned that he would be killed by his best friend. The friar was duly poisoned in his turn. Escovedo's family pursued Pérez. It appears that he had his own reason for disposing of the junior secretary.

For Pérez had become something of a double agent, having intrigued both with the Flemings and with the Portuguese, who were now to become Philip's subjects. He might, of course, have again been acting as *agent provocateur*, or fifth-columnist to the anti-Spanish groups in these territories, but the King had not been so informed; while Escovedo knew it through his Flemish connections. After Don John's death on 1 October 1578 these betraying documents went to the King at Madrid and disclosure must have followed. Escovedo's death had not concealed the fact that Pérez also had been copying and sending to Don John and others the confidential letters of the monarch – which was treason. On the other hand, he himself held in his own hands documents incriminating Philip II in matters which could not be made public, including more than one assassination.

The power of the King of Spain over his subjects was tyrannical and open: his confessor told him that 'a secular Prince has right over the life of his subjects'. After some manœuvres, suddenly, in the middle of the night of 28 July 1579, Pérez was arrested. Simultaneously the guards seized Doña Ana de Mendoza, Princess of Eboli, widow of Pérez' first patron, who had died in 1573. Doña Ana was one of the greatest and also the boldest and most outspoken of the grandees. She was confined, without trial or indictment, in a strong fortress, and, though never charged, never emerged from captivity. Her imprisonment, at the sole will of the King, lasted more than a dozen years.

The explanation officially given was that she had fomented discord between the two secretaries. The leader of Escovedo's assassins had indeed made his escape with papers describing him as her steward. He was Pérez' cousin, Gil de Mesa. By the mere will and motion of the King the Princess of Eboli suffered civic death. She was deprived of the guardianship of her children and her estates were put under the management of the King's new secretary: Matheo Vásquez, her enemy and that of Pérez also.

Philip was absent for some time, consolidating his claims in Portugal. Meanwhile Pérez was at first treated quite leniently, and, though confined, was not deprived of office. The King obviously needed to extract any papers (kept by Pérez) incriminating him. Pérez did not disgorge. A trial of investigation began early in 1584, followed in 1588 by a criminal trial. Pérez denied everything relating to the death of Escovedo. Only after being tortured on the rack (he had been shackled and otherwise maltreated already) did he on 23 February 1590 confess and incriminate a noble, who was dead, sparing the King. Two months later, with the help of his devoted wife and friends, he broke prison and escaped to his native country of Aragon, where the separate legal constitution offered him protection. The Aragonese swore allegiance to the King only after he had in turn sworn to observe the laws of their land. Moreover, they swore with the proviso that if he did not keep the law, they were absolved of any loyalty to him: 'si no, no.'

In July the Castilian courts condemned Pérez to death. The King at first pursued a civil action against Pérez in Aragon; in 1591, since certain things had better not be disclosed, his confessor instituted an action by the Inquisition and Pérez was accused of a variety of new crimes, from heresy to sodomy. After Pérez was condemned, the King's special representative was killed during a popular riot which resulted in the town of Saragossa, and on 24 September a second revolt freed Pérez from the coach of the Inquisition and propelled him eastward on the road to exile. Two months later, on 24 November 1591, in the disguise of a shepherd, he had crossed the Pyrenees to Béarn, to the Court of Catherine de Bourbon, sister of Henry IV, King of France.

Pérez was still a person to be reckoned with, for he carried his

secrets with him. The Princess of Eboli however had been elimi-
nated. In the first years of her widowhood she had indeed been
a formidable power. On the death of the Prince of Eboli she had
tried to take the veil, but Philip ordered her to uncloister herself,
to the relief of the Carmelite nuns in the convent she had founded,
whom the personal intervention of St Teresa d'Avila alone had
rescued from her dominating presence. For she was imperious,
as well as passionate: in 1576 she came to Madrid from her country
estate at Pastrana and attempted to intrigue for the throne of Portugal on behalf of one of her children; her grandchild was indeed
to ascend the throne as first ruler of the House of Braganza.

The house of Eboli had led the more liberal section of the
nobility against the war party, headed by the great Duke of Alva
(who in turn succeeded to power by 1578); thus Pérez, as the follower of La Eboli, was involved in their factions. It gave him
powerful friends and the control of more lives: the Archbishop
of Toledo, a Jesuit, had been nominated through Pérez' influence.
A Dominican, Fray Hernando del Castillo, knew of the secret trial
and private strangling of the Baron de Montigny in the fortress
of Simancas, for in the unfortunate noble's last hours he had heard
his confession. (Strangling was the method Philip was said to have
employed for the execution of his own son, Don Carlos; it was
a suitable death for those who knew too much of the King's secrets.)
The absolute monarch could therefore be put under pressure –
especially by the Church, though he also ruined several prelates.

The Princess of Eboli was permitted to survive in prison, but
her durance grew progressively more severe. At last, through
the intervention of her son-in-law, the powerful Duke of Medina
Sidonia, commander of the Armada, she was confined to one room
in her palace at Pastrana. After the escape of Pérez however the
room was completely sealed off, heavy bars were placed over the
window and the window was darkened, so that she ended her days
in perpetual night as a 'close prisoner',[4] supported by one faithful
daughter, who afterwards took the veil, and some waiting women.
The end came in February 1592, when the Princess died and was
buried tranquilly beside her husband, with no outward indication
of her faults or her fate.

The Princess of Eboli exerted the same charm as Antonio Pérez
– her ally and, as the story went, her lover. There is no doubt
she dominated him, or that the secret and enigmatic character of
Philip II ensured that the ferocious frankness of the Princess both

attracted and appalled him. Popular legend asserted that he too
had been her lover, and that he punished her for betraying him
with Pérez. Her son believed in the liaison, and that this dishonour
precluded any open charges. La Eboli is credited with saying to
the King that she would have his new secretary, Matheo Vásquez,
stabbed in his presence; and her answer to Escovedo, when he
threatened to disclose her relations with Pérez, had become
notorious: 'Do what you will, Escovedo, I love Antonio Pérez'
arse better than the King's face.'

After the death of the Princess, Pérez himself confirmed the
story of their love. The fact that modern historians have decided
that their relations were a game of power politics does not preclude
this further aspect; in fact, liaison was a way of securing adherence
not unknown both to men and women who played the power
game.[5]

When Pérez reached Béarn, his conversation was reported by
Jean de Gaufretau, who remarked that Antonio was so enamoured
of the Princess that he spoke of the fair lady on every possible
occasion, exalting her, with tremendous Spanish bombast, above
all beauties who had ever lived or would ever live. Gaufretau replied that she could not be so beautiful, having only one eye, the
eye being the chief seat and evoker of love. Pérez replied with a
resounding oath, 'Juro a Dios que si huviese dos ojos, huviere que-
mado toto el mundo.' ('By God, if she had two eyes she would
burn up the whole earth.')

Portraits of the Princess of Eboli shew her with her left eye
covered by a black patch; she was reputed to have lost the eye,
when a girl, whilst fencing with a page. The violence of Philip's
punishment, and his unrelenting, progressive vindictiveness towards the Princess, might suggest that his own personal feelings
had been involved; his last words to Pérez, on the eve of arrest,
had been charged with an irony that a dramatist could scarcely
have bettered: 'Your own particular business will be dispatched
before I leave, at least that part of it that lies with me.'

Soon after Pérez arrived in Béarn, and in the month of the Princess of Eboli's death, the King of France sent a reconnaissance
force across to Spain. Philip was moving his army against the
rebellious Aragonese, but the French were concerned lest this
might be a prelude to a Spanish invasion of France; whilst
Antonio, naturally, was hoping for some success in Aragon that
would restore him to Spain. The French expedition was a costly

failure, and Philip next bloodily revenged himself upon his own subjects. The Chief Justice of Aragon (who had upheld the country's law against the Castilian decree) was executed summarily, and his severed head displayed; many nobles were slaughtered and the liberties of Aragon curtailed. This cruel revenge became a political weapon for others to turn against Philip. It was used in this way as propaganda by the English and the Dutch, to deter their own subjects from any trust in his clemency, and to contrast his regime with their own.

Now over fifty years of age, twisted by the rack and suffering from the great hardships of his flight, including the crossing of the Pyrenees in winter time, Pérez showed extraordinary resilience. He became a compulsive letter writer and author. His *Relaciones* were first published in Pau in 1592. Having cast off the anonymous power of the King's secretary (whilst retaining the valuable papers still in his private possession), he now sought a dramatic public rôle for himself – ostentation meant survival. His wife and children had been imprisoned by Philip, and he went in constant fear of 'a titbit' or a sword thrust, and so he let out enough of his story to involve the dead but remained vague at this time about the rôle of the King himself.

Meanwhile he was offering counsel to the King's enemies. Virtually every spy at some point seems to have become a double agent. The network ran through great merchants and international financiers (in England Sir Horatio Palavicino assisted the Queen) down to wretched unemployed soldiers, religious exiles, the offscourings of debtors' prisons. The lives of the lesser fry were usually short: assassination was generally accepted as a means of political adjustment.

The metamorphosis from utter secrecy to utmost ostentation was a complete metamorphosis in one sense, but in some respects Pérez also maintained the secrecy of the spy – and went on spying.

In the spring of 1593 Henry IV sent Pérez to England. He himself was about to abjure Calvinism on political grounds ('Paris vaut une messe'); by supporting 'the Spanish traitor', he perhaps wanted to show that he was not aligning himself with Spain, and to reassure the Protestant Elizabeth. Pérez may have felt he would be safer in England than in France. He arrived in the middle of the greatest outbreak of plague known for many years, and so, after a brief stay at the French Embassy, was lodged in various country houses near the City or the Court, under the patronage of the Earl of Essex, whom the Queen had deputed to support him. She would not herself give any open acknowledgement of his presence. He had a private audience; on 23 April 1593, with the Ambassador of France, he attended the Garter Feast; in June and July he was at one of the Sidney houses, Gaynes Park, in Epping; then he was at Sunbury (near Windsor and Hampton Court), where he met the Portuguese Pretender, Dom Antonio of Portugal, and Dr Lopez, the Queen's Portuguese physician. Later he went to Barn Elms; in January 1594 he lodged with Francis Bacon at Gray's Inn, then he lived in the house of John Harrison, High Master of St Paul's; finally, in March 1594 he was given rooms at Essex House, the plague abating; and here he maintained a small but costly household, including a priest for mass.

He almost certainly saw the Christmas Revels at Court, where the Queen danced, and those of the Prince of Purpoole at Gray's Inn; on 5 February he attended the wedding of Elizabeth de Vere, Burghley's granddaughter, with the Earl of Derby, and in March he went with some of Essex's followers to Cambridge, where, at Trinity College, he saw *Laelia*. He was given to the drama and could have attended the theatres in London when late in 1594 they reopened; but as his languages were Spanish, Italian and Latin, a play in English could have conveyed but little. (No doubt he learnt enough kitchen English to seduce a chambermaid.) However, when in France he certainly attended plays, although without any capacity to write French. Enough of the English nobility knew Spanish or Latin to make his situation tolerable; he wrote to the Earl in Latin, spoke to the Queen in Italian, but the Earl's sister, the Lady Penelope Rich, could read Spanish, and he addressed her with particular devotion. Since she was of a proud and imperious temper, she may have reminded him of La Eboli, and he would instinctively have fitted her into his version of the politics of the English Court.

The psychology of the exiled and discredited double agent is familiar enough; Antonio Pérez, though used by the enemy rulers as part of their game of chess, commanded no direct power in himself. He remained useful through his old network of agents, but everyone remained also a little suspicious that he might again be playing a double game – which indeed he was, in the sense that his ultimate hope was always to return to Spain, or at least to rescue his family. He helped in recruiting an Italian branch of intelligence for the Queen, and of course, by placing his own agents and friends in positions of this kind, he was gaining leverage for himself. But his chief work was to take part in Essex's private intelligence service, which at this time rivalled the Queen's. Essex kept his agents partly to outstrip his Court rivals, delighting to outplay Burghley[6] and gain the first news of danger. He had at Essex House a group of intelligent young men, headed by Anthony Bacon, brother of Francis, who was an expert linguist and cryptographer. With them Pérez soon grew intimate, in particular becoming deeply dependent from the first on Anthony.

The great triumph of Essex's intelligence came in the spring of 1594, with the uncovering of Dr Lopez' alleged plot to assassinate the Queen; to this Pérez made an active contribution. It has already been mentioned that Lopez and Pérez lived together near Windsor. Lopez, a Portuguese Jew, was himself acting as an agent for the Queen, as well as being her physician. He had lived in England since 1559, and supplied a fellow Jew, one 'V.E.', who, in the household of Antonio Pérez, acted as a spy on the Spaniard's movements.

Essex had suggested that Lopez might improve his contacts by pretending to open communications directly with Spain in his own interest. Unfortunately, whilst at Sunbury, the physician incurred the extreme displeasure of Essex by talking about some of the Earl's own medical problems. This medical betrayal was his downfall.

Essex set to work, and soon claimed to have uncovered a Spanish plot, led by Lopez, which involved the intended poisoning of the Queen and also the planned murder of Pérez. Two members of the household of Dom Antonio of Portugal, aided by two Irish soldiers, were to have carried out the work. The soldiers had been in the Netherlands and it was supposedly the Spanish government in the Netherlands which had planned the whole affair.

Elizabeth and Lord Burghley at first refused to credit the suspicion thrown on Lopez, a harmless old man, and Elizabeth took rather a sharp tone with Essex. Absolutely determined to prove his case, Essex interrogated mercilessly the wretched Lopez, who denied everything, till finally, under torture, he gave the expected answers. On 28 February 1594 he was tried at the Guildhall before a panel which included Essex himself, Lord Rich, the Lord Mayor, the Lord Admiral, the Vice-Chamberlain of the Royal Household, the Chancellor of the Exchequer (Robert Cecil), with Coke, Solicitor-General, prosecuting. On 14 April a decree was signed by which the wretched old man suffered the full horrors of a traitor's death – to be hanged, drawn and quartered. His accomplices, so-called, were also executed, and Pérez saw their heads above Ludgate.

The unmasking of the Lopez 'conspiracy' marked the zenith of Pérez' career in England. It was presumably as a result that he was given rooms and special privileges at Essex House. His part in the affair was doubly gratifying. He had saved the Queen, assisted Essex, and had himself been proved to be of such importance that plans for his assassination were coupled with those for the assassination of Queen Elizabeth! For this proof of his standing, as well as for the confirmation of his fears, the betrayal of one who had been his friend was regarded as fully justified.

Lopez' death may also have ministered to an obscure desire in Pérez to inflict on others the tortures he had suffered himself. He is said personally to have given the torture, whilst in France, to a miserable Spaniard who was captured there.

His friendship with the Essex household, cemented by this demonstration that Essex was right and his enemies, the Cecils, wrong, did not completely allay his fears or correct his devious habits.

Enmity towards the Cecils, who remained suspicious of him, was both a duty and a pleasure. On the other hand, the extreme Puritans never accepted Pérez, and at the height of his popularity, in April 1594, Lady Bacon wrote to her son Anthony in voluble disapproval:

... surely though I pity your brother [Francis] yet so long as he pities not himself but keepeth that Bloody Pérez, as I told him then, yea as a coach-companion and bed-companion, a proud, profane, costly fellow, whose being about him I fear the Lord God doth mislike and doth less bless your brother in credit and otherwise in his health, surely I am utterly discouraged and make a conscience further to undo myself to maintain such wretches as he is, that never once loved your Brother indeed but for his own credit, living upon your Brother, though your Brother will be blind to his own hurt, and picking such vile his wicked countrymen to supply in his absence.

[Ungerer, I, no. 106 pp. 219–20

and a little later: 'I would you were well rid of that old, doting, polling papist. He will discourse out of season to hinder your health ... some do think your Brother and you do make too great note of the Earl's favour' (*Ibid.*, p. 221). Mindful that she was writing to an experienced cryptographer, the learned lady put the Earl's name into Greek characters.

In November 1594 Pérez' own account of his life was printed by Richard Field; the cost, some said, was met by the Queen. A false imprint disguised its origins and it was not licensed; it was destined for the foreign markets, especially for the Netherlands and for English renegades abroad – to serve as a warning. The purpose was to stress the tyranny of Spanish rule, the ingratitude of the King towards those who served him, and the merciless nature of his vengeance.

Pedaços de historia o Relaciones was an enlargement of a work of 'Raphael Peregrino', Pérez' pseudonym, which had appeared in France. Purporting to be a third party's narration, it told the story of the Princess of Eboli and presented Pérez in his two favourite rôles: the Pilgrim and the Monster of Fortune. His seal was a Minotaur standing in the midst of a labyrinth, and this image was used with ingenuity in a variety of ways. Copies of the work were dispatched by Pérez, with effusive epistles, to all his influential friends. Whilst one of Essex's secretaries, Arthur Atey, prepared a translation into English, another friend, Sir Henry Wotton, wrote an elaborate review in English of the whole work. Neither of these were printed; it seems that the government did not want the subject publicly discussed. Pérez himself deeply offended and alienated the Queen when she received a report in which he had been accused of discussing at table whether a king might justly be killed by his subjects. Though his life story was in one respect a good cautionary tale, in another it provided a dangerous example of revolt against royal sovereignty, and Elizabeth would not offer public favours to one who, however provoked, had turned against his own country.

In June 1595 he was recalled to France by Henry IV, and although he tried hard to stay in England, in October, to the relief of many, he left for Rouen.

Pérez was the first Spaniard of any note to have appeared on the English scene for a long time; the urgent need to make himself important meant that his letters were a means to this end, so that his literary reputation was of the first importance to him. He had begun with the introductory epistle which he sent to Catherine de Bourbon and which was supposed to have been composed on the perilous journey over the Pyrenees. This was translated into

English as part of the *Relaciones*, and later was to be cited as a high example of the Spanish style by no less an authority than Gracián; the art of letter-writing, particularly in Italy, established it as a literary genre almost as defined as the sonnet:

Most gracious lady... since there cannot be on earth any corner or hiding place whither the sound of my persecutions and adventures, according to the great noise of them, hath not come, it is to be thought that the know-ledge of them hath ascended to such high places as Your Highness.... Princes have and ought to practise on earth the nature of the Elements; which for conservation of the world, that which one element refuseth and persecuteth, the other embraceth and defendeth. And as beasts rare and monstrous in nature are presented to princes and admitted favourably, with their curious desire to see them, so before your Highness shall be presented a Monster of Fortune, which hath always been of more admiration than the other, as effects of more violent causes.

[Ungerer, II, pp. 373-4

This translation by Essex's secretary, Arthur Atey, reveals the cosmic metaphors by which Pérez enlarged his destiny and himself. The Monster of Fortune and the Peregrino gave two images by which he characterized first his devout and blameless exile, and next the extraordinary, outrageous fascination of his victimization. The labyrinth of statecraft had transformed him – as his tortures had permanently marked him – so that he became comparable not only with the Minotaur but with the dwarfs of the Prado (that collection of natural monsters kept for the amusement of the Spanish Court), or with the monsters which Ben Jonson supplied for his Machiavellian Volpone. On one occasion he compared himself with an ant, and in a letter to his wife signed himself, 'Your milk, Antonio.'

When he came to England, Penelope Rich, Essex's sister, replaced the sister of the French King as the particular object of Pérez' devotion. To her Pérez addressed a number of letters in Spanish; in one, which acquired enough fame to be translated, he offered himself to her as a dog (in English the play upon *perro* and Pérez is lost, but we may remember that Romeo wished himself a glove upon Juliet's hand, and Pérez, as the dog, exemplified another of his mottoes – Faith and Love). At the same time he is like the grotesque figure from a carnival in Madrid.

I have been so troubled not to have at hand the dog's skin gloves your Ladyship desires that, pending the time when they shall arrive, I have resolved to sacrifice myself to your service and flay a piece of my own skin

from the most tender part of my body ... in my case this is nothing, for
even my soul will flay itself for the being it loves....

The gloves, my lady, are of dog's skin, though they are mine, for I hold
myself a dog, and hold myself bound also in your service in faith and
love.

Your ladyship's flayed dog, Antonio Pérez

[Ungerer, I, p. 199

Pérez was accustomed to bestowing special Spanish gifts upon his
patrons: perfumed gloves, fine stockings, medicinal recipes or
horoscopes – to which he was much addicted. He sent another pair
of gloves to Penelope's mother, Lettice, Countess of Leicester
Penelope was an angel; she restored life to his dead carcase. In
a letter to Essex however his conceit is that he has been brought
to the verge of extinction by the kisses of seven ladies, the Pleiades
of the Court. (The English habit of greeting with a kiss was the
delight and surprise of all foreigners.)

Essex of course could revive him again. Essex was his Apollo,
his Plato, his Saviour, his Bread, his Light; he was the infant Her-
cules strangling the serpents sent by Juno (Penelope's name for
Elizabeth). Pérez himself characterized his style as obscure and
melancholy; it was the obscurity and melancholy of the Hermeti-
cist (as displayed, for example, in Chapman's *Shadow of Night*),
and with the same fantastic emblematic images.

Even the leading figures of his past life could be transformed
for the occasion, as it suited. Whilst the dedicatory letter to Penelope Rich which accompanied the *Relaciones* spoke with pathos
of the Princess of Eboli, on writing to Essex, in complaining that
the Queen ignored the services done for her, he said that even
La Eboli, 'that Cyclops', could see better than this Sybilla.[7]

For the editions of his letters published later, Pérez amplified
and improved his material, often extending the conceits. His *Century of Letters* to Essex was printed in Paris in 1601, with his
Aphorisms; other material in his *Works* had appeared in 1598, the
Aphorisms from the *Relaciones* being appended.

At first the Essex group admired Pérez unstintedly, as Lady
Bacon's protests testify. The Earl termed him 'fons concilii' in
a highly complimentary letter (Ungerer, I, no. 204, p. 319). As
late as 28 January 1595 one 'A.B.' was writing in secret dispatches
to Spain that Pérez was highly esteemed, though he adds that all
intelligence from Spain comes by way of Horatio Palavicino and
the Dutch merchants.

Despite the high-flown mannerist style characteristic of his *Letters*, Pérez was master of quite another style – that of the condensed political aphorism – which was sprinkled through the *Relaciones*. Although his practices may suggest the name of Machiavelli, Pérez was not a student of the Florentine; he was, on the contrary, a most intent student of Tacitus, having acquired a taste for him through his master, Justus Lipsius, whose two famous books *Of Constancy* he also drew upon. Pérez was one of the leading Spanish authorities on Tacitus, and corresponded with a follower who was engaged in translating the Roman historian. In his *Lodestar for Princes* he openly compared Philip II to Tiberius and himself to Sejanus, and he observed that in the translation of Tacitus his friend 'touched on many points in history ... and that the sign would be a star in the margin'. The devious ways of Tiberius had been exemplified in his own downfall.

The curt and epigrammatic style of Tacitus became fashionable at the end of the 1590s, and is best exemplified in the *Essays* of 1597 by Pérez' friend, Francis Bacon. Pérez' own style however provided earlier examples, as witness the translation by Arthur Atey, which was current in Essex's circles from 1595. So Bacon learnt from Pérez: 'Severity in princes is like many deaths to a physician; it takes away their credit.'[8] These biting aphorisms alternate with the swelling mannerist style, as his ostentation alternated with his obsessive secrecy. Pérez' failing influence is rather cruelly suggested in a letter which in May 1595 one of Essex's secretaries, Anthony Stanton, sent to Anthony Bacon. Stanton was at supper with Pérez, Lady Rich and Sir Nicholas Clifford, when the Earl entered, announcing that next day he would take Pérez to Court, and afterwards visit the Countess of Essex (who lived quietly at Walsingham House, Seething Lane, to the east of the City). They would call on the way at Anthony Bacon's house in Bishopsgate. Lady Rich decided to join them, so it was planned that she would ride straight to Walsingham House in the coach, which would then return for the Earl. Stanton however thought she might change her mind and wrote to warn Bacon of the impending visitation: 'Now it is resolved that Mr Pérez shall not depart, for that my lord hath provided him here of the same office those Ennuches or Enukes have in Turkey, which is to have the custody of the fairest dames; so that he wills me to write that for the bond he hath with my lord he cannot refuse that office' (Ungerer, I, no. 118, pp. 232–3). This cruel joke suggests that Pérez would accept any insults and even turn them to advantage in his desperate attempt to stay.

The return of Pérez to France in the autumn of 1595 saw him accompanied by a bodyguard and secretaries supplied by the Earl of Essex and wearing his livery. Pérez was still part of the Essex intelligence service; but he was of course himself being shadowed. There was apparently an attempt on his life, by a Spaniard named Penilla, who was broken on the wheel and afterwards hanged. One bodyguard, Edward Wilton, described Pérez as 'exceeding timorous and will not stir abroad without us'; 'there is not any man more fearful', wrote the other. Pérez insisted on their company, even when he went to church to see a play on the twelve Apostles. Henry IV eventually supplied four Switzers as bodyguards.

Through the correspondence of his entourage with the secretariat of Essex, the first return to France has provided a dramatic and full portrait of Pérez. His first amanuensis provides also an interesting link with the players.

Godfrey Aleyn, of Windsor, was the son of John Aleyn, who had been a messenger to and from the friend of Essex, Sir John Bowes. Whilst living near Windsor, Pérez evidently became friendly with the Aleyn household, especially the thirty-year-old Godfrey, who, on his recommendation, was taken into Essex's service and assigned to himself, for service in France. Infected perhaps by example, Aleyn took to copying confidential letters between Essex and Pérez, which he sent home for distribution by his father to Bowes and others. It was crudely done, perhaps only to enhance his own importance, but the intelligence net soon hooked Aleyn, who was quietly given a summons home, then arrested, together with his father, and thrown into the Clink, the prison on the Bankside, charged with petty treason against his lord. Pérez raged at the behaviour of this 'Judas'.

The prisoner's examination revealed his folly and his disgraceful betrayal of trust, whilst from the Clink Aleyn wrote grovelling appeals to Anthony Bacon and the Earl. Eventually Pérez wrote also, asking for his release, alleging that he did so out of love for Aleyn's sister, a young girl who lived at Windsor – though, he added, he had not seduced her: 'Benigne ... te gerito cum illo ... scito enim me illius sororem amasse, sed sine tactu illius pudoris' (Ungerer, I, no. 248, p. 386). Aleyn was freed, but, to his evidently shocked surprise, was told he could now look for no more employment from Essex.

In 1642 Edward Aleyn, the son of Godfrey, claimed the War-denship of Dulwich College, through being kin to its founder, Edward Alleyn, the great actor, who had in fact taken him in 1622 into his foundation and admitted him as apprentice to himself – the articles being witnessed by a very distinguished company, among them Sir George More, Sir Edward Bowyer, Lord Howard of Effingham and the Sheriff of the county.

This may represent only the company at one of Alleyn's festal meetings, and Edward Aleyn did not substantiate his claim; but the connection seems firm enough. This link with the players would enable them to learn about Pérez; and if his love for the wench at Windsor was nothing but a diplomatic invention, yet it bears a surprising likeness to Armado's passion for Jacquenetta. A further link with Shakespeare is provided by the printer Richard Field, who was setting up *The Rape of Lucrece* in the same year as the *Relaciones* – both perhaps at the behest of highly placed members of the Essex circle.

After the defection of Aleyn, Pérez eventually received the most observant and intelligent of his companions, Robert Naunton, future Secretary of State to James I, who was to marry Penelope Rich's niece and namesake, Penelope Perrott. To the sharp eyes and ready pen of Naunton we owe the remarkable portrait of Pérez contained in his many dispatches to the Earl, which cover two years – February 1596 to February 1598. Pérez was changed from the man they had known by 'the conflicts and encounters of a troubled spirit'. There was talk of going to the Low Countries or to Venice, but devotion to Essex still ruled Pérez; it is obvious that he himself inspired affection in Naunton, who shelved his own future to return with him to England in May 1596, when Pérez tagged along with the French Ambassador, sent to negotiate the Treaty of Greenwich.

During this brief visit Pérez was disconcerted to find himself shunned. Essex being engaged on preparations for the raid on Cadiz, Anthony Bacon suffered so severely from Pérez' reproaches against himself and his master that, as his mother had foreseen, his health was undermined, and he fled to Twickenham.

From the port of embarkation Pérez had written on 26 March 1596 to Lady Penelope Rich:

Most excellent Lady; Senor Wilson hath given me news of the healths of your Ladyships, the three sisters and goddesses and in particular that all three have drunk a carouse unto Nature in thankfulness of that you all owe

unto her; for that she gave you not those delicate shapes to keep them idle
but rather that you should push forth unto us here many buds of those
divine beauties. To those Gardners I wish all happiness for so good tillage
of their grounds. Sweet Ladies mine, many of these carouses! O what a
book I have full of the secrets of the like tillage and trimmings of gardens!
If I return again to England, I shall have no need to seek my living of
anybody, for my book will serve my turn. But I will not sell so good cheap
this second time. My receipts will cost ... dearer; therefore let everyone
provide. Of your Ladyship, her Anthony Pérez.

[Ungerer, I, no. 521, pp. 91–2]

Pérez indeed had books of recipes; what he is suggesting here is
a book of diplomatic secrets. Although Lady Rich was in the
country at Wanstead, the bawdy innuendo, which escapes the editors of Pérez, can refer only to an expected child by Charles Blount
(their first son was born that year). Whether Dorothy, Countess
of Northumberland, and their sister-in-law, the Countess of Essex
herself, had also enjoyed such 'tillage' is more doubtful. In an
attempt to claim his privileged position as their 'guardian', Pérez
was overreaching himself.

On 13 May Penelope wrote from 'this solitary place', Wanstead,
to Anthony Bacon for news of her brother, adding in a postscript,
'I would fain hear what becomes of your wandering neighbour' –
that is, the Peregrino. To which, on 15 May, Bacon replied:

Your Ladyship may well call my neighbour wandering if you knew, as I
do against my will, what strange bypaths his thoughts walk in, which fester
every day more and more in his mind by my lord's silence and the continual
alarms that sound in his ears of the Queen's displeasure. The D. of Bouillon
presseth him to be in readiness to return with him but he refuses to go
without my lord's privity and consent.

[Ungerer, I, no. 175, pp. 276–7]

By the same post he wrote frantically to Essex, asking for some
word to pacify Pérez, who 'cannot himself nor will not let me rest',
and from Plymouth Essex replied that he had done so.

Pérez was to describe Elizabeth as having 'used him as an
Orange to be first sucked and then cast away' (Ungerer, II, p. 88).
It was fairly obvious to him that he had been dropped, and, returning to France after this brief second visit to England, he com-
pounded with Henry IV.

He maintained a lordly front, however. Writing from France,
he protested to the Bacons that loyalty could never be estranged
nor grief dissembled except by 'un bas maistre de comptes', like
Robert Cecil (Ungerer, I, p. 225). The Bacons were still his good

friends, although Anthony had felt himself but 'a cistern to receive his Spanish exclamations and scalding complaints'.

Pérez' conditions for swearing allegiance to France and becoming one of Henry IV's Council were offered haughtily and their extent was staggering. He asked for twelve thousand crowns in ecclesiastical preferment, which was also to be transmittable to his heirs; for his present pension to be raised to six thousand crowns; for a Cardinal's hat (his wife being rumoured dead) or else one for his son; and that his family's release, as French subjects, should be part of any French treaty with Spain. His oath to France would bind him to that country, but he protested to Essex his greater love to England, saying that he was like a man forced to marry a rich widow, whilst his love lay elsewhere. He tried to maintain his English connections, though very loath to write directly and very insistent that anything he had already written should be either destroyed or returned. He hoped Essex would finance the great expenses of his being installed as a Knight of the Saint Esprit (an honour Henry never accorded him).

He feared that his letters might be opened, and a note by Essex indicates that the Earl feared this also. At one point Lord Rich wrote to the Earl, saying he had been given a very secret letter which he himself was to bring home. Everyone held a wolf by the ears, so that every action became loaded with menace.

Pérez' confederates had accused him of still being secretly in touch with Spain. The English, who indirectly continued to profit from his intelligence, must have realized that this violated what was now his primary allegiance – sworn to France. After a few months Robert Naunton returned to his company, and a certain Marenco also carried news. On the rumour of his wife's death Pérez described himself, in his favourite image of a divided soul and body, as being but a ghost; Naunton disliked this playing with phrases. Pérez tried to probe Naunton about Essex's opinions of himself; and Naunton offered to explain his troubled mind to Essex for him, for he found him 'many ways discontented and utterly uncertain how to betake himself, to what course, to what country' (Ungerer, II, p. 101). Naunton glances at Pérez' passion for horoscopes: if he gets all he asks from Henry IV, 'I shall then *ex eventu* cognize with him the partial respects and favourable influences of the heavens in his nativity, which have so perfected his imperfections, even by his follies to improve his fortunes, as his greatest vanities are proved not in vain and to have been practised not altogether in vain' (Ungerer, II, no. 399, p. 105).

Naunton hated his own role: 'the best allowance of credit I can have is but in nature of betwixt a Paedagogue and a Spy, both trades I know not whether are more odious or base' (he was tutoring Essex's cousin, Robert Vernon).[9] Pérez was 'a very Proteus' who, when he got the special messenger he had demanded, took umbrage because the man's comings and goings would themselves betray him – he wanted so much 'as I think Mercury himself would scantly be wary enough to serve all turns'. 'A Man must be more than a prophet to divine what will best content him' (Ungerer, II, p. 135). Like the 'Emperor' of the mental hospital who turns to beg a little tobacco, the magnificent Pérez was really desperate for money.

When some 'leak' of the secret letters to England reached France, Naunton was appalled. He knew himself to be innocent but demanded to be relieved: 'Cupio dissolvi. I desire to go hence and be seen no more' (Ungerer, I, p. 144).

Pérez was then encouraged by the French to 'leak' the news of the coming Treaty of Vervins, to be signed by France and Spain, since it would involve a breach of the offensive and defensive Treaty of Greenwich, by which England and France were bound not to make a separate peace with Spain.

After the Treaty of Vervins was signed in 1598, even the generous Henry IV grew weary, and Pérez' fortunes went into irrevocable decline. The death of Philip II of Spain later that year gave Pérez some hope of restoring himself in Spain, which came to nothing. (After Philip's death, he published further papers, implicating the King in Escovedo's death.) Next year the Earl of Essex was disgraced by Pérez continued to correspond with him. Later he attempted, without success, to treat with his former enemies, the Cecils. He had characterized Robert Cecil by a variety of names, from 'Microgibbous' ('the little dwarf') to 'Roberto il Diabolo', and the Cecils never trusted him.

Following the accession of James I, peace with Spain was signed at last and Pérez desperately hoped to get something from the negotiations. The Spanish Ambassador to England, the Constable of Castille, gave Pérez a kindly word on his way through Paris, and, encouraged also by the English Ambassador, Pérez set out. Since the fall of Essex, the Embassy had been his link with England and he had passed on intelligence through this channel. James sent peremptory orders that he was not to land, but, relying on the assurances he had received, Pérez crossed and reached Canterbury, where the Earl of Devonshire (Charles Blount), one of the Commissioners for Peace, was sent by James to turn him back. From the family he trusted most, the hard command came which denied him even the courtesy of an escort, and cut his last links. He had renounced his pension before setting out, because it had not been paid in full, and now had to beg again of the always generous Henry IV. He sold his coach (the finest in Paris) and later even his bed. But he kept the incriminating Spanish papers.[10]

James knew, as his Ambassador did not, that the Spanish government would not want Pérez on the scene; moreover, to obviate suspicion of his entering a Protestant country, Pérez had brought a priest, an act which was forbidden. He always hoped to have the sentence of the Inquisition reversed; this was finally achieved in 1615 by the devoted efforts of his wife and son. Doña Juana died a few weeks later, knowing that her children had been cleared of dishonour, if burdened with debts of the costly Trial of Rehabilitation. Posters proclaiming Pérez' rehabilitation were set up in the streets of Saragossa.

Pérez lived on until 1611. Unexpectedly, in the years immediately following his death, his story was to be reanimated, in a different form, in a tragedy by John Webster.

Analogies between this story and Webster's *The Duchess of Malfi* include the arbitrary imprisonment of the Princess without trial, and ultimately in darkness, till her death. The King of Spain used the church courts, as Webster makes the Cardinal's denunciation the undoing of the Duchess; the King's methods of attack included espionage and counter espionage, and of course the public disclaiming of responsibility – indeed, the punishment of those who carried out his secret orders, as Ferdinand punishes his agent Bosola.

The King of Spain hounded Antonio Pérez, as the princes hounded Antonio Bologna, who, like Pérez, put his trust in horoscopes. The Princess of Eboli came of royal blood, like the Duchess, and even in prison maintained her pride and her defiance; her faithful attendants and her youngest child shared her imprisonment.

Deeper than any analogues is the 'absurdist' attitude, the belief that the world does not make sense, which underlies the fantastic conceits of Pérez and the tragedy of Webster. Pérez' favourite image of the labyrinth appears in Webster as a maze or mist or a 'deep pit of darkness'. The black storm is another image used by both, in a situation where no one wins, where the spy expects to be betrayed, where any figure may change into its opposite. The Church alone is constant in evil. Pérez' towering assertions of Spanish pride, alternating with the bitter sharpness of his political aphorisms, present the contradictory life of the Court as Webster conceived it.

PART TWO

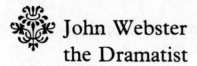

John Webster
the Dramatist

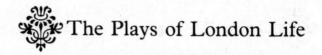 The Plays of London Life

From the first appearance of public playhouses in London in 1576, London citizens enjoyed the dramatizing of their own legends. The majority of the surviving plays dealing with London life – over a hundred from the period 1580–1642 – are comedies aimed at flattering the citizens, and making merry with the tricks of petty crime. London's part in national affairs was celebrated in the chronicle histories, and the City had its own martyrology, to which Webster's earliest surviving piece contributed.

The orthodox historic picture of London in the late sixteenth century – the Court supporting plays against a Puritan opposition from the City – is now in need of revision.[1] The facts appear to be more complex. When profits were found to be substantial, City men began to invest in the theatre, whilst some players established themselves as citizens of good standing. Webster's family trade of coach-making, another new luxury business, had itself been used as a symbol of vanity; yet if the streets were blocked by coaches, or by dangerous crowds assembled for plays, authority was powerless against force of opinion. Today, London traffic jams, or riotous Cup Finals, offer modern parallels for a situation to which, by the 1590s, the City had more or less resigned itself.

The appearance of playhouses in the late seventies and early eighties was followed by the incorporation of stable companies, and the embodiment of their playing in great poetic drama – that of Marlowe, Kyd, Greene. A sharp break occurred in the years 1592–4, when plague shut down all London playing, but in the years following this, different literary traditions became associated with certain houses, and with leading players. Around the turn of the century, in a period of great excitement, the players, having won their fight for survival, began to dispute between themselves;

it was at this point that Webster first came on the scene. His in-
volvement was probably greater than can be estimated from the
surviving documents and his printed plays. Much has been lost
from these years; the records of one theatre only (Henslowe's
Rose, on the Bankside) have been partly preserved: we have his
own word that of the work of one of Webster's friends and collaborators – admittedly a full professional – only ten per cent survives.[2]

The master of the little choristers of St Paul's first started a
playhouse just after the Merchant Taylors had recorded their disapproval of Mulcaster's money-making venture; here John Lyly's
delicate comedies, fresh from the Queen's household, were shewn
to a select audience of about a hundred.[3] In the following year,
1576, James Burbage, of Leicester's Men, built his theatre outside
the north-east gate of the City, in Shoreditch, with a capacity of
two thousand spectators. Opposition to this 'gorgeous playing
place erected in the fields' rose among clerics, inspired by the City
Fathers; but next year an actors' syndicate built another playhouse, the Curtain; also the Children of the Chapel Royal joined
the Paul's boys in the nearby ecclesiastical Liberty of Blackfriars,
where the Lord Mayor could not intervene; and around the walls,
various inns sheltered performers for the winter.

After a serious wave of opposition (1583) had been triumphantly
surmounted by courtly support from the Queen herself, two
wealthy citizens, John Cholmley, a Grocer, and Philip Henslowe,
a Dyer (also owner of property in Southwark, mining prospector
and master of the Royal Game of Bear-baiting), opened in 1587
the Rose Theatre in Southwark. Four years later Henslowe
married his step-daughter – whose father's money had launched
him – to Edward Alleyn, the leading tragedian of the Lord
Admiral's Men, so beginning a partnership which for some years
rivalled the Lord Chamberlain's Men, led by Burbage. In 1594
the last group were joined by William Shakespeare. These two
companies led all the rest.

An unfortunate venture by Francis Langley (Draper, nephew
of a former Lord Mayor, Lord of the Manor of Paris Garden and
City Alnager) produced in 1595 yet another theatre in Southwark.
Langley's trade record was far from spotless, and he certainly did
not represent the City at its best. In two years' time a libellous
presentation, *The Isle of Dogs*, at his Swan Theatre nearly shut
down all playhouses; he retreated from plays. In June 1597 the

Privy Council intervened with an Order licensing two playhouses only – one north of the river for Burbage, one south of the river for Alleyn; since their Orders usually represented a target aimed at by the Council rather than a *fiat* which must be obeyed, several other theatres persisted. Yet status and recognition had been given to the cream of the profession. They evolved specialities to suit their special talents for 'comedy, tragedy, history, pastoral'. When at Christmas 1599 Burbage's company crossed the river and settled on the Bankside to build their own Globe, Alleyn's troupe moved away from the competition and succeeded in finding a site in the fields outside Cripplegate, nearer to the Inns of Court and to the Court itself, for their Fortune playhouse. Although the City Fathers had closed inn-yard theatres within the walls (including one, the Bel Savage, which had belonged to the Cutlers' Company), the little choristers of St Paul's (whose performances had ceased in 1590) were happy to fill the gap, being soon rejoined by the boys from the Chapel Royal at Blackfriars. These two private theatres were privileged, elitist and expensive.

It has already been mentioned (see page 42) that although some courtiers were interested – Lord Derby helped to finance the theatre at St Paul's – it was the Inns that provided new playwrights for the choristers, as well as a critical audience. A young man might now increase his fashionable reputation by writing for the stages – and when John Marston at the end of 1599 inherited his father's fortune, he also took shares in the Choristers' Theatre, first Paul's and then Blackfriars.

Fortified by new blood and much attention, the different groups began to compete, trying to copy one another's successes, and engaging in cross-debate. Playwrights had their personal following; they defined their audience's expectations and tastes. In a debate, with John Marston and Thomas Dekker on one side, Ben Jonson on the other, Shakespeare intervened with his players' scene in *Hamlet* (1601–2). This misnamed 'War of the Theatres' repeated the kind of duelling that lawyers and poets were accustomed to practise; even schoolboys were licensed to dispute in Smithfield at Bartholomew Tide. If the ridicule, which was part of the technique, led to 'purges' and 'emetics' being administered on stage, players felt confident enough to challenge each other, which implied that no one else was threatening their existence. This independence had grown gradually over a quarter of a century.

In 1578 they had still hardly been thought of as citizens, when John Stockwood, Master of the Skinners' School at Tonbridge, preached the Bartholomew Tide sermon against them at St Paul's Cross,[4] before the Lord Mayor and Aldermen. He begged the nobles, whose servants the City players claimed to be, not to keep men who went 'with long blades by their sides, with slashing and cutting and ruffianly quarrelling ... and for never so little word speaking, imitating the speech of the devil to our Saviour, If thou be a man of thy hands, come meet me in Smithfield'.

Condemnation of profane sports by the Church reinforced the bureaucratic objections to riots and tumults, which might erupt in any kind of assembly. The futility of the constable was a standing joke; apprentices, who were supposed to quell tumults, were quite likely to start one. Yet in the year 1579 Stephen Gosson, while attacking plays in general for their bad effect upon the young, admits some actors are 'properly learned, honest householders and citizens well thought of among their neighbours at home'; the pride of their 'hangbyes' – that is, their hired men – 'cause them to be ill talked of abroad'. It was no small advantage for actors to enjoy full trading rights in the City – to achieve which, they had to be Citizens and Freemen of a Guild. Even Hunnis, Master of the Chapel Boys, became free of the Grocers.

John Heminges, the future leader of Burbage's troupe, and editor of Shakespeare's plays, was also made free of the Grocers in 1587,[5] having been duly apprenticed to James Collins (who later remembered Heminges in his will). But he married the widow of a famous actor Knell, and stayed in this profession. Later, Robert Armin belonged to the leading Company of the Goldsmiths; Ben Jonson was free of the Tilers and Bricklayers and rather irregularly paid his dues; Anthony Munday was a 'citizen and Draper'. Henslowe and Alleyn, Heminges and Condell became churchwardens or sidesmen in their parishes, and therefore undertook a measure of civic duty (for the City delegated to the parish in certain matters). Henslowe maintained a soldier for the militia, supplying his arms and drinking money. By the end of the century Shakespeare had acquired a coat-of-arms from the Heralds' office, Alleyn and Henslowe each had theirs, and players might even be gentlemen. Yet under the Act of 1572, players could be classed as vagabonds.

The citizens had still felt in 1584 that Christmas plays acted by amateurs were the only proper form of playing;[6] some of the tradesmen still performed plays, and the players also gave performances in special honour of the Companies. Wentworth Smith, one of Webster's collaborators, wrote in 1615 that his *Hector of Germany* had been given by tradesmen at the Curtain and the Red Bull, but that he had also written *The Freeman's Honour* to the glory of the Merchant Taylors, and the Lord Chamberlain's Men acted it.

The first great celebration of solidarity came in Armada year, 1588, when, as part of the triumph, Robert Wilson, of the Queen's Men, wrote *Three Lords and Three Ladies of London*. As preface, in dumb show, a lady, very richly attired, representing London, advanced with two angels before and two behind, having bright rapiers in their hands. The prologue explained that God would protect London for the love He bore the Queen. In tradesman's language he then switched to the matter in hand:

> Your patience yet awhile we crave till we have trimmed our stall,
> Then young and old, come and behold our wares and buy them all.
> Then if our wares shall seem to you well woven, good and fine,
> We hope we shall your custom have, again, another time.

Since they maintained morale, plays are listed by the Three Lords (Pleasure, Pomp and Policy) as part of the campaign against the Three Lords of Spain.

Eventually it was realized that some subsidiary trades were dependent on the great companies of actors; their good word or their ill word could have its effect upon employment. 'Blackfriars hath almost spoiled Blackfriars for feathers' – that is, the feather-sellers of Blackfriars have been ruined by a playhouse jest by John Webster, in the Blackfriars Theatre, that 'every fool has his feather'.[7]

The actors turned a critical eye on the details of City life; some of their satire on usurers and the tricksters of the underworld was as conventional as that of the pulpit. Yet a certain generosity to prodigals and a certain harshness towards Puritan hypocrisy in tradesmen might still be considered evidence of the 'presumption' and 'contempt' with which players had been charged in early days, as usurping the right to moralize.

Inevitably some voices continued to be raised against them, and in the year that Webster wrote *The White Devil* a country preacher at Paul's Cross was still classing players as drones of the commonwealth, with gamesters, coney-catchers (or city cheats) and 'Epicures' in a Bartholomew Tide sermon: 'Yea, plays are grown nowadays into such high request (*Horresco referens*) as that some profane persons affirm, they can learn as much both for example and edifying at a play as at a sermon. *O tempora. O mores*, O times, O manners, tremble thou earth, blush ye heavens ... to compare the idle and scurrill invention of an illiterate bricklayer to the holy, pure and powerful word of God. ...'[8]

Three years later, the illiterate bricklayer (Ben Jonson) was to celebrate the same feast with his *Bartholomew Fair*, and to produce his preaching baker, Zeal of the Land Busy, worsted in his dispute with the puppets of the Fair. Busy quoted the Old Testament against man putting on woman's attire, to be confuted by the leading puppet giving an ocular demonstration that it was innocent of sin.

The other side of the coin appears in the dedication and prologue to Wentworth Smith's *The Hector of Germany or the Palgrave Prime Elector, a new Play; an Honourable History*, which came out the following year. It is dedicated to Sir John Swinnerton, Merchant Taylor and former Lord Mayor – 'I have received some favours from you, in private things, thought it might be acceptable to give you some honour in print'. The play had been given 'by a companie of young men of the City' at the Red Bull and the Curtain, as the prologue explains:

> If you should ask us, being men of trade,
> Wherefore the players' faculty we invade?
> Our answer is, No ambition to compare
> With any in that quality held rare;
> Nor with a thought for any grace you give
> To our weak action, by their course to live:
> But as in camps and nurseries of art
> Learning and valour have assumed a part
> In a Cothurnal Scene their wits to try,
> Such is our purpose in this history.
>
> Emperors have played, and their associates too –
> Soldiers and scholars; 'tis to speak and do.
> If citizens come short of their high fame,
> Let citizens bear with us for the name,
> And gentlemen, we hope what is well meant
> Will grace the weak deed for the good intent;
> Our best we promise with a dauntless cheek,
> And so we gain your love, 'tis all we seek.

In the dedication it is reported that the company of young men 'did it well', and may therefore be presumed to have honoured the Lord Mayor. The very respectful tone in which they disclaim any attempt to compete with the actors accords full professional recognition for the 'faculty'; the tradesmen are willing to be compared with those who act 'in vacant times of recreation' – especially if these are their social superiors – but, as craftsmen, they recognize fellow-craftsmen in the players of the Red Bull. The leading poet there had just published his *Apology for Actors*.

Attempts have been made to compare the structure and organization of the actors' companies with those of the trade guilds. There was of course a rough correspondence between those who held shares in the company, and therefore determined its policy, and the masters in the guild; between the journeymen and the hired men who were qualified workers but employed by others; and between the apprentices and the players' boys. But the parallel otherwise is not very close; joint financial responsibility of the theatre 'sharers' was more like that of shareholders in a modern trade venture, and the working collaboration far closer than that of members of a guild. On the other hand, the players as such could claim no part in civic government; the guilds were to a large extent the executive arm of the City. They bought corn in times of dearth, for which the City arranged distribution; they organized the militia, and their charity made up a substantial part of Health and Welfare. The working collaboration of the guilds now lay less in production of goods than in civic administration and large-scale financial ventures.

The players would certainly to some extent take their model from the organizations they knew best, and with which they were linked through individual members. Certain guilds, particularly the Drapers and the Merchant Taylors, might be expected to have closer ties than others with the players, for gorgeous costumes were the players' most striking property, and their greatest financial outlay was often the costuming of a play. When, at the accession of James, three London companies were given royal patronage, this must have made them feel grander in social terms – it was almost like the modern theatrical knighthood. Although only troupes under royal patronage were supposed to perform, the powers of enforcement were weak, and it is rather unlikely that all the lesser groups were rooted up. If no longer 'vagabonds', now, as traders, they were 'rogues'.

If, at moments of national festivity, good players were still able to give expression to national feeling, it was evidence of their growing professionalism that such expressions should be not merely traditional but specifically fitted to the particular moment. Indeed, in their quick power to extemporize news flashes from the countryside, they were in a sense forerunners of the modern journalist. Tragedies on the 'Latest Horrible Murder' were a regular feature of the London stage, *Arden of Faversham* (1591) and *A Yorkshire Tragedy* (1606) being the best known. *The Late Lancashire Witches* (1634) was among the last.

In February 1603 Chapman wrote a farce, *The Old Joiner of Aldgate*, in which he chronicled the efforts of a London barber to sell his daughter to the highest bidder, with his eventual defeat at the hands of an unscrupulous cleric; the case was still *sub judice* and it was alleged that Chapman had been paid to stage the story in order to shame the plaintiff into withdrawing his action.

Twenty years later John Webster was to combine with others, including his friend John Ford, in staging another farcical matrimonial adventure, together with a local murder – the alternative title to *Keep the Widow Waking* (1624) being *The Late Murder of the Son upon the Mother*. The widow, a foolish old woman intimidated into marriage, lived in Webster's own neighbourhood. The murder was committed in Whitechapel.[9]

Within two years, in *The Staple of News* (1626), Ben Jonson was to attack the embryonic industry of news sheets, or *corantos*; his view was that the stage, which combined recent history with interpretation, was a higher and nobler form than direct reporting. He did not think mere information was desirable.

An attempt to turn the edge of rancour was the will of Nicholas Tooley, Gent., made on 3 June 1623. He was an actor who had played a minor rôle in Webster's *The Duchess of Malfi*, having started as an apprentice to Richard Burbage and risen to be one of the chief players. He left a sum for a funeral sermon to be preached by the Rev. Thomas Adams. Thomas Adams was a most dramatic preacher, and in 1612 he preached a sermon entitled *The White Devil*, on religious hypocrisy. The text was St John 12: 5, Judas' hypocritical protest against the anointing of Christ's feet. Adams goes through the sins of the City, the real waste of riches:

Our monstrous pride, that turns hospitality into a dumb show; that which fed the belly of hunger, now feeds the eye of lust; acres of land are metamorphosed into trunks of apparel; and the soul of charity is transmigrated into the body of bravery ... shall I say our upholding of Theaters, to the contempt of religion, our maintaining of Ordinaries, to play away our patrimonies; our four-wheeled Porters; our Antick, the fashion; our smoky consumptions; our perfumed putrefactions; *ad quid perditio haec*?[10]

He attacks the City's sins under twelve heads, all of which might be found in the City comedy. City hypocrisy is his White Devil. And Tooley expects this denouncer of sin to preside at an actor's funeral!

English history was presented to Londoners from the first in terms of their own city – less in terms of the chronicles than of the ballads and legends. In Peele's *Edward I* (1591) the Lady Mayoress is murdered by the wicked Spanish Queen Eleanor, who is punished by sinking into the earth at Charing Cross and emerging at Potter's Hithe (Scenes 18, 20).

In the Shakespearean play of *Sir Thomas More*, the witty Londoner, friend to players, fills the scene with merry jests at the expense of learned judges. London was also warned by examples, ranging from Nineveh to Antwerp, against the vengeance that overtook sin; but after the Privy Council's Order of June 1597, with characteristic audacity, players began again to stage comedies in which London's worthies indulged in sports. Dekker's *The Shoemakers' Holiday* (the Rose, 1599) shows the fifteenth-century Lord Mayor, Simon Eyre, in a species of city pastoral, leading his band of journeymen in gambols, enriching himself by trickery, abetting true lovers to outwit parental authority, endowing a feast for all the 'prentices of London, and a market in Leadenhall. In a vigorous (and plainly Tudor) London he bounces along, 'a comic Tamburlaine', as a form of encouragement spouting out incessant abuse, like Tamburlaine whipping on his jades. He shouts to his wife, 'Away, you Islington whitepot, hence, you happer-arse, you barley pudding full of maggots, you broiled carbonado.... Sim Eyre knows how to speak to a Pope, to Sultan Solyman, to Tamburlaine' (V. iv. 46–53). He really behaves more like a player than a tradesman and his wife's constant unintended bawdry is kept always in view, like the knickers of the pantomime dame. Finally the King appears to approve all that is done, and to frolic with Simon Eyre.

City disapproval is subverted by fun here; but more serious plays reflected the grave problem of the succession and the coming change of rulers, which the Queen's decline, as she approached her seventieth year, made inevitable. This forbidden subject was

'shadowed' in the succession politics of her father's reign, where
London's rôle was emphasized. Henslowe put on an expensive
play on Cardinal Wolsey; the Lord Chamberlain's Men staged
one on Thomas Cromwell,[11] and among such plays is the first surviving text with which Webster's name was associated. Henslowe,
on 22 May 1602, and again on 29 May, paid Munday, Drayton,
Middleton and Webster for a play at first named *Caesar's Fall* but
afterwards *Two Shapes*; they received £9 in all. This was for the
Admiral's Men. At the start of the autumn season, on 15 October,
for his second company, Worcester's Men, Henslowe made a
token payment of a shilling to 'Harry Chettle, Thomas Dekker,
Thomas Heywood and Mr Smith and Mr Webster' for a play
called *Lady Jane*; but on 2 November Heywood and Webster received the handsome sum of £3 in earnest of *Christmas Comes but
Once a Year*.[12]

Henslowe's record stops soon after this; but Webster appears
as an apprentice playwright, supplying piece work as his father
might supply chariots for the Lord Mayor's Show. It used to be
fashionable to try to sort out plays among collaborators, line by
line; but that is not how collaboration works in the theatre.
Webster was involved in the whole thing, and its significance lies
in what it contributed to his personal development.

His fellow-workers included the experienced Henry Chettle, a
printer by trade, and author that same year of a revenge tragedy,
Hoffman; Munday, an old hand who had also penned attacks on
plays and been satirized by Ben Jonson; Dekker, whom Jonson
had likewise satirized but who was to be Webster's collaborator
again, and a most faithful delineator of the London scene; Thomas
Heywood, to become the leading playwright of Queen Anne's
Men, and a friend of Webster; Drayton, the lyric poet, who wrote
plays as pot-boilers; and Wentworth Smith, who, like Webster,
is dignified with a respectful 'Master'. He may have been a fellow-
tradesman, for his connections seem to lie with livery-companies.
Lastly, Middleton, a young beginner trying his hand at poems,
plays and pamphlets, the son of a London bricklayer, who was to prove
one of the future leaders in satiric City comedy, and, twenty years
later, Webster's successor in tragedy.

The printed play *The Famous History of Sir Thomas Wyatt with
the Coronation of Queen Mary and the Coming in of King Philip*
appeared in 1607 as given by the Queen's Majesties' Servants (that
is, Worcester's Men), written by Thomas Dekker and John

Webster. This must be a reshaping of *Lady Jane*, which had been successful enough to warrant a second part and was being played again in 1604 at the Boar's Head in Aldgate. The book had not been licensed and presents a very short text.[13]

Lady Jane Grey, executed at the age of seventeen, six months after her nine days' reign as Queen of England (9–19 July 1553), stood as surrogate for Elizabeth, a Protestant martyr to the claims of Catholic Spain; her execution was precipitated by the rebellion of Thomas Wyatt against the Spanish marriage of Mary Tudor. This rebellion had remarkably foreshadowed the rebellion of the Earl of Essex in 1601, so the relation to current politics was clear. It was a dangerous subject even to hint at in a play; but after the succession of James I, who looked on Essex as a martyr for his own cause, the theme of Sir Thomas Wyatt's rebellion would have been quite acceptable. Just as in 1602 there had been a group of plays involving succession to the Crown, so in 1604 another group directly shewing Elizabeth appeared: the Queen's Men put on Heywood's *If you know not me, you know nobody*, the first part of which was a continuation of *Sir Thomas Wyatt* (with some of the same characters), dealing with Elizabeth's trials as Princess. The Admiral's Men, now Prince Henry's, replied with Rowley's *When you see me, you know me*, in which Cardinal Wolsey (still alive at the end of Henry's reign) plots against the Lutheran Queen, Katherine Parr! In 1606 Dekker's very noisy and triumphant allegory on Queen Elizabeth, *The Whore of Babylon*, was staged at the new Red Bull Theatre by the Queen's Men; the historic deviations were defended in the preface.

The dilemma of *Sir Thomas Wyatt*, a more thematic and serious drama than most, turns on the question 'What is treason?' In the name of lineal succession, Wyatt at first defends 'the Princely Maids' – that is, Mary and Elizabeth Tudor – against the arbitrary bequeathing of the Crown by the boy King Edward to his cousin Jane Grey. Wyatt's later revolt against Queen Mary's Spanish marriage was implicitly in Elizabeth's favour – but in this play she does not appear; Jane however goes to her death denounced by Bishop Gardiner of Winchester as a heretic, and clasping a prayer book. Gardiner, who appears in all these plays as the arch-villain (he is responsible for the death of Thomas Cromwell, and for the trials of Princess Elizabeth in *If you know not me, you know nobody*), stands for the political threat in the relation of Church and State, and the events recounted would have been within living memory.[14]

The guilt lies with the older men: the Duke of Northumberland, who marries his son to Lady Jane and leads her father Suffolk in the crime against the sacred principle of lineal succession. Jane and her husband are shown as victims and true lovers whose only wish is to die together.

In the opening scene Guildford Dudley, Jane's husband, protests that his wife, if crowned, will be a usurper:

> Our fathers grow ambitious
> And would force us sail in mighty tempests.
> [I. ii. 9–10

The young pair are as much victims of their elders' evil ways as were Romeo and Juliet. Jane replies, 'Who would wear fetters though they were all of gold?' (I. ii. 25)–a line the author of *The Duchess of Malfi* (cf. IV. ii. 216–23) would not have disowned. As Arundel hails her Queen she resists:

> O God, methinks you sing my death in parts
> Of music's loudness, 'tis not my turn to rise.
> [I. ii. 39–40

Next, as the two hapless young creatures are royally escorted to the Tower, they lament:

Dudley.   Some lodgings in it will, like dead men's skulls,
        Remember us of frailty.

Jane.   We are led with pomp to prison.
        O prophetic soul,
        Lo, we ascend into our chairs of state
        Like funeral coffins, in some funeral pomp
        Descending to their graves.
        [I. ii. 60–66

Finally, before the lords, who subsequently try them for treason, they plead:

> It was imposed upon us by constraint,
> Like golden fruit hung on a barren tree.

and this by the very men who now sit to try them!

> Who cried so loud as you, God save Queen Jane?
> And come you now your sovereign to arraign?
> Come down, come down, here at a prisoner's bar.
> [V. i. 87–9

Claiming the Queen's pardon, the 'great men, like flies, through thin cobwebs break'; whilst most are remorseful, Stephen Gardiner forces the death penalty.

Webster's interest in the law may have given him composition of the trial scene, which was to remain a feature of his later plays. Jane holds up at the bar

> A hand as pure from treason, innocent
> As the white livery
> Worn by the angels in their maker's sight.
>   [V. i. 19–21

Her betrayal is re-echoed in the betrayal of her father, a starving fugitive, by a servant who afterwards, like Judas, hangs himself. Again, it is echoed by the treachery of the comic London trades-men towards Wyatt. Led against him, on encounter they take his part, because 'Wyatt is up to keep the Spaniard down'. (Webster might have had a special interest in the event because the Lord Mayor whose action halted Wyatt at Bridgegate was a Merchant Taylor; but this scene, if originally depicted, has not survived.) Historically, Wyatt then crossed the Thames upstream of the City and marched down upon Ludgate, as Essex did in 1601. At Ludgate he was repelled by the Earl of Pembroke, retreated down Fleet Street, was wounded and captured – the jolly enthusi-asm of Brett, the Londoner, and his 'mad' flat-caps evaporating here. Exactly so had the Londoners failed to support Essex; the ground traversed is the ground of his advance and retreat, a very short distance south of Webster's own home.

A London audience must have drawn the parallel with these events, only a year old at the first staging of *Lady Jane*. The cause for which Wyatt died was Essex's cause; his last words are a warn-ing:

> Had London kept his word, Wyatt had stood
> But now King Philip enters through my blood.

The play was restaged as peace was being signed with Spain, and Spanish emissaries in the City were attended by the King's Men to wait his pleasure (Worcester's/Queen Anne's men were sent to wait on the Archduke from the Netherlands). Such words might still ring ominously in 1605.

Thematically well planned, with the clowning closely related to the main action,[15] this short version could be simply staged; there are no fights and the only property required is the head of Jane, which is brought on in the last scene, where, contrary to history, her execution precedes her husband's. In his lament he imagines her beauty still alive.[16]

Since two collaborators' names only appear on the title-page, this version could represent an abbreviated form for a company of London tradesmen, such as those who put on Wentworth Smith's *Hector of Germany* or Taylor's *The Hog hath Lost His Pearl* (which landed its performers in Bridewell). Such private performances might lead to rather dangerous discussion or comment. This is most decidedly a play for a London audience. Its religious bias is emphasized by having Queen Mary appear at first, quite unhistorically, in the garb of a nun.

Thomas Heywood, of the Queen's Men, produced his very popular and gorgeously staged *If you know not me, you know nobody* in 1604. The first part opens with a number of courtiers discussing the overthrow of Wyatt and the marriage of Queen Mary. A vision of bright angels appears to the captive Elizabeth in the Tower. The last scene shows her triumphantly rewarding her faithful friends, pardoning her jailer with an angry quip, whilst the wicked Gardiner expires. On the title-page she wears her gorgeous 'Armada' dress; this victory climaxes the second part of the play. Part 2, however, is mainly a London frolic about Sir Thomas Gresham, his extraordinary financial resources, and the prodigal career of his nephew,[17] who is apprenticed to another frolicsome figure, Hobson the Haberdasher, built on the familiar model of Simon Eyre. London citizens had already been complimented by Heywood in *Edward IV* (1599), a two-part play, where the pathos of Jane Shore, the nobility of her husband, and the humours of Hob the Tanner of Tamworth (a madcap, again modelled on Simon Eyre) are fitted to a very slight historical frame. Both these actions are based on ballad material. Preaching the safe doctrine that a de facto ruler must always be obeyed, throwing in a few compliments to the London 'prentices for their valiant defence of the City against Falconbridge's Lancastrians, Heywood also boldly condemns the treacherous attitude of the Court and even the Council, as Webster and Dekker had done.

London's sense of its own identity and the continuity of its history had been popularized by the great *Survey* of John Stow (1598). The little London tailor had devoted his whole life to this work, which became a quarry of legends. Since so many Londoners came originally from the country, the London legends would play an important rôle in making them feel part of the City, giving it identity and the kind of cohesion that was found in country places and more stable communities. One success story, popular on stage then, still survives in pantomime – *Dick Whittington.*

Webster's share in the City's welcome to James I is marked by the verses he supplied for Stephen Harrison's *Arches of Triumph*, the account of the City's magnificent series of triumphal arches built for the coronation entry in March 1604. Webster makes the point that these celebrate not war but a peaceful accession, and thereby London becomes more glorious than Rome. The fact that his verses were called for implies a modest reputation in the City as a loyal Londoner.

Moreover, the coach-makers, who were also builders of pageant waggons, would have been vitally interested in the dimensions of those arches, through which the whole procession had to make its way.

Webster's next collaboration with his friend Dekker in the season 1604–5 resulted in two successful comedies for the Children of Paul's: *Westward Ho!* and *Northward Ho!* These were of a quite different order from his previous work, and put him with the avant-garde; the first of the comedies provoked a riposte, *Eastward Ho!*, from a very strong team, Chapman, Jonson and Marston, which caused a major scandal and landed the first two in jail. Webster and Dekker returned the ball rapidly, for the opportunity was too good to miss.

The themes treated were in one form or another to remain Webster's particular province; they were the relations of marriage and money, of different classes in one complex society, and the relation of the play world to the real world. Here the society is London – citizens, courtiers and the underworld. The first theatrical season of the new reign, when the theatres reopened after another long closure for plague, brought renewed excitement and new daring in the treatment of London life. The pace of evolution was fast; *Westward Ho!*, *Eastward Ho!* and *Northward Ho!* each take a different approach, use a different set of conventions or combine conventions in a different way. So the titles do not only represent the cries of the Thames watermen advertising voyages upstream or downstream, they also suggest different points of direction in a critical sense.

The variety required and achieved is described in the induction to a play that appeared at Blackfriars next year; the discoverer of a new-found land, the Isle of Gulls, is 'A stranger? the better

welcome; comes he Eastward, Westward or Northward Ho? ...
what method obtains he in his play, is 't anything critical? are
lawyer's fees and citizen's wives laid open in it? ... is there any
great man's life character'd in it? ... is there any good bawdry
in 't? any cuckolding?'[18] Satirist and amorist are joined by a third
spectator, the ranter; I like neither railing nor bawdry; no, give
me a stately penned history as thus

> The rugged winds, with rude and ragged ruff....'

Westward Ho! seems to be the first play to satirize – and at the
same time to give the victory in marital contest – to City wives.
It was to be followed both at the Choristers' and the Men's theatres
by a range of variations. Its basis, ultimately, is *The Canterbury
Tales*, with their London Merchant, the Host of the Tabard Inn,
the Woman Merchant from Bath, the Guildsmen.

The theatre at Paul's was very small, being in a private house
in the cloisters, but there were seventeen actors, ranging at first
in age from ten to fourteen, who resided in the precincts under
the direction of their Master, Edward Peers, a former Gentleman
of the Chapel Royal – one therefore well acquainted with the rival
troupe at Blackfriars. The play might be no more than a sequel
to a chamber concert, where some of the best music in Europe
might be heard. Consequently it needed to be pungent and sharp;
to this end, the choristers' poets developed and heightened the
'gamey' style of the old private plays at colleges and Inns of Court.

The comedy was here 'framed' in a melodramatic action that
parodied several recent revenge tragedies. The hero of this part
of *Westward Ho!*, an Italian merchant resident in London, bore
the name of the chief agent of Sir Horatio Palavicino, the financier;
whether Signor Justiniano was really 'characterized' in this Proteus is not clear. A wicked old Earl pursues with villainous intent
the chaste Mistress Justiniano; seemingly deserted and left to
poverty, she appears to yield. The mute but splendidly arrayed
figure who awaits the Earl in Mistress Birdlime's bawdy house
appears at first, when unveiled, some kind of devil; but the appari-
tion emerges later as Justiniano himself in his wife's attire. The
dead body of the lady is then produced, and Justiniano claims to
have poisoned her to preserve her chastity. When the Earl has been
publicly shamed by a powerful denunciation before the other visitors to the bawdy house, the lady is briskly commanded to rise,
which she does. The Earl departs and her husband congratulates

his wife on obtaining her rich garments and jewels without any payment. His high moral tone is therefore rather abruptly abandoned.

Virtue besieged, and the resurrection of supposedly dead characters, are familiar themes in Dekker's plays; but this play also contains a parody of Tourneur's *The Revenger's Tragedy*, played by the King's Men, and of Marston's tragedy of *Sophonisba*, played by their Chapel Boys at Blackfriars. Mistress Justiniano, lamenting her poverty, is eloquent enough:

> Poverty, thou bane of chastity,
> Poison of beauty, broker of maidenheads,
> I see when Force, nor Wit can scale the hold,
> Wealth must. She'll ne'er be won, that defies gold.
> But lives there such a creature; O 'tis rare
> To find a woman chaste, that's poor and fair.
>
> [II. ii. 142–7

To ensure that we are not in the presence of the tragic Mistress Jane Shore, or of Castiza, she is instantly deflated by the entrance of Mistress Birdlime: 'Now, lamb! has not his Honour dealt like an honest Nobleman with you?' (II. ii. 248). Justiniano's vision of the universal state of sin may echo the tragic speech of Vindice but it is actually part of his temptation of a City wife: 'Why, there's no minute, no thought of time passes, but some villainy or other is a brewing; why, even now, now, at holding up of this finger and before the turning down of this, some are murdering, some lying with their maids, some picking of pockets, some cutting purses, some cheating, some weighing out bribes. In this city some wives are cuckolding some husbands....' (II. i. 185–90).[19] And when his scholar says, 'Troth master, I think thou wilt prove a very knave,' he retorts, 'It's the fault of many that fight under this band.' (He is wearing Puritan bands instead of a ruff.)

The main action (framed by melodramatic parody) concerns a game of catch-as-catch-can between three tradesmen's wives, their husbands, and three gallants who are wooing the wives, assisted by Justiniano, here in disguise as a writing-master and Puritan but really operating as a pimp. He is a version of the disguised ruler or spy or double agent, one of the most popular figures in the comedies and tragi-comedies of this season.[20]

The full obscenity of Justiniano's new name, Parenthesis, is not revealed;[21] but in contrast to the melodramatic assaults on Mistress Justiniano, the pursuit of Clare Tenterhook, Mab Wafer and

Moll Honeysuckle by the Earl's nephew and his boon companions gives the Wives' City League a chance faithfully to copy the trading skill of their husbands. In putting up the only commodity they have for trade – their favours – the wives show themselves expert; the scene itself is brought very close to the playhouse. Their first treat is a glass of Rhenish wine and a Dutch bun at the Steelyard. The next assignation is to be in St Paul's, and at prayers: 'Through Paul's; every wench take a pillar, then, clap on your masks; your men will be behind you, and before your prayers be half done, be before you and man you out at several doors' (II. i. 220–23).

The wives continue holding back, manipulating their clients and deceiving their husbands, whilst they take a jaunt by water to Brentford, with the prospect of a good supper and a night's lodging at a famous inn. But like the merry wives of Windsor, the three City wives preserve their virtue. After boasting, 'We are furnished for attendance as ladies are, we have our fools and our ushers,' they contrive that while one woman feigns sickness, the other two rush off to attend her and they lock themselves in: '[We] have wit enough to outstrip twenty such gulls ... the jest shall be a stock to maintain us and our pewfellows in laughing at christenings, cryings out, and upsittings these twelve month' (V. i. 159–73). They are more skilful than the Young Lady of Kent in Victorian times:

> There was a young lady of Kent
> Who said that she knew what it meant
> When an elegant sinner
> Would take her to dinner –
> She knew what it meant; but she went.

Finally, they coolly join forces with Mistress Birdlime and her resident damsel, Luce. With such allies, the wives confront their husbands (as they arrive at midnight in pursuit to charge them with infidelity), bringing counter charges that cannot be denied. The men have visited Mistress Birdlime, given tokens to Luce. All parties return to London, to the words of a song incorporating the pun still heard at Boat Club suppers: 'Oars, oars, oars, oars!' The whore and bawd are indeed the most interesting and fully developed characters here. Mistress Birdlime had predecessors on the Choristers' stage[22] – and in the law students' revels too, perhaps – but her account of her highly professional work on behalf of the Earl brings the spectators back once more to the cathedral church of St Paul's – 'now, now, at the lifting of this finger' – the scene might be enacted in real life: 'The troth is, my lord, I got her to my house. There she put off her own clothes, my Lord, and put on yours, my Lord, provided her a Coach, searched the middle aisle in Paul's and with three Elizabethan twelve-pence pressed three knaves, my Lord, hired three liveries in Long Lane, to man her; for all which, so God mend me, I'm to pay this night before sunset' (II. ii. 42–7).

Extreme wickedness is still liable to be fathered on someone Italian, or Italianate; Birdlime appeals to Mistress Justiniano: 'This Italian, your husband's countryman, holds it impossible any of their ladies should be excellent witty and not make the utmost use of their beauty, will you be a fool then?' (I. i. 91–4). But Justiniano himself compares her defence of chastity to London salesmanship – a piece of Puritan hypocrisy. It is obvious that the Italian colouring is simply a certain approach, or way of looking at London; this 'Italy' is a country of the mind, not a region on the map: 'Ay, ay, provoking resistence, 'tis as if you come to buy wares in the city, bid money for 't, your Mercer or Goldsmith says, truly I cannot take it, lets his customer pass his stall; next, nay perhaps two or three, but if he finds he is not prone to return of himself, he calls him back and takes his money....' (I. i. 168–72). Another comparison brings in the clientele of the playhouse; Birdlime philosophizes: 'A woman when there be roses in her cheeks, cherries on her lips, civet in her breath, ivory in her teeth, lillies in her hand and liquorish in her heart, why she's like a play. If new, very good company, very good company but if stale, like old Jeronimo, go by, go by' (II.ii. 181–7). She does not spare the law students who formed the main part of the Paul's audiences:

Civil gentlemen without beards, but to say the truth I did take exception at their knocking; took them aside and said to them, Gentlemen, this is not well that you should come in this habit, cloaks and rapiers, boots and spurs, I protest to you, those that be your Ancients in the house would have come to my house in their caps and gowns, civilly and modestly. I promise you they might have been taken for citizens, but that they talk more liker fools.

[IV. i. 11–19]

Countries other than Italy might be represented much more realistically, to make up the international flavour of metropolitan society. Dekker, who was of Dutch origin, generally fits in a Dutchman somewhere or other; others patriotically contrast foreign styles of wooing, making play with broken English or scraps of a foreign tongue. But whilst lesser foreigners (including

Welsh, Irish or Scots) might enhance the self-importance of the City, Italians offered means to question and criticize. Similarly, two angry or merry women, four 'prentices, six clothiers or whatever other band might be selected for roving adventures must be adventurous, cannot be really wicked; they may be allowed the huntsman's ruthlessness, but they must also keep the solidarity of the pack. On the other hand, the ruler-in-disguise, whether Italian or not, but especially if Italian, presents conflict or questioning, if not between his different rôles, then between himself and his society. Justiniano, afflicted with the Italian disease of jealousy, spies on his wife, but also, to protect his self-esteem, attempts, in disguise, to undermine the wives of other men. He plays in this rôle the part of the 'clever servant' from classical comedy, a character that had been successfully used by Chapman (who scored several popular successes in the Men's theatres before transferring to the Choristers). The jealous husband and the pimp are kept strictly apart.

Attempts to define *Westward Ho!* as a parody of romantic journeying plays or an inferior brand of City comedy do not allow for the complexity of its double plot. The 'moral' is shattered not only by its context, but by the double character of Justiniano. In the same way Chaucer would present all sides of the case in his marriage sequence of tales – the tale of patient Griselda (which Dekker had borrowed for an early play), followed by its highly subversive *envoi*: 'Griselda is dead and eke her patience....'

Some time in the summer of 1605 *Eastward Ho!* landed Jonson and Chapman in jail; King James severed finally the connection between the Chapel Royal and the boy players of Blackfriars. Sir James Murray considered himself insulted and King James was mimicked – all of which did not prevent the play, suitably amended, being given at Court on a later occasion. It is the supreme example of collaboration in the Jacobean theatre, combining Jonson's vivacity of individual speech, Marston's unnerving switches of mood, Chapman's sense of pattern, and the example offered by *Westward Ho!*, which is greeted respectfully in the prologue:

> Not out of our contention to do better
> Than that which is oppos'd to us in title,
> For that was good; and better cannot be....
> Only that Eastward still Westward exceeds –
> Honour the sun's fair rising, not his setting.

The less respectful conclusion, 'We only dedicate it to the City,' is a taste of the well-pitched insults that were to be administered to citizens under the guise of a Prodigal Son's story – although, in effect, it was the Court that erupted with rage.

Touchstone, the hero, a Master Goldsmith, abounds with moral maxims, his favourite saying being 'Work upon that, now!' as accompaniment to his thrusts. His Idle Apprentice, Quicksilver (who goes to old-fashioned plays), ends in the Counter prison, where he experiences a conversion and edifies all; his Industrious Apprentice is promoted Alderman's Deputy and marries Touchstone's virtuous daughter. Her foolish sister weds a Knight who promises her a coach to take her down to their country estate (see page 12 but, with all her fortune, absconds on a voyage to Virginia. This ends in shipwreck (owing to the drunken state of the crew) at the Isle of Dogs, and the Knight ends up in jail. James was about to give a Charter to the Virginia Company (April 1606) and the City would not relish this jest any more than the Court.[23]

Tender treatment of the prodigal had been customary in the immediately preceding plays of 1604, as has been seen (page 103); the prodigal here, far more engaging and less criminal, is matched by the charming absurdities of Touchstone's foolish daughter, set adrift in London with her waiting-maid, Sin-defy: 'Good lord, that there are no fairies nowadays ... to do miracles and bring ladies money.... I'll sweep the chamber soon at night, and set a dish of water o' the hearth. A fairy may come and bring a pearl or a diamond. We do not know, Sin' (V i. 75 ff.). Although the worthy characters may be laughed at, this is not a cynical play; cupidity and recklessness get a gay run for their money, but Touchstone wins, even recovering his daughter's dowry; the Usurer, Security, who is cuckolded and cheated by his wife, is the real villain and victim.

Northward Ho!, setting off in quite a new direction, came out within the year. The type-casting includes some rôles for the boys who had played *Westward Ho!*,[24] but a helter-skelter chase leaves little room for the local colour of the earlier plays. 'Cry Northward Ho! as the boy at Paul's says,' the merchant of this play admonishes his wife and his 'little hoary poet' (another pun may be suspected, the poet being afflicted by the whore Doll having conceived a passion for him). So northward to Ware, a point of leave-taking for those setting out on the Great North Road, where the final imbroglio involves, with all the main participants, 'a whole regiment of horse', consisting of Doll's cheated clients. It is like the roof-top chase of early comic films, doublings and redoublings being the essence of it. But there is no representative of the law, all the penalties being self-devised. The old outwit the young, the tricksters are tricked by cheating games thoroughly familiar, whether from Italian *novelle* or English jest-books. In marriage, cheating is a rule of the game. The two gallants who aim to mock the City are married off to whores, and each philosophically accepts his fate: 'It's better to shoot in a bow has been shot in before, and will never start, than to draw a fair new one that for every arrow will be warping' is a stock ending for those prodigals who are not already married to patient wives.[25] The 'frame' of virtue in distress is far less significant than in the previous play, the point of view being more consistently caustic.

There are several open reminiscences of Chapman's comedy of *All Fools but the Fool*, given at Blackfriars this same year. Moreover, the trickster-in-chief, who is a poet, bears a strong likeness to Chapman himself. The 'perspective' of this play is not between Italianate vice and English folly but between the play world and the everyday world. The curtain line sardonically hails promiscuity, as all the couples are challenged by the triumphant merchant:

> This night ... we'll dare
> Our wives to combat in the great bed of Ware.

This famous marvel, capable of holding six couples (it is now in the Victoria and Albert Museum), was a favourite object of visitation; by it hung a large horn from which visitors drank. The Great Bed would certainly give chances of wife-swapping far beyond the dreams of Chaucer's Reeve or Miller; but Chaucer is the model invoked: 'A comedy, a Canterbury tale smells not half so sweet as the comedy I have for thee, old poet ... thou shalt write upon 't, poet' (IV. i. 208–10) cries the merchant Mayberry to his venerable friend Bellmount; and the comedy envisaged at the beginning by Bellmount, who has just returned to Ware from Stourbridge Fair, is a comedy of cuckoldry with Chaucerian overtones.[26]

The play is morally neutral; if you prick these characters they do not bleed, though if you wrong them they will most certainly revenge. The exception to this is the chaste Mistress Mayberry, falsely accused to her husband by the gallant whose advances she has repelled; she is vindicated by the simple method of her husband's friend, the poet, reassuring him that the charge is inherently improbable – 'Pray God they do not borrow money of us between Ware and London' (I. i. 187–8). Later, he assures Mistress Mayberry that her husband's elaborate plan of revenge does not include an intrigue with another woman. This must be almost the sole example in all Elizabethan drama where slander is rejected without hesitation on the grounds that it is unlikely to be true.

The poet mocks his jealous friend with 'Sfoot, you talk like a player', to which Mayberry retorts, 'If a player talk like a madman or a fool or an ass, and knows not what he talks, then I am one; you are a poet, master Bellmount, I will bestow a piece of plate upon you to bring my wife on the stage, would not her humour please gentlemen?' (I. iii. 30–33). To which the poet replies that it would be worth *two* pieces of plate to him 'to have you stand by me, when I write a jealous man's part'.

In a later scene, composing at night (as Chapman did), the poet is shewn brooding on his own capacity to be a statesman: 'I can in the writing of a tragedy make Caesar speak better than ever his ambition could; when I write of Pompey I have Pompey's soul within me and when I personate a worthy poet, I am then truly myself, a poor unprefer'd scholar' (IV. i. 6–10). This (though inconsistent with Bellmount being able to bail his prodigal son out of prison) is true enough of Chapman.

It was natural enough that the translator of Homer should be engaged on *The Tragedy of Astyanax*, Hector's small son (Chapman's tragedies were written for the Chapel boys). He dreamed it was to be given at the French Court, and to earn the poet a post in the government, at the personal request of 'the Marshal de Biron or some other great minion of the King'. (On the contrary, Chapman's *The Tragedy of Byron*, 1608, which he was already perhaps talking of, was to bring about a general shut-down of London theatres.) On the way back to Ware, the poet is committed to Bedlam by a trick of his friends, but he hits back by the jest that 'your best poets are mad for the most part'. As Chapman had been to jail for writing *Eastward Ho!* the jest is a little sharp. Later still, one of the *filles de joie* decides that if the fashion of his beard marks him as a gentleman, he only sports with the citizens because he is in debt to them. He is not above taking small commissions from Doll to write sets of verses for carving on cheese trenchers. The contrast between grandiose dreams and petty activity is pitiful: this portrait is far subtler than Dekker's earlier caricature of Jonson.

There was a jest at the expense of Macbeth and the 'big company'. One of the wives goes sleep-walking – into the bedchamber of her favourite gallant. This parody of Lady Macbeth was a joke well suited to the 'little apes', who might all have been stowed away in the Great Bed of Ware like puppets in a box.

> Why do men say to a creature of my shape
> So soon as they see him, it's a pretty little ape?
> And why a pretty ape? but for pleasing imitation
> Of greater men's actions in ridiculous fashion?
>
> [*Volpone*, III. ii. 11–14

Blackfriars faintly echoed back the success of this third comedy in Edward Sharpham's *The Fleire* (1606): 'And will you to the Southward, i' faith? will you to the confines of Italy, my gallants? take heed how ye go Northward; 'tis a dangerous coast; jest not with 't in winter. Therefore go Southward, my gallants; Southward ho!' (II. 397–401). Southward only to the Red Light district on the south bank, for here the two daughters of an Italian duke, in reduced circumstances, have set up a London bawdy house, and their own father, in disguise, acts as their pander. Sharpham had a capacity for carrying any situation to extremes. In another of his plays, the jealous man had himself gelded, so as to assure himself that if his wife bore any children, they must be bastards.

Webster and Dekker had certainly set a fashion. In *Westward Ho!* the virtue of the City wives is maintained; in *Eastward Ho!* the sardonic and the fantastic are not relieved by any contrast. In *Northward Ho!* the perspective shifts to a view of poet and plays, but the citizens are drawn with greater malice. Written within a single season, these comedies volleyed back and forth between the two Choristers' troupes, and were imitated by other writers with suitable variations.

Henslowe and Paul's gave Webster his apprenticeship to the craft of playwright, but as a poet his master was John Marston. He was associated with Marston's finest work, *The Malcontent*, in the delicate task of adapting a play, originally written for the Choristers, to be performed by the leading company among the adult troupes, the King's Men.

The influence of *The Malcontent* may be felt throughout early Jacobean theatre – particularly in Shakespeare's *Measure for*

Measure, written in the same season as his company put on Marston's play (and in which he may have taken part). *The Malcontent* itself was a response to *Hamlet*, defined by the author as a bitter comedy ('aspera Thalia'), and would now perhaps be assigned to the Theatre of the Absurd.[27]

In form an adaptation of the Italianate Revenge play, of which Marston had already composed one specimen, it was acted at Blackfriars in 1604 and appeared in print, with preface and dedication by the author, in the same year. Clearly he was proud enough of this work to dedicate it to Ben Jonson, in firm proof that the 'War of the Theatres' was ended, in which they had been so impolite to one another; this was especially generous, because Ben Jonson's latest play, his tragedy of *Sejanus*, had been theatrically a failure, although in literary terms its wide influence is evident. It was generous too to allow Webster's name on the title-page; most authors shed their collaborators when it came to print.

The Malcontent's two rôles in one character must have presented an obvious opportunity for the vocally trained boy player ('Malevole shifteth his speech' as his enemies approach), but the opportunities for Burbage, who had been playing Hamlet and knew his 'antic disposition', must have been of a different kind. Malevole the Malcontent is a duke-in-disguise, a 'duke of dark corners' who takes up the rôle of a professional railer. The third printing, which contains the 'augmentations' of the author and the 'additions' of Webster, expanded the bawd's part, created a new bitter fool (presumably to be played by Robert Armin), included further passionate speeches (for Burbage) and added an induction which explains what the King's Men's version will be like. The induction is generally held to be Webster's contribution. It opens with one of the chief actors – therefore easily recognizable – entering in the guise of a foolish citizen trying to play the courtier:

Enter W. Sly, a Tireman following him with a stool

Tireman. Sir, the gentlemen will be angry if you sit here.

Sly. Why? we may sit upon the stage at the private house. Thou dost not take me for a country gentleman, dost? Dost think I fear hissing? I'll hold my life thou took'st me for one of the players.

Tireman. No, sir.

Sly. By Gods lid, if you had, I would have given you but sixpence for your stool.... Where's Harry Condell, Dick Burbage and Will Sly? ...

[Induction, 1–13

This was in the style Jonson had used in the private houses; Marston had also used it there. The self-satisfied youth knows the boy attendant would expect a big tip beyond the sixpence fee. He is joined by his cousin, son of Master Doomsday, the usurer, cousin to a woollen draper. He himself knows the play well and has been copying down the jests, expatiates freely on his own talents and tastes, even takes the feather out of his hat because there will be a jest against feathers, and instructs his kinsman in the manners suitable for playhouses. He goes on to insult the common audience, 'crammed in the horse-belly' like the Greeks before Troy, their presence betrayed by the garlic they have eaten. He likewise insults the players; Burbage and Condell, with Lowin, have come on to try to placate this difficult customer, but also to make the point, for the real audience, that no particular applications are intended. This is neither Satire nor Moral but to be played 'straight'.

Sly asks, rather menacingly, 'I would know how you came by this play?' to which Condell answers jestingly,

> Faith, sir, the book was lost; and because 'twas pity so good a play should be lost, we found it and play it.
> *Sly.* I wonder you would play it, another company having interest in it.
> *Condell.* Why not Malevole in Folio with us, as Jeronimo in Decimo Sexto with them? they taught us a name for our play: we call it *One for Another.*
> [Induction, 74–80

This has been taken to mean something like filching on both sides; but the plays in question were *in print*. (No one in their senses would advertise a shady action in an induction.) The boys could use the 1592 quarto of *The Spanish Tragedy*; what the King's Men 'found' was not a manuscript, but one or other of the previous issues of the quarto.[28] While it might be thought unusual for the 'big company' to take something from the Choristers, the Choristers had been burlesquing the Men, so the Men were now readapting 'bitter comedies'. The additions are 'not greatly needful', only 'to entertain a little more time and to abridge the not-received custom of music in our theatre'. The incidental music in the play remains in fact just as it was; it is the entr'acte and the preliminary concert that have been replaced by a new induction. The effect of the original music, an hour's concert by some of the finest voices in Europe, perhaps performing some church music by Merbecke, Tallis or Byrd, would have roused the audience to feelings that would receive from the actors shock upon

shock. *The Malcontent* opens with 'The vilest out of tune music'
being heard and two boys bawling '... you think you are in a
tavern, do you not?', 'You think you are in a brothel house, do
you not?' Then the voice of the Malcontent offstage: 'Yaugh, god
a' man, what dost thou there? ... shadow of a woman, what
wouldst, weasel? ... ah, you smooth-chinned catamite?...' (I.
iii. 5–9).

The voice of Burbage would make a very different effect in the
composite offering of induction and play. He first appears in his
own person, grave, courteous, restrained, but says, 'I must leave
you, sir,' and, as he goes, the foolish citizen demands whether he
plays Malevole – 'I durst lay four of my ears, the play is not so
well acted as it has been.' To which Condell retorts ironically, 'O,
no, sir, nothing *ad Parmenonis suem.*' (Parmeno, according to
Plutarch, was skilled at imitating a pig, so that when a real pig
was smuggled in, his claque cried, 'Nothing to Parmeno's pig.')
The boys parodied the men – the men were taking up the parody
and giving it added resonance. They are the assured gentlemen
of this induction: it is the citizen who has been filching feathers,
which he picked up in the tilt-yard, where they had fallen in a
joust; his memory consists of telling the signs along Goldsmiths'
Row, where he goes to borrow money. He is altogether inferior
to the players.

Such scenes were 'invented merely to be spoken', as the address
to the Reader insists, and are to be read 'only for the pleasure it
once afforded you when it was presented with the soul of lively
action'. This is poetry for performance and for performance in
a particular context – by the King's Men, who had just been waiting on the Spanish Ambassador and could give lessons in decorum
to tradesmen. It is Burbage who now, as Malevole, anatomizes
the world of the City in a style that no Paul's Cross sermon could
improve on:

Mendoza. Wherefore dost thou think churches were made?
Malevole. To scour plough shares. I ha' seen oxen plough up altars *Et nunc
seges ubi Sion fuit.*.... I ha' seen a sumptuous steeple turn'd to a stinking
privy; more beastly, the sacredest place made a dog's kennel; nay most
inhuman, the stoned coffins of long-dead Christians burst up, and made
hog's troughs; *Hic finis Priami.*

[II. v. 124–32

The steeple was St Paul's; the Blackfriars itself was a desecrated
building. 'I shall rise ... at the last judgment,' cries Malevole and

several times re-echoes this in the course of his earthly elevation back to the dukedom.

The perspective supplied by Webster's induction was an addition to the many perspectives supplied by the play itself: by its disguises, by its Italian setting and by the ironic reversals and echoes in the plot. With the boys, Webster was to gain further practice in building plays through contrasts, but it was from the transposition of Marston's masterpiece into a major key that he learnt most.[29] He became a dramatic poet incomparably greater than Marston, but he built on Marston's foundation.

Webster's theatrical activity between 1602 and 1606 belongs to a period of unequalled theatrical change, the first part ending when the playhouses were closed in March 1603, not to reopen for a year. The years 1604–6 saw the excitement of James's coronation, with its national celebrations and international visitors – years of such excitement that each season, each playhouse had its own particular flavour. Even a young man, silent or withdrawn, might be pressed to contribute at such times, and Webster had tasted every kind of theatre: he had worked for both the leading adult companies, and for the Choristers, each time, it would appear, with considerable success. His sketches of Burbage and Chapman, player and poet, combine comedy with insight. Interesting psychological development lies in the contests between the citizens and their wives. Domestic life in the City provided the most intimate form of marital companionship, for in the country each sex worked at really different tasks, whether it be the lady in her still-room and the squire as Justice, or among the farms and cottages where the men tilled the land and the women dealt with milking, chickens, spinning, cooking. The great household, by its very size, kept husband and wife apart; indeed, they often had quite separate establishments. But the citizen's wife lived over the shop, with the 'prentices to mother – and occasionally to sport with; she had not such extensive occupations as the countrywoman. Maids had to be supervised, but her life was considered a pampered one; she was free to move outside her home, her children were sent into the country to nurse, and, if widowed and well endowed, she was in the most privileged position of all. The City men were supposed to be doting husbands, often cuckolded, sometimes by wild young prodigals. In this society the rôle of the woman was of quite especial interest, and Webster would have learnt to use the women in his plays as the real agents of the comedy.

He was much more of an innovator in placing them at the centre of a tragedy. Yet, in his two great tragedies, and in the plays which he wrote at the end of his career, one continuous thread may be followed: the rôle of women in society, the relation of marriage to money, the mutual rights and obligations of women to their original family and to their husbands.

CHAPTER SIX

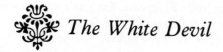 *The White Devil*

Webster was slow in advancing to be Master in the craft of playing; in the winter of 1612 with *The White Devil*, he once for all 'crossed the Alps', and crossed also the boundary into a modern world. In his two masterpieces, at the very centre, without implanting any social doctrine, he placed two women and two servants, one a secretary, one a spy. Vittoria and her brother Flamineo, like the Duchess of Malfi and Daniel de Bosola, belong heroically with the people that things are done to – yet, in their moodiness, their quick response to threats, their ironic self-appraisal, they exemplify and expand that freedom to be a self first met in Shakespeare's *Hamlet*.

Since he was working now not only for particular theatres but to suit the individual styles of particular actors, Webster's large design is united with close poetic texture, action with words. 'Poetry is a deed,' as the first of Elizabethan actors had proclaimed;[1] by 1612 the actor's 'deed', no longer the grand soliloquy or the acrobatic flourish, meant the 'personation' of 'passion'. 'There you may show a passion, there you may show a passion,' cried old Hieronimo, describing the discovery of his murdered son to the painter in the new additions to *The Spanish Tragedy*. The actor needed to respond or react to his fellows; play was *inter*play.

Webster also shewed, in a series of perspectives, 'motion' – the ebb and flow of passions. He used very subtle variations of distancing and closing in on the violent moments of his close-packed story of crime. Dreams, mimes, ceremonies and pictures frame or sharpen certain acts; so too do brief, highly concentrated, pungent epigrams or metaphors define a mood, paint a fellow-actor's rôle or deflate his grandeur.

Richard Perkins, the young leading actor of the Red Bull

Company, received special mention from Webster in the postscript
he added when he himself put his first tragedy into print. It was the
first time that any individual actor had received such a tribute;
since he 'crowned' both the beginning and the end, Perkins had
evidently played the Protean Flamineo. Perkins's career was as
significant for Webster as Burbage's for Shakespeare.

A square inn-yard, open to the weather, had been converted
in 1605 when the Queen's Men moved in from the old Boar's Head
in Whitechapel. The Red Bull Theatre was given to all kinds of
spectacle: fireworks, big built-up displays. It was a sort of poor
man's Lord Mayor's Show, as the Lord Mayor's Show was a sort
of poor man's Court masque, and as James's Court masques were
a sort of poor man's copy of the Medici's festivities at Florence.
The capacity of the Red Bull was said to be three thousand.

The Red Bull was also what today would be called a 'neighbourhood theatre'. It lent properties to the young gentlemen of Lincoln's Inn, and probably helped with their shows. It allowed
young groups of 'prentices to put on amateur plays. The actors
were residents of the parish of St James Clerkenwell, respectable
local people. Learned and more dignified actors often jested at the
expense of the Red Bull entertainments – especially in later days,
when the stratification of the acting profession was complete – but
the troupes there (often led by the chief clown, Greene or Rowley)
were thoroughly professional, as is witnessed by the opening four
lines of the prologue of amateurs for *The Hector of Germany*, 'a
new play ... as it hath been publicly acted at the Red Bull and
at the Curtain', the oldest playhouse still standing, built in 1577
(see page 95). This play, published in 1615, had been written
for the Mayoralty of Sir John Swinnerton, Merchant Taylor, in
1612, and was therefore contemporary with *The White Devil*.

Webster's own play was evidently a risky attempt to give the
actors at the Red Bull a chance for fine character parts, with an
especially strong lead. They were trying to 'trade up' – to move,
as it were, from the Charing Cross Road to Savile Row, with this
scion of the Merchant Taylors. The performance was remarkable
enough to gain the professional congratulation of other players,
but, as Webster records in his note 'To the Reader', being shown
'in so open and black a theatre' and 'so dull a time of winter', it
did not draw a full audience, nor did they who came understand
it. 'Ignorant asses,' cried Webster; he had foregone Chorus and
the Nuntius but the 'uncapable multitude' were still unresponsive.

He could console himself with the thought that in the previous year Ben Jonson's tragedy *Catiline*, acted by the King's Men, had fallen completely flat – as indeed had his *Sejanus*, some years before.

The White Devil, after the fashion of plays written for the public theatres, is not divided into acts, but runs straight through, cumulatively, until the finale, the masque-like scene where Vittoria, together with her brother and her waiting-woman, are murdered in ritual revenge for the lady whom she had supplanted. The play opens with her seduction by the Duke of Brachiano, Paolo Giordano Orsini, planned with the help of his secretary, her brother Flamineo. The centre-piece, headed 'The Arraignment of Vittoria', presents her trial for adultery in an ecclesiastical court. Vittoria. like Shakespeare's Cleopatra, far outshines the Duke's virtuous wife, Isabella, who, together with Vittoria's own husband, Camillo, has been murdered, ostensibly to prevent their revenges upon the adulterous pair. The high comedy of her quarrel and reconciliation with Brachiano, followed by the momentary triumph of their marriage, is abruptly transformed by the secret revenge of the Medici (Duchess Isabella's family), who poison Brachiano in the midst of his wedding festivity.

'The true imitation of life, without striving to make nature a monster,' which Webster praised in his actors, had been considerably heightened by him from the historic events. He may have first heard of these (later culminating in the assassination of the new Duchess of Brachiano on the night of 22 December 1585) from John Florio,[2] translator of Montaigne, Italian tutor and secretary, who, in the year of Vittoria's death, had translated *A Letter lately written from Rome*, which omitted that catastrophe. He also knew an account given in a Fugger newsletter, of Vittoria's assassination, and he would certainly have remembered Brachiano's heir, the gallant young Virginio Orsini, who in January 1601 had paid a private visit to London, after escorting his cousin, Marie de Medici, on her way to become Queen of France. The young Duke stayed with an Italian merchant in the City; he would have needed an interpreter, and Florio would have been an obvious choice for his friends, the Cecils, to supply (as he had worked for that family). The Queen sent special coaches to convey the Duke to Court for a Twelfth Night feast, followed by a play and a ball. This young man appears at the end of Webster's play, to give judicial sentence on the murderers.[3] Earlier he has appeared in armour, proudly announcing his martial ambitions; then he makes a dramatic entrance in a suit of black, accompanied by the villainous Lodovico to bring to the Duke of Florence the news of his mother's death. For a minor part it is strongly high-lighted.

The first half of Webster's play is centred on Vittoria, the second on Florence's vengeance; he has heightened the first by having the two spouses killed at the same time, and heightened the second by having Brachiano murdered on his wedding-day, destroyed first by a poisoned helmet, then strangled in a parody of confessional rites. Webster also added the fratricide of a younger brother, Marcello, by Flamineo, and the madness of their mother, Cornelia; but he transformed into a blameless character the first wife of Brachiano. In history she had been strangled four years before the Duke met Vittoria – it was reputed, with the connivance of her brother, Francesco de Medici, Duke of Florence – for her life had been far from blameless, and it is by no means certain that Virginio was really Brachiano's son.

The implications of witchcraft, even of diabolic possession, are suggested in Brachiano's first words on entering, 'Quite lost, Fla-mineo!' (I. ii. 3). His absolute surrender to the beauty of the 'white devil' is shewn as her sinister black waiting-maid spreads the rich carpet and cushions for their encounter; Flamineo, the Mephisto-pheles who does not believe in the happiness he trades in, has anti-cipated this moment with an elaborate suggestion to his sister of magical powers to compel love; but the opulence becomes ironical, since it is given in the presence of her wretched husband, who thinks that Flamineo is referring to himself. So while love is made to seem inevitable, it is also presented as an illusion:

He will give thee a ring with a philosopher's stone.... Thou shalt lie in a bed stuff'd with turtle's feathers, swoon in perfum'd linen, like the fellow was smother'd in roses. So perfect shall be thy happiness that as men at sea think land and trees and ships go that way they go, so both earth and heaven shall seem to go your voyage. Shalt meet him, 'tis fixed with nails of diamonds to inevitable necessity.

[I. ii. 150–59]

As his lord and his sister 'close', Flamineo adds his malicious in-nuendoes to their exchanges. '"His jewel for her jewel" – well put in, duke.... That's better, "she must wear his jewel lower"' (I. ii. 225, 228).

But Vittoria's macabre dream of the graveyard by moonlight,

of the 'hellish' activity of her husband and the Duchess, the vengeance of the almost equally sinister 'yew tree', bring from Flamineo a direct tribute, 'Excellent devil!' (I. ii. 256). The hidden
dread that Vittoria perhaps really feels, here becomes for the
audience also a dread of Vittoria. She insinuates a need for protection; the Duke is at the same time being manipulated. She is a
woman who needs to dramatize herself, and therefore, literally,
a *hyprocrite*; this was a 'figure' which Webster took from a sermon
by a famous London preacher, and one particularly popular with
dramatists.[4]

> Webster was much possessed by death
> And saw the skull beneath the skin,
> And breastless creatures underground
> Leaned backwards with a lipless grin.
> [T. S. Eliot, 'Whispers of Immortality'

During the years of silence, Webster had had reason enough to
be possessed by death, for, with the rest of the Londoners, he had
survived nearly five years of plague. When reported deaths rose
beyond fifty a week, playing was banned, which may be the
explanation of his long intermission. The record speaks for itself:

1603   Playing stopped on 19 March because of the Queen's sickness; from
       8 May till Christmas, playing banned because of plague
1605   Playing banned 5 October and 15 December because of plague
1606   Plague from March till December (playing banned)
1607   Plague from July till November (playing banned)
1608   Plague from July till December (playing banned)
1609   Plague from April till December (playing banned)
1610   Plague from September till November (playing banned)[5]

In plague time London was deserted by all who could flee. The
coach-builder was almost as busy as the gravedigger, and the price
of coaches to hire or sell rose very sharply. Since the plague was
a poor man's disease, in the crowded district round St Sepulchre's
the mortality rate was always amongst the highest. Players left in
hired waggons, with hired horses, as we know from the will of one
of Pembroke's Men, who died of plague in 1592.[6] The City had
built a pest-house, for those found homeless and wandering; infected houses were sealed up, with the red T-shaped cross and
'Lord have mercy' written on their doors. Crime flourished, for
malefactors were not likely to be taken, and the dead and dying
fell easy prey to robbers. Dramatic stories of sudden death (the
girl who died on her wedding morning) and hideous privation in

the prisons, where some perished of starvation, grew like the grass in Cheapside. Newgate was one of the worst jails, with its cramped chambers and underground dungeons. St Bartholomew's Hospital saw a former dramatist, Thomas Lodge, now a physician, standing at his post; but many, including some of the clergy, betook themselves to friends or relatives, if they could be received.

John Donne published his 'Anatomy of the World' (1611), supposedly an elegy for a girl of fifteen, Elizabeth Drury, but rather a poetic statement of what this scene of death, 'Sick world, nay dead, nay putrified', becomes – 'fragmentary rubbish'. Donne dramatically enacts the process of dying:

> Think thee laid on thy death bed, loose and slack,
> And think that but unbinding of a pack,
> To take one precious thing, thy soul, from thence ...
> Think that thou hear'st thy knell, and think no more,
> But that, as bells call'd thee to church before,
> So this to the Triumphant Church, calls thee....
> Think that thy body rots, and (if so low,
> Thy soul exalted thus, thy thoughts can go)
> Think thee a prince, who of themselves create
> Worms which invisibly devour their state.
>   ['The Second Anniversary', 1612

The body, 'this curded milk, this poor unlittered whelp', took its natural revenge, so that visions or dreams of luxury and pleasure compensated for daily horrors. Dekker, Webster's collaborator, in his immensely popular _Bellman of London_ (1608) describes an idyllic country feast – to which come all the beggars and rogues. His is not 'the fatal Bellman' of Newgate but a genial character who enjoys the roguery he dissects. Dekker, who had often called upon London to repent, dropped his preaching style in this time of plague. He became a comedian, a pastoralist, dispensing consolation in country joys.

Webster's tragedies give the brilliant physical impact of the outer world that comes on recovery from deep sickness or escape from deadly peril. It is as if a veil or shade, dimming the scene, had been withdrawn. The figures glitter as if in some great Court festivity; yet there is always a feeling that the brilliance may vanish, like those visions at Court constructed by the art of Ben Jonson and Inigo Jones, in which the Websters may have had a share. The great wheeled chariots for _The Masque of Blackness_ (1605) must have been specially built; Webster quoted from the text of

The Masque of Queens (1609). The contrast of the witches coven – a grotesque introduction or Antimasque invented at the Queen's request – and her own dazzling appearance as Goddess, gives the effect of paradox, of two incompatibles meeting. In 1611 the opening scene of rough rocks was split asunder to reveal the Fairy Palace. Webster's poetry, like the spectacle of Inigo Jones's masques, unites extremes, and produces an Epiphany – without invoking the supernatural, a supernatural colouring shimmers. In the Infernal Paradise where Vittoria and Brachiano unite formal language with intimate physical wooing, Webster may add a shudder for some of the audience by delicately bringing in echoes from a famous English murder;[7] he might himself recall from the layers of his memory this or that instance, but the thickly laminated dramatic poetry, built with alternating views, shifting perspectives, allows the audience to insert any variations they wish; the actor can 'breathe' inside his part. Webster does not enforce any readings. With a stage device, the old-fashioned dumb show, he gives a distanced effect to the two spouses' murders, watched by Brachiano as if he were watching a play; it is as if they were illusions by a conjurer. ' "Twas quaintly done' is Brachiano's approving comment on Camillo's end; the word is to be heard again when he himself is strangled with 'a true love knot'. A painting of Brachiano is used for the murder of his wife; Isabella is poisoned by taking from the portrait the kiss which Brachiano had denied her in their last meeting.

Webster himself lived surrounded by painters, who, like most professional practitioners, had their own quarters in London, chiefly in the parishes of St Sepulchre's, St Andrew's Holborn and St Anne's Blackfriars.[8] Imagery of painting occurs throughout this tragedy, down to the last boast of Lodovico, as he contemplates the triple murder: 'I limn'd this night piece and it was my best' (V. vi. 247). Moreover, in his 'Character of an Excellent Actor', Webster was later to insist that the actor must be a painter himself.

The grand procession of Lieger Ambassadors suggest the larger political dimensions of the story; ambassadors became frequent only during the reign of James, and they were always present at Court masques, rituals of international concord. By contrast, the small enclosed tableau of mourning revealed when Cornelia is seen winding Marcello's corpse gives a sharp contrast, in its humility, as epilogue to the macabre death scene of Brachiano, with its

parody of the last rites carried out by the murderers disguised as
Franciscan friars (they have come from quite a different Francesco, the Medici, to whisper threats of damnation as they kill him).

Very early in the play Flamineo ironically warns against perspective instruments:

I have seen a pair of spectacles fashion'd with such perspective art, that
lay but down one twelvepence o' the board, 'twill appear as if there were
twenty – now should you wear a pair of these spectacles and see your wife
tying her shoe, you would imagine twenty hands were taking up of your
wife's clothes ... jealousy ... presents to a man, like so many bubbles in
a basin of water, twenty several crabbed faces....

[I. ii. 100–22

One type of 'perspective painting' presented two images which
could alternate: 'Though he be painted one way like a Gorgon, /
The other way 's a Mars' (II. v. 116–17) cried Cleopatra of her
faithless Antony. The other kind of perspective would contain
some apparent monstrosity which came into focus only if viewed
from one particular angle.[9] The use of perspective in Court
masques heightened the chief figures; Webster uses this art both
for presenting his figures, and for their inter-relations, their views
of one another. Such paintings force the spectator to review them,
rebuild them; the activity of interpretation exercises him in a kind
of action, as well as in solving a kind of puzzle.

Vittoria and Isabella change aspects, replacing each other in
Brachiano's soul. After Vittoria has become to him his 'dukedom,
health, wife, children, friends and all', Isabella turns physically
loathsome, so that when she attempts to kiss him he repulses her:

> O your breath!
> Out upon sweetmeats and continued physic!
> The plague is in them.
>   [II. i. 163–5

Then, in the scene at the house of convertites, where Vittoria
seems faithless, he reverts:

> O my sweetest duchess,
> How lovely art thou now.
>   [IV. ii. 99–100

The poison he had used on her ('equally mortal with a winter
plague'), and the practices of the pesthouse, were to be returned
upon himself;[10] but when he already sees his fate as brought down
on him by Vittoria, it is her fatal beauty that he dwells on. She

is a beautiful reliquary – such as one of those made by Cellini, encrusted with gold, enclosing some fragment of a saint's severed finger – but here a devilish one:

> Your beauty! O ten thousand curses on it!
> How long have I beheld the devil in crystal?
> Thou hast led me like a heathen sacrifice,
> With music and with fatal yokes of flowers,
> To my eternal ruin.
> [IV. ii. 87–91

Brachiano suddenly sees the alternative form of his perspective, but the intimate broken appeal (the familiar 'thou') betrays deeper, hidden dread within, the sudden realization of where he is standing, as mere stripped victim. ('O whither hast thou led me, Egypt?' Antony had cried to Cleopatra.) Depth of passion, shewn through the quarrel, brings up into action all the underlying contradictions. The actor gets his opportunity for passion whilst he is kept faithful to his 'conceit' or realization of the part as a whole.

The 'perspective picture' was the Jacobean way of defining and drawing attention to this internal quality of the actor's art, as Shakespeare made clear by using the simile of a perspective painting to describe the subtle varieties of grief in *Richard II*:

> Each substance of a grief hath twenty shadows
> Which shows like grief itself but is not so,
> For sorrow's eye, glazed with blinding tears
> Divides one thing entire to many objects
> Like perspectives which rightly gazed upon,
> Show nothing but confusion – ey'd awry,
> Distinguish form.
> [II. ii. 14–20

From his portrait it is possible to deduce the fluid, graceful style of Richard Perkins – as he was playing Flamineo, in this part the alternative rôles are more consciously assumed; he first feigns madness, and then feigns death. Francesco also, like a true Medici, enjoys masquerades, and puts on a whole set of attitudes, from Christian resignation to carnal infatuation:

> My tragedy must have some idle mirth in 't
> Else it will never please.

His sister's spirit appears to him, an embodiment of his melancholy mood, as Flamineo's fears of being often named by Brachiano on his death-bed conjure up the Duke's ghost, bearing a pot of lily flowers, with a skull under the flowers. This formal

emblem of love and death entwined is of course a small 'perspective' in itself which could have been copied out of a book. It has
no relation to the howling ghosts of early Revenge plays.

But a deeper laid perspective, involving the inwardly felt
expression of a human being, is suggested by Isabella – 'our phlegmatic duchess', as Brachiano terms her – after ranting through
her 'part' of divorcing Brachiano, repeating his exact words but
adding '*Manet alta mentem repostum*', to imply that she has inner
depths, where things may look different. She is deliberately enigmatic here, but the stately Virgilian form of her oath underlines
how this daughter of the Medici is sacrificing herself to maintain
peace between the two dukes. Vittoria is afraid of 'the Duchess',
with whom her mother has threatened her; Brachiano, in spite
of his bold defiance of Florence, is in no way equal to the Medici,
and knows it.

Woman's self-assertion in a male-dominated society is mocked
at the end of this scene by jesting exchanges between Isabella's
husband and her reconciled brother. The surface pattern of a
social hierarchy which dominates women and servants is clearly
articulated, but underneath it lies 'the heart of the mystery' (as
Hamlet termed it). Here the individuals confront their destiny,
as they have made it, at the moment of death, when true identity
is finally visible. Webster's relating of these two levels, so that a
character is seen or sees himself first in one relation and then in
another, means that, with his tragic pattern, he works in the social
developments of family structure as he saw it evolving around him,
with the competitive struggle of the underling who must acquire
some hold over his lord if he is to feel secure. This was to be a
matter which his successor Middleton was to develop in his two
tragic masterpieces as an explicit theme (*Women Beware Women*,
c. 1621; *The Changeling*, 1622). De Flores is the descendant of
Flamineo; and the Duke of *Women Beware Women* is Webster's
Duke of Florence.

The bitter comedy which Webster sets in his tragedy – Flamineo's laughter or the laughter of the two murderers as they prepare the poisoned picture for Isabella's kiss – derives from those
earlier plays in which some disguised ruler, playing the servant's
rôle, can allow one of his rôles to 'mock' the other.[11] Flamineo
is not, like these, a double character, but a single integrated one.
Two halves of a divided self, he is an egoist forced by simple need
(as he savagely insists to his mother) to act the Proteus. This shift

alters the whole perspective; the critic, instead of being a disguised prince, is an accomplished actor, a hypocrite who despises his own arts. He has to appear less intelligent than he is, so that his lord shall not suspect how he is being manipulated. The wit that allows him some enjoyment of his punishment is his inner resource.

Nevertheless, Flamineo is also the head of his own family, Vittoria being in some sense his property even before she ceases to be the wife of Camillo. If Florence is grey-haired, most action still rests in the hands of the younger group. Cornelia's attempt to interfere is attacked:

> I would the common'st courtesan in Rome
> Had been my mother rather than thyself.
> Nature is very pitiful to whores.
>
> [I. ii. 333–5

Flamineo's 'policy', which is to be like 'the subtle foldings of a winter's snake', includes using 'old odds and ends' of proverbs picked up from dull dramatists, which he then turns round and derides to the audience, exposing his tricks to them:

> It may appear to some ridiculous
> Thus to talk knave and madman and sometimes
> Come in with a dried sentence, stuffed with sage;
> But this allows my varying of shapes,
>   '*Knaves do grow great by being great men's apes.*'
>
> [IV. ii. 243–7

When, at last, with his sister's marriage, Flamineo becomes his lord's brother-in-law, and achieves security – 'In all the weary minutes of my life, Day ne'er broke up till now' – he immediately develops the gentleman-like humour of quarrelling with his brother and suddenly stabs him treacherously. This violent release of resentment is quite gratuitous[12] and reduces him to a worse degree of servitude, for he is told by Brachiano he will have to sue for his life day by day. He may think he knows how to handle women, but he does not know how to handle Zanche, the Moor. Whilst recognizing the sin of it, Marcello has accompanied Vittoria in her flight from Rome, but, haughtily objecting to Zanche joining the family, he finally dies repentant, confessing their solidarity: the Church witholds Christian burial from him.

> There are some sins which heaven doth duly punish
> In a whole family. This it is to rise
> By all dishonest means.
>
> [V. ii. 20–22

Cornelia, at this fratricide, 'grows foolish', her protest peasant-like –

> Why, here's nobody shall get anything by his death.
>> [V. ii. 28

Webster had changed the original pattern of Vittoria's family (reducing her first husband to a cipher); in the other family, that of the Medici and its dependants the Orsini, he has reshaped the character of Lodovico, Vittoria's assassin, a minor avenger who is left to face the music by Francesco, and who actually counsels this course to his Prince. He is Brachiano's cousin; his hot fury, like his cool appraisal of the final murders, reveals an artist in crime:

> I'll make Italian cut-work in their guts
> If ever I return.
>> [I. i. 52–3

The original Lodovico confessed that in his lifetime he had personally been responsible for killing forty persons. In discussing alternative methods with Francesco, who would really like to inflict a military defeat, Lodovico suggests some ritual humiliation:

> 'Have crown'd him with a wreath of stinking garlic
> T' have shown the sharpness of his government
> And rankness of his lust.
>> [V. i. 82–5

In his disguise as a Moor (the devil's hue) Francesco stresses military glory; the military ambitions of the young Prince afford some suggestion of the larger military world outside the palace walls. Cornelia's dirge over her slain soldier redresses priestly severity with Nature's piety – 'the robin redbreast and the wren'; Flamineo now senses for the first time the 'maze of conscience' and applies his mother's grief to himself:

> We think caged birds sing, when indeed they cry.
>> [V. iv. 122

The image of the caged bird appears again and again in Webster.

Women expected to be controlled by some male or another – but Webster's women refuse to be so controlled. The intolerable position of being at once enmeshed and uncomprehended becomes Vittoria's when, after the trial (not in a civil court, for adultery was not a civil crime), she is sent to the house of convertites and then attacked by her lover for infidelity. Their quarrel scene, an explosion of fire between two totally committed to each other – whatever they say – sparkles with the high comedy of parts of Shakespeare's *Antony and Cleopatra*. The rôle of a woman, even when, like Vittoria, she initiates so much of the action, is one of frustration in each of her five scenes. Vittoria is cursed by her mother in the wooing scene; facing a hostile court, she next combines a womanly respect for the Ambassadors with a truly masculine display of 'virtue', as, in defence of her womanhood, she outfaces the Cardinal and gives as good as she gets. Later, in the lovers' quarrel, she resorts to the strong language of religion (compare Mark 9: 45)

> I had a limb corrupted to an ulcer
> But I have cut it off; and now I'll go
> Weeping to heaven on crutches.
> [IV. ii. 121–3

But she can also simulate 'Popish' devotion, as when later she pretends to be ready to commit suicide:

> Behold, Brachiano, I that while you lived
> Did make a flaming altar of my heart
> To sacrifice unto you, now am ready
> To sacrifice heart and all.
> [V. vi. 83–6

Through much of Brachiano's death scene she preserves an appalled silence; at her own death, though she trembles, she is Duchess of Brachiano still, successor to a Medici:

> I will be waited on in death; my servant
> Shall never go before me.
> [V. vi. 216–17

And, baring her breast, she advances 'as princes greet some great ambassador'. If enigmatic, she is consistent. She looks on her dying body as something almost to be wondered at:

> O my greatest sin lay in my blood,
> Now my blood pays for 't.
> [V. vi. 239–40

And then looks forward in sudden realization of far regions of the spirit:

> My soul, like to a ship in a black storm,
> Is driven I know not whither.
> [V. vi. 248–9

Finally, in words that faintly echo Brachiano's greeting of his
'happy lady', by their flatness and simplicity – 'O happy they that
never saw the court / Nor ever knew great man but by report' (V.
vi. 261–2) – she becomes once more Flamineo's sister, victim of
circumstance; the trite words are loaded with all that has preceded
them, and her life is summed up in a 'moral sentence', with envy
of the simple lot.

The Cardinal Monticelso's attempt to do as much in the trial
scene, with his Character of a Whore (preceded by the ludicrous
court rhetoric of the advocate), defeats itself, as the judgment of
the Ambassadors confirms:

French Ambassador.   She hath liv'd ill.
English Ambassador.   True, but the Cardinal 's too bitter.
                                                    [III. ii. 106–7

Here all the suggestions of diabolic infiltration, poison, the sale
of her person produce only a judgment of the tabulating kind.
Monticelso three times refers to his definition of her as her
'picture',[13] which she as steadily rejects:

> These are but feigned shadows of my evils:
> Terrify babes, my lord, with painted devils.
>   [III. ii. 146–7

Yet in her very denial we can hear the voice of Lady Macbeth,
the murderess.

The comparison of the defined 'Character' of a Whore with that
of a Wife, of the Bad Woman with the Good Woman, is exploded,
but this means that Vittoria can be found neither innocent nor
guilty. Although the evil powers may be sensed, they always
remain just beyond the range of the visible and the palpable; and,
in so vivid a world, what is seen and touched will triumph. The
Cardinal's formula of possession – 'Next the devil, adultery /
Enters the devil, murder' (III. ii. 108–9) – is dissolved by Vittoria's
power to transform the Cardinal's trial of her into her trial of the
Cardinal. This is not the reward of innocence but of courage. Prisoners may gain ascendancy over their jailors, and Vittoria demon-
strates the disgraceful political rôle of a corrupt Church, leaving
a sceptical gap that is to be unresolved even in the final scene.
The Cardinal exemplifies precisely the worst kind of White Devil,
as listed by Thomas Adams – the hypocritical churchman, the
Judas of the faith.

We see Vittoria at her prayers; we shall also see her, instigated by her 'infernal' attendant, Zanche, ready to threaten Flamineo with damnation as well as death: herself dying in spiritual blindness.

It has often been noted that Webster's characters almost never soliloquize, but neither do the later heroic figures of Shakespeare: Antony and Coriolanus are enigmatic, yet they are revealed even by the gaps in the parts, such as Antony's decision to return to Egypt or Coriolanus' to defect to the Volsces. The old form of soliloquy went out in *c.* 1609.

The perspective of madness or dream releases the character from ordinary dialogue and sometimes produces almost the effect of a soliloquy – or a chorus. Yet, even in moments of communication, opacity may descend. For the rest, the characters magnetize each other, but egoism keeps them afloat in their uncomprehended several orbits. Each moment is fully lived and the whole play exists in that moment:

> I do not look
> Who went before nor who shall follow me,
> No, at myself I will begin and end.
> [V. vi. 256–8

The units of action are short, and the units of speech are often no more than a single sentence, after which the actor must change his tone. These small packets of energy, implosive rather than explosive, drive the action forward; the actor works with a very small energy charge, but because this is constantly renewed, the total effect is of very great energy indeed.

There is no doubt of the depth of their sensibility. A 'dried sentence' of Flamineo at the beginning of his pretended distraction reveals vulnerability behind endurance:

> We endure the strokes like anvils or hard steel,
> Till pain itself make us no pain to feel.
> [III. iii. 1–2

Isabella, feigning jealousy, releases her hatred of Vittoria in appalling visions of torture; she is not phlegmatic when her own 'plaguey breath' becomes Vittoria's rotten teeth:

> To dig the strumpet's eyes out, let her lie
> Some twenty months a-dying, to cut off
> Her nose and lips, pull out her rotten teeth.
> [II. i. 245–7

Francesco is not interested in Zanche's confession of the murders by Brachiano which Lodovico takes as justification for their revenge; his curt 'Tush for justice!' sets the royal will above all.

What kind of people, then, are these? The fire of life burns high; they are fuelled by a spirit more powerful than that which consumes ordinary mortals. Even old Cornelia, in her madness, burns with this pure concentration. More like the lives of angels or devils than of human beings, theirs are devoid of daily trivialities. The world they live in, like that of the drug-addict, is brilliant, compulsively attractive or repulsive. Moods shift abruptly, so that their speech is full of sharp breaks; in the death speeches this may appear as delirium or wandering, yet through their constantly nervous, staccato rhythm these disjointed speeches reveal identity more strongly than ever. The death speech was the natural climax for any Elizabethan or Jacobean tragedian. Compare the methods of dramatic projection in the eloquent last speech of Chapman's Byron, written for a boy, and the last speech of Flamineo (see page 140):

> And so farewell for ever! never more
> Shall any hope of my revival see me;
> Such is the endless exile of dead men.
> Summer succeeds the spring; autumn the summer;
> The frosts of winter the fall'n leaves of autumn;
> All these, and all fruits in them yearly fade,
> And every year return; but cursed man
> Shall never more renew his vanished face.
>
> [*The Tragedy of Byron*, V. iv. 245–52

Master Chapman's 'full and heightened style', as Webster termed it, is here at its highest; yet the grand Marlovian sweep of these lines does not make such demands on the actor as the free, shifting technique Perkins used in Flamineo.

The breaks or jumps in the verse (and Flamineo's death speech is even more varied in direction and mood than Vittoria's) act like trills or shakes or the warbling that Monteverdi used in his operas; this allows the actor to display his control in a virtuoso's flourish. Bernard Beckerman has described this technique in the scene of Hamlet's first encounter with the Ghost, and Oliver Neville sees it as the basis of the structure in Jonson's *Sejanus*.[14]

Such gratuitous violence as Cornelia's in striking Zanche, her son's whore, or Flamineo's stabbing of his brother, or Zanche's betrayal of the whole series of murders to Florence, appear almost inevitable outbreaks, when life is lived at such a pitch.

However, the interpretation of what Webster is aiming at by his disjunctive technique has ranged from nihilist scepticism to didactic optimism. Gunnar Boklund followed the picturesque account of Rupert Brooke – 'grubs writhing in an immense night' – by asserting that the 'tenacity of his artistic purpose' conveys 'the extraordinary sense of a world without a centre'. David Gunby and Dominic Baker-Smith have presented religious interpretations that differ widely. The Augustinianism of the Jacobeans, a mood rather than a dogma, was shared by such different men as John Donne and William Perkins, the Puritan: 'We are all conceived in close prison; in our mothers' wombs we are close prisoners all; when we are born, we are born but to the liberty of the house; prisoners still, though within larger walls; and then all our life is but a going out to the place of execution, to Death' (Donne, *Sermons*, vol. 11, p. 197). Perkins sees every man by nature 'not only chained and fettered in his sins' but 'stark dead therein ... not having any ability to move or stir; therefore he cannot so much as desire to do anything that is good of himself' (*Works*, I, p. 559).

But whilst for Baker-Smith, Webster's is Montaigne's 'incomprehensible God', a *Deus absconditus*, a hidden God set against the visible world which exists *in* and *per se*, Gunby sees so clear a Providential design that even the triumphant Francesco de Medici only *seems* to conquer, since his evil exists only in time, contingently. It may be that Man could shape himself. The old conflict of Fortune and Virtue revives, depressing the rôle of Providence.[15]

Theatrical images allowed just such a wide interpretation of the play's emblematic tableaux. Cornelia mourning over Marcello, in her songs and her gestures of distraction may recall Ophelia; but the posture recalls King Lear mourning Cordelia, as both recall the Catholic *Pietà* of the Mother with her dead Son. Even the simpler members of the audience were used to interpreting images of daily life (for instance, inn signs and tradesmen's signs), and this 'language' of posture or grouping would be as current at the Red Bull as in the Court masque.

Some effects, like the solo entry of young Orsini in his mourning suit (III. ii), were commonplaces of the stage and can readily be understood today. The election of the Pope, on the other hand, a central moment, would be 'darker' in Jacobean England. The most difficult form of emblem is Webster's narrative fable. Vittoria's dream plainly hints at witchcraft; the emblem of the stag weeping for the loss of his horns (II. i. 325–7) is briefly and neatly dealt with; but Flamineo's long, ambiguous fable of the Egyptian crocodile and the little bird who acts as a 'pretty toothpicker' (IV. ii. 221–35) is so suddenly attached at the end of a deeply emotional scene that the opportunities for Richard Perkins's irony do not exist for the modern actor – he could not 'work' this narrative's insinuations. It would be in keeping with the Red Bull tactics if, in a modern production, some kind of transparency or screen image were to be flashed on to give the two contradictory interpretations of this 'tale for the children': either Brachiano is not rewarding him for his devotion, *or* Vittoria is not rewarding Brachiano for *his*.

The simpler the story, of course, the more it might be used as a means of conveying dangerous and subversive messages. Fable is aggressively unpretentious, and Webster was later to employ tactics of implicit comment for political ends.[16]

The gnomic couplets of Flamineo, his 'dry sentence stuffed with sage', may have served to replace the Chorus that his theatre denied Webster; biting comments on the action by some detached onlooker, or the snarling match between Lodovico and Flamineo, display self-conscious verbal artifice, which is mocked at the same time that it is indulged. Whilst the strength of such lines implies that even the most negative attitude is based on commitment ('I am' is defined by what 'I lack'), yet Webster resists the temptation to dogmatism or edification. He kept at the level of proverb, stage image, demonstration: substitutes for Nuntius or Chorus. Current stage images, and the practices of other tragic writers, were directly employed; it was plain truth when Webster declared ('To the Reader') that he desired to be read by their light, and that he also desired to be watched by their light too.

From Shakespeare he took the iterative imagery, such as the caged bird or savage predators, that link his play together (like the images of blood and darkness in *Macbeth*). He also borrowed from particular scenes, as has been said; he could have read *Hamlet* and *King Lear*, but can have known *Macbeth* and *Antony and Cleopatra* only from the theatre. From Chapman he took a conception of character, in which energy carries charges both of good and evil:

> Give me a spirit that on this life's rough sea
> Loves t' have his sails fill'd with a lusty wind,

Even till his sail yards tremble, his masts crack,
And his rapt ship run on her side so low
That she drinks water and her keel ploughs air.
[*Conspiracy of Byron*, III. iii. 135–9]

He also took from Chapman the transformation of dumb shows and emblems into complex perspective art.

From Jonson he took the technique of moving forward by action and reaction, and some details of trial scenes from *Sejanus*. From Marston he took most – the Italianate Court life as another form of 'perspective', the use of contrasted rôles in one character, the epigram as malicious comment, the 'horrid laughter'. Verbal fireworks spurt most brightly in Flamineo.

The most fully annotated and most badly misunderstood feature of Webster's style however is what used to be called his verbal borrowings, but which I should prefer to call laminations or bondings of other men's images and short sayings into his text. Here he should be compared with those modern exemplars, Eliot – who used Webster himself for this purpose – Joyce and Lowry. The method allows – indeed, demands – constant elaboration and revision. Webster spent a long time writing this play, as he confesses in his preface; the method of slow, careful composition had been one of Mulcaster's precepts. It is at the polar opposite from the copybook habits of keeping elegant extracts. Unfortunately, Webster's method was discovered before the modern investigations of the Renaissance habits of training the memory – or, indeed, the principles of its rhetoric – were generally understood.

Webster seems to have confined himself to modern authors, to phrases that were already part of an English tradition (here again the influence of Mulcaster may have been responsible). They were often already highly polished and pointed, the final density of reference being a way of concentrating ironies, and of stating paradoxes that 'outrun the pauser, reason'. He may have expected some, but not necessarily all, of his quotations to be recognized; all derive from the common tradition, the rich collective subsoil of European poetic accumulations, and each image may work differently for different readers, 'multiplying variety in a wilderness of mirrors'.

Chapman is the only contemporary who practised anything like Webster's bonding; the discovery of their method led at first to rather scandalized assumptions from scholars who ignored the evidence of the theatre and the evidence provided by contemporary writers.[17]

Yet, as the commentary will show, it is becoming increasingly evident that Webster did not employ even the commonest proverbs without the stimulus of some specific work. . . . Webster's sources are in some measure determining the dialogue . . . sometimes working directly from his source, but more often employing a commonplace book . . . probably every repetition in Webster, including those not yet traced, stems from this notebook method . . . he composed the work bit by bit from sources . . . a . . . line or two at a time, with a commonplace book open.

[R. W. Dent, Introduction to *John Webster's Borrowing*, 1960

This is to confuse the mnemonic device of *making* a commonplace book with the habit of referring to it continuously. The Merchant Taylors scholar would work under Rules of Allusion, as in *Scholar's Guide from the Accidence to the University* (1665), where Ralph Johnson wrote, 'We may allude to sentences of authors, applying them to another matter. . . . We may say of drunkenness as the poet did of love, *raptam tollit de cardine mentem*' (page 9). And Jonson, in his *Discoveries*, telling the story about Euripides that Webster was to use as justification for his own slow composition,[18] comments:

Indeed, things wrote with labour deserve to be so read and will last their age . . . the third requisite in our poet, or maker, is imitation, to be able to convert the substance or riches of another poet to his own use . . . not as a creature that swallows what it takes in crude, raw or undigested; but that feeds with an appetite, and hath a stomach to concoct, divide and turn all into nourishment . . . turn all into honey, work it into one relish and savour; make our imitation sweet; observe how the best writers have imitated and follow them.

When T. S. Eliot remarked that 'Bad poets imitate; good poets steal', he was perhaps recalling his own transformational uses in *The Waste Land*; as of Goldsmith:

> When lovely woman stoops to folly and
> Paces about the room again, alone,
> She smooths her hair with automatic hand
> And puts a record on the gramophone.

This was Webster's transformational habit; however rich the elements, they are always modified; he does not quote exactly, but makes his own very subtle adjustments. When he is making a popular stage 'bonding', he presumably means the theft to be recognized, and its often ironic application savoured.

On the other hand, like Eliot, he himself may not always have been conscious of his verbal borrowings. The art of memory trains recall, not recognition; the associative powers, that have summoned up one image, then summon up another (less consciously), thus forming a cluster. The classic method was to impose images on some imaginary building; this was Cicero's method of training the orator.[19] Webster's very individual results should make it obvious that he was working not so much on a copybook basis as in the manner used by great preachers – Thomas Adams, or Lancelot Andrewes, or John Bunyan. Bunyan knew his Bible so well that 'still I pulled, for still the numbers came': the relevant passages recalled themselves. Sometimes scattered, sometimes bunched, Webster's verbal echoes recalled his very close reading of his favourite books – the *Arcadia*, Montaigne, William Alexander. Adams in return used Webster – see p. 182.

It has been mentioned that, in common with nearly every satirist of the Inns of Court, Webster himself, in the induction to *The Malcontent*, had satirized the kind of activity with which he was at one time credited – by Dent: sitting copying 'sentences' out of a commonplace book, and building a dialogue around them. His foolish playgoer declared he could have prompted the actors: 'I am one that hath seen this play often and can give them intelligence for their action; I have most of the jests here in my table book' (*The Malcontent*, induction, 15–17). Though he never 'studied the art of memory', this same gallant, after one saunter down Goldsmiths' Row, can recite all the signs. 'I do use to meditate much when I come to plays, too,' he added (*Ibid.*, 110–11).

Whilst the modern actor may find the staccato style difficult, this was one of Webster's assets for the Jacobean actor,[20] and resulted from his many bondings. Nevertheless, when he defended himself in the note 'To the Reader' – which is a rebuttal of all the charges he can imagine being brought – his haughty 'I confess I do not write with a goose quill, winged with two feathers', with the comma pause, puts the accent on *goose*.

The thick incrustation of other men's jewels upon the fabric of his play, like the thickly encrusted pearls and diamonds that were worked into patterns on the state dresses of the Court masquers, offer always a design and many times an emblematic significance of their own. 'O Lucian thy ridiculous purgatory,' cries Flamineo, evoking the whole concept of Lucianic tragi-comedy (the kind which Hamlet uses in the graveyard scene).

Since the death scene is the final definition of any character –
existential presentation of his final 'shape', the Jacobean index to
his eternal destiny – the final scene of *The White Devil* may serve
as an example of bonding, or 'digested' citation.

Vittoria and Flamineo greet each other, not quite seriously, as
devils; threatened with death by him, she preaches to him sound
doctrine against despair, which he counters with his Lucianic
mockery. He ends with a choric statement from the classical
William Alexander, changing the praise however of 'unlooked for
death' into 'violent death'. After they have 'shot' him, Vittoria and
Zanche, excited by his ferociously exaggerated account of his own
death pangs, turn upon him with threats of damnation, after
which, his 'revival' and taunting – modulated into the beautiful
lament which Eliot borrowed and wove into *The Waste Land* –
present a death-bed which recalls a bride-bed, with its thick cur-
tains, and which sums up a strong line of imagery running through
the entire play:

> O men
> That lie upon your death beds and are haunted
> With howling wives, ne'er trust them – they'll remarry
> Ere the worm *pierce your winding sheet*, ere the spider
> *Make a thin curtain* for your epitaphs!
>
> [V. vi. 154–8

As the second group of murderers, still masked in their friars'
habits, break in, Flamineo greets them with a bitter jest out of
Florio's Montaigne, sandwiched between some 'dried sentences
stuffed with sage' from Alexander. Then his last display begins:

> I recover like a spent taper for a flash
> And instantly go out.
> Let all that belong to great men remember th'old wives' tradition to
> be like the lions i' th' Tower on Candlemas day, to mourn if the sun
> shine, for fear of the pitiful remainder of winter to come.
> 'Tis well yet there's some goodness in my death,
> My life was a black charnel; I have caught
> An everlasting cold. I have lost my voice
> Most irrevocably; farewell, glorious villains –
> This busy trade of life appears most vain,
> Since rest breeds rest, where all seek pain by pain.
> Let no harsh flattering bells resound my knell,
> Strike thunder, and strike loud, to my farewell.
>
> [V. vi. 263–76

A reflection of the playhouse itself as the actor finishes his part,
and then an old wives' tale which brings the event unashamedly

into the City of London. Another of Sir William Alexander's 'sentences', completely inverted, laments that permanent theme in Flamineo's part: the underlying 'pain'. Then comes the last bravura flourish, challenging Heaven's judgment of thunder.

The death of Flamineo is followed by the last resolute challenge of Lodovico, his murderer:

> I do glory yet
> That I can call this act mine own – for my part
> The rack, the gallows and the torturing wheel
> Shall be but sound sleeps to me.
> [V. vi. 293–6

This comes as pure defiance, for the thunder of Heaven *has* already been heard – Lodovico has been killed by firing directed from off-stage.

The various ceremonies of death in this tragedy are confidently recommended for 'use' by the boy prince, who had earlier put his uncle the question

> What do the dead do, uncle? do they eat,
> Hear music, go a-hunting and be merry,
> As we that live?
> [III. ii. 323–5

It is the question Webster's art puts to his auditory. For this young Duke of Brachiano, who had so captivated London, had died young – before Webster wrote the tragedy of his parents.

The year 1612 was a festive one for the Merchant Taylors Company, since one of their number, Sir John Swinnerton, was Lord Mayor. Webster's former collaborators, Thomas Dekker and Wentworth Smith, produced works which were published with dedications to him as a lover of plays. *The White Devil* may have been intended as part of the celebrations; tragedies were performed even at weddings. The ironic motto on its title-page, 'Non inferiora secutus' (from *Aeneid*, VI. 170 – 'following no inferior standard') recalls the fate of Aeneas' trumpeter, slain by the Tritons because his music rivalled theirs; it may stand in lieu of dedication – which in all his later works Webster provided. Since the play had been a public failure, Webster proudly offered it, not to the Lord Mayor, but to the judgment of future times. He must almost immediately have started on his second masterpiece.

CHAPTER SEVEN

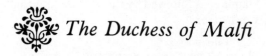 *The Duchess of Malfi*

In the one predominant perturbation; in the other overruling wisdom; in one the body's fervour and fashion of outward fortitude to all height of heroic action; in the other, the mind's inward constant and unconquered empire, unbroken, unalter'd with any most insolent and tyrannous afflic- tion.[1]
[George Chapman, letter dedicatory to his translation of Homer's *Odyssey*, 1614

Chapman's comparison of the *Iliad* and the *Odyssey* would serve for Webster's two great tragedies; though each might be subtitled 'A Woman at Bay', Vittoria's 'heroic action' serves her worldly ambition, whilst the courage of the Aragonian princess gives her fortitude to endure the consequences of her bid for feminine happiness and fulfilment.

The similarities in structure (Duke and Cardinal combining in punitive alliance) should not disguise the differences. Since they have been revived, the superiority of *The Duchess of Malfi* has ensured half-a-dozen revivals for every one of *The White Devil*. The play was probably acted in the winter of 1613–14, and cer- tainly before 12 December 1614, for on that day William Osler (who first played Antonio) died. In Webster's own day the play was from the first regarded as his masterpiece and seems to have enjoyed a continuous stage success. It was one of the opening plays for the Cockpit in Court in 1635, a command performance for royalty.

The crowds who thronged to Blackfriars, where the play was put on by the King's Men, were recalled nearly twenty years later by the son of old John Heminges, leader of that group. In a macabre mock-elegy for the amputation of a duelling finger, he sets a procession of poets escorting it to the banks of the Styx:

It had been drawn and we in state approach,
But Webster's brother would not lend a coach,
He swore that all were hired to convey
The Malfi duchess sadly on her way.[2]

Webster, if only temporarily, had transferred himself from the
company of his old acting friends, to regain the kind of conditions
in which he could succeed. The Blackfriars (opened only three
or four years earlier) led as the first indoor theatre for an adult
company – one which had held together for nearly twenty years,
and which cultivated a long tradition in revenge plays. Burbage,
creator of *Hamlet*, was in the cast. Webster made full use of the
intimate setting of this hall for another family tragedy – indeed one
family more significantly than before, including the Household.

Throngs of coaches crowding to Blackfriars were a common
cause of complaint. Visiting dignitaries, even royalty, had been
seen there. What could have brought Webster to the attention of
the King's Men? Possibly the printed edition of *The White Devil*,
with its generous tribute to the actors and its lament for conditions
at the Red Bull. Possibly the disappearance of some of their playwrights – the retirement of Shakespeare and Beaumont.

When Webster published the tragedy, the names of all the actors
(with their parts) were prefixed – the first example of such a tribute.[3] John Lowin, as Bosola, was recognized as the leading actor;
Burbage played Ferdinand, Duke of Calabria, and was later succeeded by Taylor; Henry Condell played the Cardinal of Aragon
and Richard Sharpe the Duchess; Nicholas Tooley, Burbage's
apprentice, doubled some minor parts.

This team included both high and low in their audiences. They
were used to playing at Court, but they also kept their old theatre
on Bankside, the Globe, and evidently transferred Webster's play
there, although some scenes needed darkness and silence. The prison scenes do not demand a small cell, but occupy the whole stage,
which implies the Blackfriars.

Webster's dedication offered this play to a grandson of Lord
Hunsdon, who had been the patron of the troupe in Queen Eliza-
beth's time. Other playwrights gave him commendatory verses;
Middleton, Rowley (leader of Prince Charles's Men and a future
collaborator), together with young John Ford, from the Middle
Temple, united to affirm that the work sealed Webster's immor-
tality, Ford comparing him with the best poets of Greece or Rome.
Middleton described the audience as being overcome by pity;

pity is indeed a key word towards the end of the play, but almost always used ironically: 'Thy pity is nothing of kin to thee' (IV. i. 135).

The story is much simpler and bolder in relief than that of Vittoria. The historic basis was at once more distant and more tenuous; Webster took it from Painter's *Palace of Pleasure* (1567), a context that did not enforce any historic stringency. This narrative source is of minimal significance in itself. The litanies of a protracted rite of royal death are built on great public occasions and draw on many literary forms, especially the two contradictory ones of funeral elegy and wedding masque. (The latter is now extinct.)

Webster developed the inverted religious ritual of the death of Brachiano and added to it complex recall not only of many books and of other literary forms, but of events from life – such great events as the funeral of Prince Henry and the marriage rites of Princess Elizabeth and the Elector Palatine in 1613, such local events as overseeing Robert Dove's charity for the condemned at Newgate. To this he joined an attention to his individual actors, and to the effects which could be achieved in his theatre, which is closer than any other dramatist, except Shakespeare, was prepared to go. He knew what could be asked of a boy who had played Hermione or Queen Katherine. Webster made his theatre into an instrument to play on, but he too had vibrated to performance before fashioning it. His use of plays that were still unpublished (*Macbeth*, *Othello* or *Antony and Cleopatra*) proves his attentiveness. Consequently, he shares with Shakespeare an openness to reinterpretation. This paradoxical result, rising from richness and complexity, allows a great variety of valid interpretation and emphasis. It is the reward of a performer's art. With Shakespeare, Webster attracts new relevances from the experience and cultural concern of modern audiences. For example, the modern view that the Duke of Calabria was incestuously fixated upon his twin sister can satisfactorily compensate for inaccessible Jacobean theological or social moods, just as, in a living organism, one part may take over the function of another. This adjustment is the mark of classic work, always renewable by transformation. Today, unless they have personally faced some extremity of horror and collective wickedness, very few believe in supernatural evil, or personal devils.

In this chapter therefore, first the social, then the psychological, and lastly the contemporary theatrical background are explored to re-establish the missing context – this, not to replace modern reading, but to enrich it.

The Duchess of Malfi is distinguished from *The White Devil*, which was firmly grounded in recent history, and the distinction produces a different conception of the play – one which was also influenced by the very different playing conditions at Blackfriars.

The story had survived only because it had been recounted by a contemporary, Matheo Bandello, who told it as Antonio's tragedy; this Italian bishop may have been the Delio of the play, as he seems to have known Antonio personally. Tragic 'shaping', carried through the French to Painter, had made it legendary in the course of one hundred years, the interval between the murder of Antonio Bologna at Milan in October 1513 and Webster's play. The secret marriage between the young widowed Duchess and the steward of her household, their five years' happiness, their flight, and the vengeance of her brothers were told through long speeches, laments and songs from the two lovers. Painter displayed what historical records fail to supply: the Duchess's imprisonment and death by strangling, together with her faithful maid and two children; he briefly ended with the record of Antonio's assassination later on the orders of the Cardinal.[4]

Into such a legend Webster was free to insert contemporary colour. The Spanish rulers of the Kingdom of Naples could be interpreted in the light of contemporary Spanish honour and Spanish pride. (Indeed, a few years later Lope de Vega was himself to write a play on the story of the Duchess.) There was freedom also to shape it in terms of the noblest theatrical form, the masque, though in an unusual and paradoxical way, turning the form and the occasion upside down. The old tale and the modern instance, eternity and time, were combined in Webster, and still without any dogmatic fixations. His negative capability, or 'power of being in doubts, mysteries, fears without any irritable reaching after fact and reason', was strengthened by contrasts of darkness and light, diamond and mist, so that his perspectives in this piece are larger, and yet his style is softened. The sharp contrasts of the central scene in *The White Devil* have become the nightmares of the Duchess's prison in Act IV. The total effect is still paradoxical – the epigrams of Bosola and the Duchess giving rise to numinous shudders, the abrupt breaks in speech to the stealthy encroachment of menacing forces, stage figures to the implications they carry. In place of the Ambassadors who represent the political aspect of Vittoria's challenge, perspectives of hell open in the Duchess's prison; since the time of Charles Lamb these scenes have been recognized as being 'not of this world'. Madness was itself thought of as diabolic possession, and the 'comic' masque of madmen prefigures the later madness of Ferdinand.

There is no single 'source'. Bandello's narrative records his extreme shock, which he dealt with by blaming everybody – Antonio for his presumption, the Duchess for her lust, the brothers for their cruelty; his position is self-contradictory. For Webster's generation, the end of Penelope Rich and Charles Blount's love affair, or the story of Antonio Pérez and the Princess of Eboli, offered possible endorsement. The modern reader is at least better equipped by this analogue from Webster's day, to gain insight into the price for private security amid Court splendour, and also into the psychology of the spy. For Webster's chief method of shaping the story was to create the single character of Bosola out of the Duchess's household servants, her prison tormentors, and the named assassin of Antonio in Milan, a Lombard captain. Bosola's insecurity, his bitter jesting and self-mockery, his constant, unremitting demands for 'reward', which is always denied him, and finally his love of disguises as a mode of psychological relief can all be found in Pérez. Better than any other writer of his time, Webster has realized the dark side of political power, the cruel grip of intelligence networks, the shocks of betrayal. In production, Bosola often dominates the play, so that the lives of the Aragonian princelings serve but as background to his self-destruction. This spy, who repents and institutes a counter-vengeance for the murder which he himself had executed on command, reaffirms the tragic fate of the servant. The great lady who ends her days in darkness, close prisoner in her own palace, shares the pride of Penelope Rich and Ana de Mendoza, Princess of Eboli.

Every Jacobean would know that madness was hereditary in the royal blood, which it was the Duchess's crime to have contaminated by a base marriage; they would also know the story of Philip II's heir, Don Carlos, strangled in prison.

The last element of public feeling which Webster incorporated into his play may not have been recognized by his contemporaries. His own mourning for England's heir, Henry, Prince of Wales, who had died in November 1612, had been set down within a few weeks in *A Monumental Column*, his elegy. Here many of the images, later closely united in *The Duchess of Malfi*, lie about as *disjecta membra*. It is not in itself a memorable achievement, but points to one of the sources of the tragedy; this widespread national grief provided some powerful emotional drives which went into the tragedy and were transformed.

It is possible to sustain a reading of the play in terms of contemporary views of social duty or social structure; it is also perfectly possible to read it as a character study of the four leading figures, with religious overtones, or as a subtle variation upon the perspectives of the masque. The story is 'open' not so much to the moral alternatives which are powerful in *The White Devil* as to differences of genre, of interpretative approach, or of emphasis, of light and shade. It has proved attractive in this way to modern poets, who have adapted it in a thoroughly Websterian fashion.

In accordance with the practice of the private theatre, Webster divides the play into five acts, centring on the Court, the bedchamber, the world, the prison and the grave. But these locations are not closely defined. In the prison scene, the waxwork show of mortification, the masque of madmen and the ritual of execution are in themselves theatrical; they belong with the hell-castle of *Macbeth*, with its porter and its alarm bell, with the shows in the witches' cave. These in turn reflect the 'great doom's image' of medieval drama – Heaven and Hell. The King's Men at this time were increasing this element in their productions – with new effects in *Macbeth*, and with Shakespeare's final plays. Their own experience of the Court masque (where they had enacted the witches for the antimasque of *The Masque of Queens*) must have affected their general style.[5] It was a secular ritual, using religious terms, but without ever introducing religious material.

The legendary, the contemporary, the dramatically ritualistic are laminated, and this inlay increases the dramatic life of the work. What now has to be substituted for Webster's contemporary lamination is something of our own day: both T. S. Eliot and Allen Tate, in their lyrics, added this perspective to the original poetry. Eliot chooses the bedchamber scene, where the Duchess is surprised, partly through Antonio's jest of leaving her, and sees in her mirror not the face of her husband but that of her brother, holding out a poniard. This is adapted so that the two figures

become two aspects of one man, who both loves and hates at once.
The effect is not pity but terror:

'You have cause to love me, I did enter you in my heart
Before ever you vouchsafed to call for the keys'
With her back turned, her arms were bare,
Fixed for a question, her hands behind her hair
And the firelight shining where the muscle drew....
There I suppose they found her
As she turned
To interrogate the silence fixed behind her.[6]

Allen Tate contrasts the tale of the Duchess with the sterility of
a modern reading:

The stage is about to be swept bare of corpses.
You have no more chance than an infusorian
Lodged in a hollow molar of an eohippus....

Now consideration of the void coming after,
Not changed by the 'strict gesture' of your death,
Splits the straight line of pessimism
Into two infinities....

And the katharsis fades in the warm water of a yawn.[7]

If the cynicism of Bosola and Flamineo is to jest about moral values
they cannot afford, Tate's *persona* in this poem fits into the play
well enough. Its own comedy starts in the opening scene at Court;
then, in Act II, Bosola uses the tone of the Malcontent in his mockery of women's painting; Ferdinand's actions begin with the
manic grandeur of forbidding his courtiers to laugh except when
he laughs. Later, as he silently confers with his brother, and someone comments, 'The Lord Ferdinand laughs', it seems

like a deadly cannon
That lightens ere it smokes.
[III. iii. 54-5

The Duchess's mirth consists of simple, rather childish bawdy
jokes with her maid and her husband, but Ferdinand's entry trans-
fers it into the bitter wit with which she enacts her play of banish-
ing Antonio. She neither employs nor suspects any espionage; her
wit serves chiefly to control her own pain and resentment and acts
upon herself (as Bosola's also acts upon himself).

Historically, the removal of Antonio Bologna and his Duchess
from this world was neatly and expertly carried out; there was
no scandal and little comment. It was a family affair; the Duchess

simply vanished and was never seen again, her secret marriage
matched by her secret death. In this play, uniquely among
Webster's works, there is no trial; tyranny is condemned by Ferdinand's self-accusation:

> By what authority didst thou execute
> This bloody sentence?
> *Bosola.*   By yours –
> *Ferdinand.*   Mine? Was I her judge?
> Did any ceremonial form of law
> Doom her to not being? did a complete jury
> Deliver her conviction up i' th' court?
> Where shalt thou find this judgment registered
> Unless in hell ...?
>   [IV. ii. 298–304

The only form of sentence we have witnessed was that of her
banishment from Ancona, carried out in dumb show, at the shrine
of Our Lady of Loretto. This was evidently staged in great
splendour, for an Italian visitor to London commented upon it
in 1618. During the ceremony the Cardinal violently took her wedding-ring from the Duchess's finger, which constituted an ecclesiastical act of nullity of the contract; punishment by the secular
arm (banishment) followed this ecclesiastical judgment. From the
comments of the two onlookers one learns also that the Pope has
seized the duchy ('But by what justice?' 'Sure, I think by none/
Only her brother's instigation').

In the case of Antonio Pérez and the Princess of Eboli the arbitrary nature of Spanish judicial procedure, with the unscrupulous
use of ecclesiastical charges in default of secular evidence, was the
whole point of the *Relaciones* being published in England. It
showed to the English (including the English Catholics) the
superiority of English justice. There is no form of justice in the
family acts of vengeance against the Duchess, who repeatedly calls
it tyranny.

If the drama were viewed simply as a family history, as it might
have been by one of Webster's young friends from the Inns of
Court, it would have been considered that the Aragonian brethren
were lacking in a proper sense of duty in counselling the young
Duchess to live unmarried, and then going off and leaving her.
It was their duty to look round the world at large, find a suitable
husband and present him to her. The absolute authority of the
head of the family over all members was not disputed, and the
natural subjection of sister to brother appears in a number of

English plays.[8] But imposing on the Duchess the heroic rôle of Virtuous Widow – a rôle which the individual could certainly choose, which was seemly for older women, which could confer extraordinary power on a Catherine de Medici – was tyrannical. Later, indeed, Ferdinand pretends he is planning a marriage with Malateste, and the Cardinal also claims to have a plan for her remarriage. Antonio, as her faithful servant, counsels marriage to her before she makes her declaration of love to him. (In all stage comedy, the remarriage of widows is a central assumption.)

Yet, whatever the value of 'a contract in a chamber', the Duchess, by failing to publish her marriage, destroys her own good fame. Antonio is aware that 'the common rabble do directly say she is a strumpet'. To her brother she claims that 'my reputation is safe', but he declares that once it is lost it is irrecoverable (III. ii. 116–35). He explains, as if to a child, that love is found only among shepherds or dowerless orphans. Marriage as a social contract, an affair of the larger family, means that if Antonio was her husband he was not her 'lord and husband'; he jests at himself as a lord of Misrule, reigning only at night. He simply does not belong with the great ones; his rôle in the marriage is passive, indeed feminine; the Duchess, acting as the masculine half in the partnership, proposes the contract, directs their action, plans their flight, faces her brothers. At the end, Antonio hopes only to ask pardon of his new kinsmen. As a member of the Household, he should have respected its degrees; since he is an upper servant, his life is held as cheap as Bosola's by the brothers.

Imprisonment was the usual penalty for clandestine marriages between a great lady and a servant. The most eminent example is John Donne, secretary to the Lord Keeper, who, after he had married the Keeper's niece, Anne More, in December 1601, was two months later committed to the Fleet Prison for conspiracy to violate the civil and common law. The cleric who performed the ceremony was also jailed, as was even the man who had 'given' the bride – a gift he was certainly in no position to bestow. Years of poverty followed. The case of Lady Arbella Stuart is more frequently mentioned in the context of this play; in that instance it was her nearness to the throne which caused her imprisonment.

One of the works that Webster was certainly reading at this time, for there are many 'bondings' in this play, was Montaigne's essay 'Upon some Verses of Virgil' (Book 3, Chapter 5), which treats of love and marriage. Montaigne assumes, without requiring any examination, the double standard by which men would face almost any crime in their family rather than the infidelity of their wives. The particular passion of the Italians, love ('Luxury is like a wild beast, first made fierce with tying and then let loose'), is stronger in women than in men. Marriage is another thing: 'Wedlock hath for his share honour, justice, profit and constancy; a plain but more general delight, Love melts in only pleasure; and truly it hath it more ticklish; more lively, more quaint and more sharp ... a pleasure inflamed by difficulty; there must be a kind of tingling, stinging and smarting. *It is no longer love, be it once without arrows and without fire.*' Webster laminates Montaigne's cool and occasionally alarming survey of the relation between the sexes with the glowing ardour of Sidney's *Arcadia*: the perfection of its two heroines in prison, their sufferings for love. In Sidney he found the device of the wax figures used as torture for his Duchess. Florio's translation of Montaigne had been dedicated to, among others, Penelope Rich; the collision between Sidney's burnished examples of Virtue and the sardonic enigmas of Montaigne must have been strengthened by bitter contrasts in the life of a woman who linked these two works.

Penelope's last battle was for the right to call herself Countess of Devonshire; the Duchess of Malfi is never given a personal name. She is always addressed by her title. Her private person is suppressed in her public rôle; we never meet Giovanna d'Aragona. Yet it is the struggle between these two elements which her maid laments in the concluding words of Act I:

> Whether the spirit of greatness or of woman
> Reign most in her, I know not, but it shows
> A fearful madness; I owe her much of pity.
>
> [I. i. 504–6

Webster was later to use another antithesis, in comparing 'The Character of a Virtuous Widow' – who never remarried – with 'An Ordinary Widow', who remarried again and again: noble and comic, sacred and risible. In this play however he showed the one character in two different rôles, overt and covert. Her public rôle as Duchess gives her no power within the family; she makes her domestic choice with a sense that she is acting like soldiers who

> in some great battles
> By apprehending danger have achieved
> Almost impossible actions.
>
> [I. i. 344–6

And to Antonio she suggests that 'love mixed with fear is sweetest' (III. ii. 66).

The Duchess of Malfi's life was cleft in two by her secret marriage; her integrity was restored ultimately by the price she was prepared to pay for it. She changes and grows, as few other characters do; and ultimately the language she uses is that of religious experience – there is nothing doctrinal about it. For she is denied the consolation of the Church (which Spaniards were always most punctilious in allowing to the victim); she has to improvise her own ceremonies. The Cardinal and Ferdinand use the ceremonies of Church and State to release their own perversions.

Tragic awakening begins for the Duchess with a pathetic variation on her brother's warning that happiness dwells only with unambitious shepherds or dowerless orphans:

> The birds that live i' the' field
> On the wild benefit of nature, live
> Happier than we; for they may choose their mates
> And carol their sweet pleasures to the spring.
> [III. v. 18–21

This is pastoral happiness that Webster drew elsewhere in his 'Character of a fair and happy Milkmaid'.

At parting with Antonio, she hopes that they will not part thus 'i' th' Eternal Church' and sees the heavy hand of Heaven in her affliction:

> I have seen my little boy oft scourge his top
> And compared myself to 't; nought made me e'er
> Go right but Heaven's scourge-stick.
> [III. v. 81–3

This is not a sustained attitude, for human pride and even religious cursing at other points contradict it. Her 'diamond' quality combats with her fragility: she is no stoic; conflicting passions succeed her initial stunned, somnambulistic calm.

The Hell, or Purgatory, which the Duchess undergoes in prison is defined by its remoteness or detachment. Her first words after Antonio has left her are 'My laurel is all withered' (III. v. 93).[9] The laurel which protected the Roman Emperors from thunder was also their emblem of good fame. In being removed to her own palace, she enters a realm darker and grander to which she provides her own choric comment:

> I have heard
> That Charon's boat serves to convey all o'er
> The dismal lake but brings none back again.
>
> [III. v. 107–9

These Roman comments transcend her own rôle; they give a godlike view.

The silence of the prison scenes is preceded by Bosola's account of her own deep and silent grief. The scene may well be her own bedchamber, where she jested with Antonio, the arms of the Duchy of Malfi still blazoned on the tester. The 'shows' of Antonio and the children, following the 'love token' of the dead man's hand, bring her to feel that living itself is hell. She invites the ritual punishment for an ill-matched marriage:

> If they would bind me to that lifeless trunk
> And let me freeze to death.
>
> [IV. i. 68–9[10]

A deep sense of unreality has come upon her; a world 'not just confused but unfathomable' is created by superimposing two images in a new 'art'; the magic ring and the dead man's hand are 'witchcraft'; the 'show' is the preparatory stage of her tomb-making. Bosola tries to convert this to penance, rites for the dying. The madmen with their mocking jests (as if from some great court antimasque),[11] 'Woe to the caroche that brought home my wife from the masque at three o'clock in the morning; it had a large feather bed in it' (IV. ii. 104–6), go on to babble of the Last Judgment. Their comments on sex and violence serve both as prelude to the 'masque' of the Duchess's execution and also as a foretaste of the supernatural evil to be let loose at the end, when Ferdinand thinks he is transformed to a wolf and when, in storm, 'the Devil rocks his own child'. For a tempest marks the final holocaust.

With the inverted three actions of a true masque – the entry of the executioners, their invitation to the Duchess to join them, and their presentation of the gifts that bring 'Last benefit, last sorrow' – the Duchess finds that the coffin has indeed replaced the nuptial bed; she has 'welcomed' ruin before, but her new perception goes deeper:

> I perceive death, now I am well awake,
> Best gift is, they can give or I can take.
>
> [IV. ii. 224–5

Bosola has stripped her title; if she declared, 'I am Duchess of
Malfi still' – perhaps glancing at the scutcheon above her bed, or
pointing to it – the audience might remember that the arms of
those condemned to die are taken down. When this happened to
Mary, Queen of Scots, she replaced her royal arms by a crucifix.
Bosola's last disguise also brings him out of history into Webster's
world, the parish charity for the poor prisoners of Newgate:

> I am the common bellman
> That usually is sent to condemned persons
> The night before they suffer.
>
> [IV. ii. 173–4

The ritual has brought her too out of the dream country of the
Revels; it is as Giovanna Bologna that she gives instructions for
the care of her children and sends a last message to her brothers
– 'Go, tell my brothers, when I am laid out, / They then may feed
in quiet' (IV. ii. 236–7) – as she kneels to 'enter heaven'. There
is almost a suggestion of cannibalism latent in the image, which
catches up an earlier one.[12] When the gruesome comedy of the
waiting-maid's death is ended, Bosola sees where he is – 'a
perspective that shows us hell' – and he names the deed as
'murder'.

'I am Duchess of Malfi still' had asserted the 'Mind's empire'
against Ferdinand's 'tyrannous affliction'; Bosola replies, 'That
makes thy sleep so broken.' Had she said, 'I am Giovanna Bologna
still,' she would have more truthfully disclosed the way in which
her marriage had severed her public rôle from her private person.
She had 'awakened' Antonio with the words '[I] only do appear
to you a young widow / That claims you for her husband' (I. i.
456–7) and 'put off all vain ceremony' – though later she had
improvised one.

For those who would see the Duchess as love's martyr, the
moment of her death is crucial. Critical judgment has placed her
at every point on the scale that separates Fair Rosamond or Jane
Shore from the Virgin Martyr (a play on St Dorothea had just
been acted at the Red Bull). The Duchess's death converts Bosola,
the expected miracle. The sight of her face also 'awakens' Ferdinand to what he has done: 'Cover her face; mine eyes dazzle;
she died young' (IV. ii. 264). In the darkness of the prison this
suggests a halo of glory; sex, violence and religion are fused in
nine short words.

Antonio's first portrait of her to his friend had enskied and sainted her; yet when she finally appears to him 'a face folded in sorrow' in the graveyard, she seems only a mournful, hovering ghost, still the wife of Antonio, still earthbound.

Giovanna Bologna is buried obscurely in the ruins of an ancient monastery; it is as 'my wife' that Antonio recognizes the voice of the Echo. The scene is highly ritualized (perhaps, as in the echo scenes in Monteverdi, Echo was sung), but this truly obscure being has been heard once before – crying out in the pains of childbirth. The unknown self within the Duchess should perhaps be heard as another voice, lacking security, a voice as homeless as the birds that once she envied for their freedom. This voice offers no comfort. He will 'never see her more'.

Theological security, 'which some call the suburbs of hell', had betrayed the Duchess. It is 'mortal's chiefest enemy'. The conviction that the future is assured, springing from the self, its good deeds or its good intentions, is the vice of the Pharisee, but also rises from that combination of Pride with Generosity that defeats Prudence. Security means an unexamined assumption of safety, privilege and stability; it makes denial or responsibility easy, being basically both self-centred and inattentive.

Antonio knows that faithful counsellors should warn the Prince of 'what he ought to foresee' (I. i. 22), but when the Duchess gives him her wedding-ring, 'to help your eyesight', he sees 'a saucy and ambitious devil dancing within the circle', which the Duchess removes by putting the ring on his finger. She senses his 'trembling'. They embrace. Her words are stately or fantastic, but her blushes grow deeper, she asks him to lead her to the bride-bed. For a foil to the Duchess, Webster invented Julia, the Cardinal's mistress, who takes a man if she feels the impulse. In a parody of the Duchess's wooing she seizes Bosola by entering with a pair of pistols and asking him what love potion he has put in her drink. Her end is another macabre jest; the Cardinal poisons her by giving her his Bible to kiss.

Had the Duchess been wanton, she would have tried her arts upon her jailers; and, indeed, the nature of Bosola's devotion is very like love when, after he thinks she is killed, he finds her still living:

> She's warm, she breathes.
> Upon thy pale lips I will melt my heart
> To store them with fresh colour.
>
> [IV. ii. 341–3

Antonio and Bosola stand almost at the same distance from Aragonian royalty; Ferdinand had thought of using Antonio as his spy, and to him there could not be very much to distinguish between the head of the household servants and 'some strong-thighed barge-man' or one of the porters who carried coals up to the Duchess's lodging. From his ducal height, he twice snubs Bosola for attempting to find any explanation of the spying he is set to do, offers his sister his hand to kiss, and even, in madness, deals ruthlessly with the familiarity of the doctor. The Cardinal, whom Antonio at the opening painted as a religious hypocrite, prepares to eliminate Bosola because he will not risk blackmail from one who knows him as a 'fellow murderer'. The hollowness of the Cardinal's priestly rôle is the latest revelation of the play. In the last scene the Cardinal and the Duke are both in prison; the Cardinal has made his own prison for himself, by locking the doors and ordering his Court not to pay any attention to cries for help. The 'accidental judgments, casual slaughters' that finally leave the stage corpse-strewn are in violent contrast to the ritual of the Duchess's 'last presence chamber', but they are taking place in a prison, and perhaps some lighting or 'blocking', or the Cardinal's scutcheon, might relate the two scenes.

The Cardinal knows already that he is in Hell; looking in his fish-ponds for his own image, he has seen 'a thing arm'd with a rake' that seems to strike at him. (It is an echo of the scene where the Duchess sees the face of Ferdinand instead of Antonio's.) The garment of those condemned by the Inquisition was painted all over with devils, to show their state within; so the devil that threatens, as it seems from outside, is really already in possession, and pulling him down. This devil takes away the Cardinal's power to pray; he is in a theological state of despair.

The Cardinal 'ends in a little point, a kind of nothing'. Bosola sees his killing as an act of justice, and, in his last words, the Cardinal echoes his sister in appealing to her executioner (now his) for 'Mercy'. Yet he acknowledges the sentence:

> O Justice!
> I suffer now for what hath former bin –
> Sorrow is held the eldest child of sin.
>   [V. v. 53–5

In a mockery of *L'uomo universale*, the Renaissance man, he has played many rôles – shed his Cardinal's robes for the sword and

armour of the soldier; endured with some boredom the attentions
of a mistress for fashion's sake. His cool manipulation of finance
– it is the Pope who gets the dukedom of Malfi, not Ferdinand
– ruins the Duchess and the experienced Antonio.

Ferdinand has but one overt rôle – the secular head of the
family, the soldier – and he plays it with gusto, ostentatiously. His
moments of silence, of playing 'the politic dormouse', and his out-
bursts of manic rage, build up to the madness that is demonic and
fatal. Burbage, who had created the rôles of Hamlet and Lear, was
playing this part.

For a Jacobean, the madness of the Spanish royal house and
the Spanish code of honour would have sufficed to explain all this;
to a modern audience, the idea that Ferdinand's driving impulse
is an incestuous fixation on his twin sister opens up a meaning
more readily available today. It explains the ceremonial forms his
persecution takes; ritual is an effective way of disguising and con-
trolling repressed desires. He sees himself as a physician
administering purges, even whilst he also sees the Duchess's behaviour as Heaven's punishment for some sin in himself or his
brother – a punishment through their common flesh:

> I could kill her now
> In you or in myself, for I do think
> It is some sin in us, heaven doth revenge
> By her.
>
> [II. v. 63–6

(The pious Marcello had the same idea; see page 129.) The Cardinal replies, 'Are you stark mad?' His attempts at control in the
scene where he meets her, coupled with his utter refusal to listen
to what she has to say, or to see Antonio, are part of the protective
design by which Ferdinand seals off the interior chaos that eventually engulfs him.[13] The ritual execution of the Duchess restores
him to a sense of what he has done to 'my dearest friend' – before
this last insight finally destroys his mental balance. Such an
explanation of Ferdinand has been found so serviceable on the
modern stage as now to be almost orthodox.

Incest was not a subject about which Jacobean dramatists felt
any squeamishness. Tourneur brings it, as a threat, into *The Athe-
ist's Tragedy*, and Webster allows the noble lover to subscribe to
it in *The Devil's Law Case*. Acting as bawd to one's own kin might
be considered 'a kind of incest', and, in basing a tragedy upon
fraternal incest, Webster's young friend John Ford some dozen

years later was to copy themes from this very play.[14] The hero and heroine in *'Tis Pity She's a Whore* join themselves together in a private ceremony which invokes the very tie that should prevent it:

> Sister ⎫   On my knees
> Brother ⎭ even by our mother's dust, I charge you
> Do not betray me to your mirth or hate;
> Love me, or kill me ⎰ sister.
>   ⎱ brother.
>
>   [I. ii. 249–55

They are two innocents in a wicked world, and their union has the isolating effect of an addiction, like the homosexuality of Edward II in Marlowe's play. Society is uniformly disgusting, and these people have isolated themselves from it, each with one who appears the mirror of his or her self. The fraternal relation serves Ford, as it served Webster, in more than one play; its stable, immutable quality (which made one French heroine prefer her brother to her husband on the grounds that the second could be replaced, but not the first) is reflected even in the final scene, for, after entering with Annabella's heart upon his dagger, in a parody of the devotional worship of the Sacred Heart, Giovanni dies with a prayer that restores a chaste remoteness, as if he were looking into a mirror:

> Where 'er I go, let me enjoy this grace,
> Freely to view my Annabella's face.
>   vi. 107–8

'Viewing' undoes Ferdinand.

There is much in the strangling of the Duchess to recall the strangling of Desdemona, not least her momentary revival after she is supposed dead. But the remorse of Ferdinand is shared by Bosola; it is he who sees the great gulf between the 'sacred innocence that sweetly sleeps on turtle's feathers' and his inner hell. Ferdinand feels his life bound up with hers; they were twins. Those who are interested to work out such matters for performance might imagine that the twins were united in enmity against their elder brother, the Cardinal; that the hidden animosity between the two men is shewn by the Cardinal's effortless use of

Ferdinand as his pawn. He even usurps Ferdinand's part as a soldier, for there is nothing priestly about him except his vestments – themselves of course a sign of diabolic intrusion to the more Puritanically minded members of the English Church.

Ferdinand shares with Bosola, his spy, a capacity for pain; the pain hidden behind an outward façade is the thread of life that runs through scenes of external violence.[15] Pain so great that it 'makes us no pain to feel' became in Ford 'the silent griefs that cut the heart strings'; in Ferdinand it emerges in images – sometimes poignant, sometimes bizarre:

> Thou are undone:
> And thou hast ta'en that massy sheet of lead
> That hid thy husband's bones and folded it
> About my heart.
>
> [III. ii. 111–14

Or 'The pain's nothing; pain many times is taken away with apprehension of greater, as the toothache with the sight of the barber that comes to pull it out' (V. v. 59–61). His last words imply that he is one flesh with Giovanna – and one dust:

> My sister O my sister! there's the cause on 't.
> Whether we fall by ambition, blood or lust,
> Like diamonds, we are cut with our own dust.
>
> [V. v. 71–3

Sensitive apprehension of pain lies behind his brutality, and sharpens it, but whilst the modern reading of his impulses as incestuous allows a valid presentation, it seems probable that in Webster's day the same effect upon the audience would have been reached by different means.

Bosola, created by fusing three historic figures in a single tragic rôle, is sometimes felt to be unconvincing, but on stage the part becomes capable of dominating the play. Bosola is a professional murderer, prepared to kill a servant to prevent him unbarring a door; he has served as a galley-slave for murders committed at the Cardinal's instigation. Yet he is also a 'fantastical scholar', slow in working, much concerned with curious learning. When he defends Antonio, as a faithful servant missing reward, and the Duchess unwarily discloses her marriage, he offers her the powerful tribute of the unbeneficed scholar's prayers. Her choice of virtue above greatness will bring her good fame from 'neglected' poets, who will presumably win their own immortality from her story.

Antonio, 'this trophy of a man/Raised by that curious engine, your white hand', will also be praised by poets when heralds have exhausted their easily bestowed nobility. Tributes to the Duchess from needy poets in England had in fact been provided by Robert Greene and George Whetstone (see Boklund, pp. 18–19).

But Bosola also counsels their flight should be disguised as a religious pilgrimage to Loreto (transport is his job). This proves the Duchess's undoing, for it is Papal territory. His praise is immediately followed by the sickening drop to his rôle as spy:

> What rests but I reveal
> All to my lord? O this base quality
> Of intelligencer!
> > [III. ii. 326–8

Bosola, the chief instrument in the Duchess's betrayal and subjection, also bears the strongest witness to her virtues. In prison he may hope, in some confused way, to save her soul if not her body from Ferdinand's damnable plan to 'bring her to despair'; but there is a collusive relation between the two men that makes the servant in some way an emanation of his lord.

Ferdinand, in such utterance – or, again, when Bosola urges the need for her penance – 'Damn her! that body of hers / While that my blood ran pure in 't was more worth / Than that which thou wouldst comfort, call'd a soul' (IV. i. 121–3) – and in the constant imagery of fire, blood and tempest that surrounds him, may be considered as diabolically possessed even before his madness takes over. This leaves Bosola also the prisoner of dark powers, tempted by devils in human form (as a 'scholar', he might have been once in holy orders).

Ferdinand has sworn in the bedchamber scene that he will never see the Duchess more. When Bosola meets her it is always in some form of disguise: 'vizarded' at her capture, dressed as an old man (the stage emblem for mortality), then a 'tomb maker', then playing 'the common bellman'. Whether for their effect upon her, or for relief to himself, these disguises enable Bosola to act as a kind of priest, even whilst he conducts the execution. Yet at the end he is still asking for reward from Ferdinand; he expects to be paid the rate for the job – a pension. He is cheated by the two devils who have brought him so low.

Bosola is not the same kind of Protean shape-changer as Flamineo; his melancholy is not assumed, and his 'antic dispositions' have more than a touch of Hamlet about them; but he is a Hamlet who cannot unpack his heart with words. However, his death speech is firmly orchestrated ('One can almost see the conductor's raised baton,' ejaculates one critic). He begins on a low note, with the unwilling murder of 'his other self', his fellow-servant and the lover of the Duchess, Antonio:

> Such a mistake as I have often seen
> In a play.
>
> [V. v. 95–6

He recollects 'the dead walls or vaulted graves' where the Duchess's voice had echoed, but he hears none:

> O this gloomy world!
> In what a shadow or deep pit of darkness
> Doth (womanish and fearful) mankind live.
>
> [V. v. 100–102

He rises to a brave sentiment, but falls away as he too feels 'Charon's boat' approach:

> Let worthy minds ne'er stagger in distrust
> To suffer death or shame for what is just –
> Mine is another voyage.
>
> [V. v. 103–5

Then, 'staggering in distrust', he ends on this faint litotes.

He can mock his own degradation wittily – 'I think I shall shortly grow the common bier for churchyards' (V. ii. 311–12) – yet, with all his many rôles, Bosola is never permitted the luxury of being a self. He is the masquer, in both senses: he comes with ceremony to his captive Duchess; he leads those scenes that have been generally understood as parody or inversion of a Court masque. Additionally, the play, from beginning to end, depends upon varying or enlarging, contracting or inverting the forms of a masque.

The year 1613 had seen a great number of masques, in particular the three given for the marriage of the Princess Elizabeth to the Elector Palatine on St Valentine's Day, 1613. Two of these masques contained antimasques of madmen.[16] The Court masque, as developed by Ben Jonson and Inigo Jones, celebrated the splendours of the royal house by the epiphany or revelation of some great personage (usually the Queen), who carried the image of a divine or heroic being, supposed to be drawn down to inhabit a mortal frame. It was a rite of cosmic harmony, linking the government of the realm with the government of the spheres, or the marriage of some great persons with the unity of the cosmos. It was a secular sacrament. It was magic. The masquers ultimately came down from their stage to join the audience; the 'revels', or dances, which ensued, preceded sometimes by the offering of gifts, were the main function of the rites.

It had long ago been a feature of revenge tragedy to end with such a masque, only to have the masquers turn upon their hosts in a bloody act of vengeance. (A masque had historically been used in the reign of King Richard II to kidnap Thomas of Woodstock, who was then murdered.) The play-within-the-play at the end of *The Spanish Tragedy*, the masques in Marston's *Antonio's Revenge* and *The Malcontent*, the double masque in *The Revenger's Tragedy* would have been known to the King's Men as well as to Webster. Excitement, surprise, the dropping of disguise were features which belonged also to secret revenge.

Webster developed the old rite, which had its own security built in, into a new drama of insecurity and scepticism. Open alternatives are left by him unresolved. His rite is not one of harmony but of disharmony, not of brilliant light but of darkness. As the ghost of the old revenge play has become no more than the active image of a mourner's fancy, so the melancholy of a Prince Hamlet is domiciled not only in the Cardinal, 'a melancholy churchman', but in Rosencrantz's successor, Bosola the spy.

At Court, the fable, however slight, must be strongly symbolic; the music, dancing and splendid costumes offered a delicate blend of homage to the King, to the Ambassadors of other kings, to the Court, and to some divine Truth which was being 'shadowed' platonically by the action.

The Duchess of Malfi opens with tilting matches and her brother's warning the Duchess to give over her chargeable revels; he characterizes them (as they were often characterized in tragedy) as breeding-places for lust. Her little masquerade with Antonio follows immediately, when she leads through a discussion of accounts and testamentary deposition to the wooing.

Ferdinand's sudden appearance in his sister's bedchamber with his gift of a poniard is a masquerade of the deadliest kind; her own masquerade of dismissing Antonio follows, but he and she cannot resist playing upon their real situation with such quibbles as 'H'as done that, alas, you would not think of' and 'You may

see, gentlemen, what 'tis to serve a prince with body and soul'
(III. ii. 183–209).

There follows a dumb show of the Duke and Cardinal receiving
the news, whilst Delio and Pescara interpret to the audience the
sinister mime:

> These are your true pangs of death,
> The pangs of life, that struggle with great statesmen.
> [III. iii. 56–7

The second dumb show (of the Cardinal's assuming a soldier's
habit, and the banishment of the Duchess and Antonio from
Ancona) is conducted before a very rich shrine. It leads directly
into the scene of the Duchess's capture, and the inverted rites of
the prison scenes, whose masque-like character has already been
shewn.

It has already been pointed out also that Webster's elegy for
Henry, Prince of Wales, who died on the eve of his sister's wedding,
provided material for *The Duchess of Malfi* (see page 3).
Laments for the Prince were often bound up with wedding songs
for the Princess. This is powerfully reflected in the elegy by a
little fable of how Sorrow is masked in the robe of Pleasure. This
fancy of ceremony being used for the opposite purpose to its original one may be taken as a clue to the way in which Webster, in
his tragedy, is using the masque – the more masterfully, since a
blending of 'mirth in funeral and dole in marriage' had actually
occurred in the winter of 1612–13.

Webster's *A Monumental Column*, registered on Christmas
Day, 1612, within six weeks of the Prince's death, was bound up
with other elegies by Cyril Tourneur and Thomas Heywood. The
religious note is here sounded clearly and unequivocally. Webster
was to remember Prince Henry again ten years later, in his very
latest production (see page 180).

Theories that Henry and his sister had often been reflected in
the drama have been put forward of recent years.[17] In this play
Webster transmuted the sorrow that rose from the failure of
national hope in one who, like the Duchess, 'died young', into a
sorrow that could not be defined, that resisted comfort. He took
his elegiac fable from an old play, *The Cobbler's Prophecy* by
Robert Wilson, which means perhaps that it was still performed. Pleasure was sent down to earth by Jupiter, but, recalled
in thunder, left behind on her ascent her 'eye-seeded robe' (a

common dress in masques).[18] Next comes Sorrow – who bears a
likeness to Bosola:

> Sorrow that long had liv'd in banishment,
> Tugg'd at the oar in galleys, and had spent
> Both money and herself in court delays
> And sadly number'd many of her days
> By a prison Kalendar.
>
> [ll. 162–6

Finding the robe, her face painted by an old Court lady, Sorrow
is disguised and courted by great statesmen, to whom she gives

> intelligence that let them see
> Themselves and fortune in false perspectives.
>
> [ll. 184–5

And 'since this cursed mask, which to our cost / Lasts day and
night' any Pleasure is false; as Robert Wilson had said, ' 'Tis pain
that masks disguised in Pleasure's weed.'

Pain is the 'disguised' feeling that unites the unsympathetic
twins, Ferdinand and his sister; pain, disguised by Bosola under
many maskings, emerges at last as welcome:

> It may be pain, but no harm to me, to die
> In so good a quarrel.
>
> [V. v. 99–100

And Antonio had suggested at parting from the Duchess (III. v.
61–5) that they are like some delicate, fine instrument, being taken
to pieces to be mended; here he echoes the elegy:

> Like a dial broke in wheel or screw
> That's ta'en in pieces to be made go true.
> [*A Monumental Column*, ll. 241–2

This hope he cannot sustain; his dying words are

> Pleasure of life, what is 't? only the good hours
> Of an ague.
>
> [V. iv. 67–8

If an overarching fable were to be sought for the whole play,
it could be a masque of Good Fame. This was a favourite figure
in masques, and the central one in Ben Jonson's *Masque of
Queens*;[19] good fame is immortality. Antonio pledges care of her
good fame to his Duchess, Ferdinand tells her that reputation,
once lost, is lost for ever. The very curious fable that she tells

Bosola on her capture implies that good fame cannot be discerned till death; only a complete life may be measured, when those who seem to have few claims may be found to have most. Bosola himself had earlier promised the Duchess good fame through the poets who heard of her story; and this was indeed the way in which it was kept alive.

The Cardinal's good fame is destroyed at his death. At the very last, the faithful Delio brings on the eldest son of Antonio and the Duchess, hoping to instate him in 'his mother's right'. This was not the Duchy of Amalfi but her personal dowry; yet such an action would involve the recognition of a legitimate marriage, for a bastard could not inherit anything. It is Delio who closes the play on the simplest of major harmonies:

> Integrity of life is fame's best friend,
> Which nobly, beyond death shall crown the end.[20]

From the complexities that negate it, this proverbial flourish may be rescued if it is applied to the play itself. It is in fact Webster asking for his reward, his applause. 'Crown the end.' On this occasion he received it.

CHAPTER EIGHT

The Citizen at Drury Lane

The death of John Webster senior in the winter of 1614–15 could not but change the lives of his sons, who would inherit a substantial estate. In February 1615 Edward renewed the lease of the Cow Lane property; in June John took out his freedom by patrimony of the Merchant Taylors. This required sufficient wealth to sustain his Freedom of the City; he would vote in Common Council and enjoy the coveted privileges of trading, for which he now presumably possessed the capital. Henceforth his work contains a steady stream of references to overseas trading, the ways of seamen, letters of marque. Perhaps he became something of a merchant venturer. His later writings belong more to theatrical history than to dramatic literature, but they carry their own significance in the rapidly changing situation of the last decade of James's reign, 1615–25. Even closer attention to the special needs of the players suggests that Webster wrote out of regard for his friends; tragic issues are replaced by those 'that make Cities and Societies live', culminating in his City pageant of 1624.

Monuments of Honour, performed 'at the sole munificent charge and expense of the right worthy and worshipful fraternity of the eminent Merchant Taylors', welcomed the installation of Sir John Gore as Lord Mayor on Simon and Jude's Day, and must have cost at least ten times all the sum of Webster's previous productions. He had the oversight of it, and would himself appear in the procession with the rest of his company. Twenty years before he had written verses of praise for Stephen Harrison's *Arches of Triumph*, celebrating James's coronation entry. He loved City pageantry. Yet fate was to turn this civic triumph into a fitting end for the ironic poet. Every prophecy of prosperity, every confident good wish was soon to be blasted by yet another outbreak of plague, the worst that had struck the City since 1603. The Lord Mayor's own home was infected and for a time his deputy took over. Once more theatres closed, law courts were transferred, grass grew in the streets. Among the forty thousand who perished of plague alone were Thomas Lodge, John Florio, John Fletcher and William Rowley, Webster's collaborator. In March the King died, and next year King Charles forbade any triumphal entry through the City, such as his father had enjoyed. Webster's pageant marked the end of an era.

The King's private bounty maintained his own players, but virtually all the other companies were dissolved. A new group, Queen Henrietta's Men, assembled at the Cockpit, or Phoenix, in Drury Lane, the scene of Webster's latest triumphs.

However, after his father's death his first incursions into the theatre world had been indirect – and anonymous. In 1615, he contributed thirty-two Characters to the sixth edition of the late Sir Thomas Overbury's collection: *Characters, drawn to the Life of Several Persons in Several Qualities*. This brought him into the orbit of the Overbury case.

Overbury had been a member of the Middle Temple, where his father, Sir Nicholas, was still a bencher. It was natural that all lawyers, but especially those of the Middle Temple, should be concerned with the most startling criminal trial of the age, and although the Earl and Countess of Somerset had not in 1615 yet been charged with the murder of Sir Thomas, the arrest of minor figures was pointing in their direction. Sir Thomas Overbury's 'Character of a Wife', which opened the volume, was supposed to be the cause of the Countess's fatal enmity towards him, since he had written it for his friend, the Earl, to dissuade him from marrying her. No wonder the book sold like hot cakes.[1] Webster appears to have overseen the printing of the sixth edition.

Friendship with Overbury (then an intimate of Robert Carr, the future Earl) may explain the dedication by Webster of his elegy on Prince Henry to Carr – who seems otherwise a somewhat unlikely recipient of it. In any case, now he was editing the *Characters* of the dead Templarian, Webster, in addition to such contributions as 'A Virtuous Widow' and 'An Ordinary Widow', slipped in a riposte to the extremely derogatory 'Character of a Common Player' that had recently come from Lincoln's Inn. He had involved himself in one of those legal slanging-matches familiar from other days.

Early in 1615 John Stephens, of Lincoln's Inn – a minor play-wright – had issued, through Webster's own printer friend, Nicholas Okes, *Satyrical Essays, Characters and Others*, to which a certain 'J. Cocke' (the name was a pseudonym) had supplied 'The Character of a Common Player'. It opens, 'A common Player is a slow Payer, seldom a Purchaser, never a Puritan. The Statute hath done wisely to acknowledge him a Rogue.' This might represent satire, of the lowest level of strolling players if Cocke did not continue, 'However he pretend to have a Royal Master or Mistress, his wages and dependence prove him to be a servant of the people. When he doth hold conference upon the stage, and should look directly into his fellows face, he turns about his voice into the assembly for applause sake, like a Trumpeter in the fields who shifts places to get an echo.' Webster sprang to the combat, ending his own 'Character of an Excellent Actor', which answers Cocke point by point, by an abusive attack on 'the imitating Characterist'. His 'Excellent Actor' – note the new honorific title – who appears to be a compound of Burbage and Perkins, 'by a full and significant action of body ... charms our attention; sit in a full theatre, and you will think you see so many lines drawn from the circumference of so many ears, whiles the Actor is the Center.' As Webster had already remarked in his eulogy prefixed to *The White Devil*, he now reaffirmed that 'he doth not make nature monstrous, she is often seen in the same scene with him, but neither on stilts nor crutches ... by his action he fortifies moral precepts with example; for what we see him personate, we think truly done before us.' The actor is even set above the poet, for he 'adds grace to the poet's labours; for what in the poet is but ditty, in him is both ditty and music'. His moderation, fine charac-terization and variety of parts are united in an enchanting pre-sence, so that 'when he dies, we cannot be persuaded any other can do his parts like him'. So the Characterist was 'extreme idle in calling them rogues ... rogues cannot be employed as main ornaments to his Majesties Revels'. Webster ends with a few de-rogatory references to his opponent's 'itch of bestriding the Press or getting up on this wooden Pacolet [a wooden war-horse] which hath defiled more innocent paper than ever did Laxative Physick'.

The furious Characterist issued a second edition of his own work, in turn attacking the unknown 'rayler' whose 'hackney similitudes' are to be found strewn throughout his Overbury volume. He makes the lame defence that he had not spoken of *eminent* actors, correcting his most outrageous statement to 'rogues *errant*', and attributing the mistake to Nicholas Okes! A year later another member of Lincoln's Inn continued this battle with a verse 'Character' of Webster himself, which identifies him as a carping critic. A 'masque' of odd madmen at Blackfriars which may glance at the masque in *The Duchess of Malfi*, includes:

> crabbed Websterio,
> The playwright-cartwright (whether-either) Ho!
> No further. Look as you'd be look'd into:
> Sit as you would be read.

To term the Websters 'cartwrights' was almost as abusive as terming Burbage a rogue. However, with the cry of Whoa! the new writer, Henry Fitzjeffrey, describes Webster's painful method of composition (the description is on the familiar model that many years before had been applied to Ben Jonson),[2] and, for a climax, he alleges his interference as a meddlesome corrector of other easier, more gracefully negligent writers:

> Lord, who would know him?
> Was ever man so mangled with a poem?
> See how he draws his mouth awry of late,
> How he scrubs, wrings his wrists, scratches his pate.
> A midwife, help! by his brain's coitus
> Some centaur strange, some huge Bucephalus,
> Or Pallas sure engender'd in his brain,
> Strike, Vulcan, with thy hammer once again.
> This is the critic, that of all the rest
> I'd not have view me, yet I fear him least.
> Here's not a word cursively I have writ,
> But he'll industriously examine it,
> And some twelve months hence, or thereabout,
> Set in a shameful sheet my errors out.
> But what care I? it will be so obscure
> That none shall understand him, I am sure.[3]

Webster took the cue. He cut the reference to the obscure 'Characterist' out of the next edition of the increasingly popular Overbury volume. But every one of his future plays contained satire of lawyers, some of it extremely pointed. However, he was now engaged in a different matter, in which Lincoln's Inn was again in opposition to his friends, the players. The campaign of Stephens and Fitzjeffrey may be explained as part of an attempt by that Inn to block the building of a new theatre in Drury Lane, the Cockpit, or Phoenix (hence, perhaps, the pseudonym J. Cocke).

Situated between Drury Lane and what is now Great Wild Street, the Cockpit, a small brick and tiled building, was the first theatre to appear on this historic site. It was to prove the chief rival to Blackfriars, and the centre for Caroline tragedy. Middleton and Rowley's *The Changeling* was played here in 1621; most of Ford was staged here; the building survived to Restoration times, and is therefore the direct ancestor of modern stages. We know more about this 'private' theatre than about any other of the time, for the plan of its interior has been convincingly identified among the sketches of Inigo Jones.[4] Thanks to John Orrell, we can say that no less a person than the King's Surveyor designed the conversion of the original Cockpit, built in 1609 by a Grocer, John Best. The lessee was Christopher Beeston, leader of Queen Anne's Men, the troupe from the Red Bull, in Clerkenwell, who had put on *The White Devil*. Sometimes the royal cockpit at Whitehall had been temporarily converted for theatricals (it was to be permanently converted by Jones in later years). Beeston first saw the possibility for a permanent conversion in Drury Lane and, by securing the interest of Inigo Jones,[5] he protected his scheme against building restrictions. For the King's Surveyor was responsible for enforcing these same restrictions; and so, although in September 1616 the Benchers of Lincoln's Inn protested against 'Converting the Cockpit in the fields into a playhouse', the Justices for Middlesex turned a blind eye to what Beeston and Jones, with the aid of John Shepherd, of Lillypot Lane, Bricklayer, were doing.

Very skilfully, Jones took the circular building (not more than forty feet in diameter), with its central pit and steeply raked galleries, and, retaining one half-circle for an auditorium pit, extended the other half into a square, providing a thrust stage, with galleries on each side, an upper stage and back-stage area. The two halves were not constructed on the same module, but the whole gave a variant on the Vitruvian design Jones had met in Italy, taking no more space than the original building, a condition for planning permission. Intended for the gentry, the Cockpit would demand a different style of acting and consequently a different style of play from the old square inn-yard of the Red Bull, where the Queen's Men had played since it was built by Aaron Holland and one of their own number in 1605. No noisy spectaculars, no crowd scenes could be staged; but fine shades of acting, elegant duelling, music and quick variety of styles came in.

Beeston moved from Clerkenwell, where most of the Queen's Men lived, to a small house on the same piece of ground, thus maintaining the fiction that the whole thing was 'private'. In spite of the efforts of Lincoln's Inn to stop it, the Cockpit opened on 25 February 1617.

In a week's time, in their traditional Shrove Tuesday rampage, a mob of apprentices broke in, destroyed the costumes and play-books and damaged the fabric of the building. The players defended themselves vigorously, and one apprentice (or, in another account, three) was killed by gunshot. The rest were committed to Newgate; shortly after, fifty persons were charged with damaging the house of Christopher Beeston, and were suitably punished. Repairs were speedily put in hand and in June 1617 the playhouse, appropriately known as the Phoenix, reopened for the season. The Queen's Men, including Richard Perkins, moved in from the Red Bull, leaving that place to Prince Charles's Men from the Rose – part of old Henslowe's theatrical empire. They had a particular reason for getting out of Clerkenwell. Webster was to write them a comedy entitled *The Devil's Law Case, or when Women go to Law the Devil is full of Business*. To this, Richard Perkins and the rest of Queen Anne's Men might have returned a fervent 'Amen, brother!' For they were suffering at the hands of the widow of their former leader, Susan Greene, now Susan Baskerville, who claimed not only her husband's share but some new and old debts which she insisted they owed to her.[6] As her reckoning rested on a proportion of the takings, they may well have hoped, by shifting their ground, to escape from the three shillings and eightpence she claimed each day. Members of a theatre company were expected (like other fraternities) to settle differences by friendly arbitration, but Susan Baskerville was seeking remedy by a Chancery suit – which is how the account of these troubles, that were eventually to bring down the company, chance to survive.

Webster's play, *The Devil's Law Case*, is dedicated to Sir Thomas Finch, whom Webster confesses he did not know; but he knew Sir Thomas had seen this play and also his earlier works, *The White Devil, The Guise* (now lost) and *The Duchess of Malfi*. Sir Thomas was the grandson of Queen Elizabeth's Vice-Chamberlain, Sir Thomas Heneage, and might have been expected to take an interest in plays. The reason for the dedication however was not his lineage but his address, for Sir Thomas lived in Drury Lane. He must have been one of those who supported the new playhouse, for it would undoubtedly have been here, and not at the Red Bull, that the Queen's Men gave it.

The Devil's Law Case has puzzled readers from Abraham Wright, who noted in 1650 that the plot was intricate but faulty, to the most thoughtful of recent editors, who observes, 'there is a mercurial, almost childish shifting of mood. It is ... most diffi-cult to see in the paradoxes some unifying pattern or point of view.'[7]

If the tragic-comedy is seen as a vehicle for bravura display of Perkins's talents in the leading rôle, in a new rival to Blackfriars, its intricacy becomes explicable and the absence of any unifying point of view a challenge to 'the Judicious' – to whom Webster commends it in the preface, adding, 'A great part of the grace of this (I confess) lay in the action.' This is the plea that Marston was accustomed to make, and perhaps Webster was harking back to the memory of that little private theatre at St Paul's of a dozen years before; in fact, he applied in fatal disjunction the farcical plot-structure of those times to the method of his later character-izations, especially for the two women, mother and daughter: the result is almost like a parody of *The Duchess of Malfi*. But the suc-cess of that play at Blackfriars made him an obvious choice for the new venture, and *The Devil's Law Case* is very stylish.

Romelio, a rich young Neapolitan merchant, blessed with what the Stock Exchange calls 'flair', is trading not by overseas ventures but with the hand of his eminently marriageable sister. He betroths her forcibly to the nobleman of his choice, regardless of her attachment to an attractive young wastrel, of equally noble lineage, whom he is fleecing. His other sinful exploits include attempted murder, fraud, slander, criminal enticement, fornica-tion and misappropriation – all committed however within the circle of those who should be his nearest and dearest. With the agility of Mr Punch, and the same contempt for the law (likewise for the ministrations of the Church), Romelio ought to end up in boiling oil, but all he is asked to do is to return some money to the man who had volunteered to fight as his second in judicial combat, and to marry a nun whom he has got with child. His élan and irreverence make him a sort of cross between Lord Byron and the Jew of Malta (one of Perkins's famous parts). His insolence however is not lordly; on the contrary, it is largely directed against the foolish spendthrift habits of the nobles.

The five acts rise to helter-skelter action in III and V, between which, in Act IV, comes the Law Case itself. Between the bouts of helter-skelter action are fixed tableaux, or emblems. In Act III, Scene iii, as Jolenta sits at a table set out with a death's head, a book and two candles, mourning for her two lovers, who have apparently killed each other in a duel, Romelio suggests that she should feign pregnancy in order to inherit the wealth of one, the other having already willed her his possessions. With one of the enigmatic riddles that seem to be the refuge of ladies in despair, she tells her brother she is already with child – afterwards explaining that, by this confession, she hoped to incite him to kill her. But his resourcefulness merely prompts the notion of her producing twins. The other baby would be his bastard by the nun. By ferocious lies, he persuades her, half mad with sorrow, to agree to his plot, and then she begins to enact the macabre details of a false pregnancy. Afterwards, when she tells one of the miraculously revived suitors that Romelio is the cause of her shame, he not unreasonably concludes this is a case of fraternal incest. Meanwhile, in revenge for his murderous plots, Romelio's mother brings a suit in court for his disinheritance on the grounds that he is a bastard. The man she designates as his father unluckily turns out to be the judge in the case, and also possessed of a cast-iron alibi. But Romelio's attempt to assassinate one of the supposedly mortally wounded duellists, miraculously effects a cure by lancing his wound.

The farcical effect of these ricochets makes it fitting for the play to echo Ben Jonson's play of 1616, *The Devil is an Ass*, in which a junior tempter is so outplayed by the wicked of the City that he has to be rescued from Newgate by Satan in person. The feeling of masquerade is sustained by such artificial devices as Romelio's disguising himself, for his murderous onslaught on the suitor, in the robe of a Jewish physician, which is afterwards donned simply as 'disguise', in a therapeutic way, by one of the real surgeons. The mother's device of calling herself to recollection by means of a portrait – the portrait of the man she decides to accuse of having seduced her thirty-nine years ago – provides another static emblematic scene, which belong particularly to the women. If this were just a farce about how young men treat their families in Naples, its intricacies would not involve a shift of mood, and, though dizzying, would not be puzzling.

But Romelio and his mother, Leonora, can make single speeches

which are quite incompatible with farce. Leonora enters, to
present Romelio (and his second in the judicial combat over the
charges for murder which he faces) with two coffins and two
shrouds. The sprightly Machiavellian, at this, suddenly breaks into
pure poetry of lament, that would not be out of place in *The Duchess
of Malfi*. His meditation is given before a devotional tableau.

> All the flowers of the spring
> Meet to perfume our burying.
> These have but their growing prime
> And man does flourish but his time,
> Survey our progress from our birth;
> We are set, we grow, we turn to earth.
> Courts, adieu: and all delights,
> All bewitching appetites,
> Sweetest breath and clearest eye
> Like perfumes, go out and die;
> And consequently this is done,
> As shadows wait upon the sun.
> Vain the ambition of Kings
> Who seek by trophies and dead things
> To leave a living name behind
> And weave but nets to catch the wind.
>   [V. iv. 114–31

In a sudden return to artifice, the mercurial young man next locks
his mother and her attendant priest into his cell: 'Wast thou not
weary of her preaching? . . . I am rid of her howling at parting.'
After this, any suggestion of overruling Providence, when he finally sends for the priest, must provoke the reflection that he is
merely taking out an insurance policy for the next world. Of
religious feeling – as distinct from ecclesiastical emblems – there is
no trace.

Leonora's law case (apart from the suggestion that she is slightly
possessed by a not very efficient devil) springs from her hidden love
for one of her daughter's suitors; she gets him in the end. Here
again, her tragic soliloquy seems incompatible with the tenor of
the tale. She is a respectable widow of presumably sixty:

> There is no plague i' th' world can be compared
> To impossible desire, for they are plagued
> In the desire itself; never, oh never
> Shall I behold him living, in whose life
> I liv'd far sweetlier than in mine own. . . .
> For as we love our youngest children best
> So the last fruit of our affection,
> Wherever we bestow it, is most strong,

Most violent, most unresistable,
Since 'tis indeed our latest Harvest-home,
Last merriment 'fore winter.

[III. iii. 242–57

After this, her introduction to her plot, designed to revenge the supposed death of the favoured young man in the duel – 'Here begins/My part i' the play' (III. iii. 358–9) – marks the transition to a fine farcical trial scene, the best drama in the play. The finale (where one of Jolenta's suitors, disguised for some reason as Prince Hamlet, is acting as second in a duel to avenge his own supposed murder) culminates with a tableau and a moral speech from Jolenta, 'her face coloured like a Moor', standing beside the wanton nun:

Like or dislike me, choose you whether;
The down upon the raven's feather
Is as gentle and as sleek
As the mole on Venus' cheek.

[V. vi. 34–7

The preposterous law case would have its own interest for the law students; it is conducted by an impeccable judge with great decorum, but some of the pleaders fall short of this: ''Uds foot, we are spoiled;/Why my client's proved an honest woman' (IV. ii. 521–2). The riddles, equivocations and disguises seem to be Webster's means of engaging the audience, as well as of giving Perkins the chance to display his virtuosity. The play would need to be acted at top speed, and only the most judicious and practised members of the audience would be able to follow its intrigue; in the manner of Restoration comedy, its speed might amuse whilst it bemused the rest. Romelio ends as brother-in-law to one of Jolenta's revived suitors, and step-son to the other, and all of them are to pay for galleys to repel the Turks.

In November 1617 the players at the Red Bull put on *A Fair Quarrel*, by Middleton and Rowley, which also combines a mother who slanders her son with bastardy and a duel of honour. This 'Red Bull version' of these themes is heavily moral and marks the difference between the two houses, but also the close connections between their two troupes.[8] After Queen Anne's death, Beeston suddenly joined Prince Charles's Men, brought them to the Phoenix from the Red Bull and ejected Perkins and his friends. There was a big quarrel, Susan Baskerville revived her claims, Perkins attacked Beeston; but eventually, after desperate efforts to hold the remnants of the old Queen's Men together (they finally gave up in the autumn of 1622), Perkins gravitated to the King's Men at Blackfriars. Webster may have retained friends in both groups and tried to help their sinking fortunes; he collaborated with Rowley, Ford and Dekker to write a lost and scandalous play, entitled *Keep the Widow Waking*, for the Red Bull, and also collaborated with Rowley to write *A Cure for a Cuckold*, presumably for the Red Bull also.[9]

In 1623 Webster published *The Duchess of Malfi* and *The Devil's Law Case*. His only later publication was the City pageant. *Keep the Widow Waking* described a local scandal, concerning a friend of Webster's father. After being kept dead drunk for days on end, a rich old woman was married to a young fortune-hunter. Her outraged daughter and son-in-law entered a petition in the Star Chamber; perhaps the play was written to enforce the need for redress. It was certainly put on at the local theatre, with a horrid murder in Whitechapel for added interest.[10]

A Cure for a Cuckold gave the star part to William Rowley, leader of Prince Charles's Men, who collaborated with a variety of writers and himself took comic leads. He was a fat man,[11] and in this play Compass, the sailor, suggests by his name a certain rotundity. He quotes an epithet from the 'roaring' part of *A Fair Quarrel* (Chough's) with the remark, 'I learnt that name in a play' (IV. i. 123–4).

This 'pleasant comedy' wrests the law to upset some traditional assumptions. Determined to claim as his own the child born to his wife during his four years' absence at sea (against the claim of the childless rich merchant who begot it), Compass also devises a ritual cure for the imputation of cuckoldry. The jest of instant divorce and remarriage allows a farcical scene of wooing between Compass and the new 'widow', his former wife, played deadpan by both – Compass loves his wife; since he had been given up as dead, and she reduced to desperate need, the fact that he also obtains the custody of a handsome settlement made on Mrs Compass's baby may be held a just reward.

The 'heroic' plot echoes in an intensified form the absurdities of *The Devil's Law Case*. Bonville and Amabel the paragons, Lessingham (that is, 'leasing 'em', or 'cheating 'em') and Clare, whose acts are so obscure as to be indecipherable, are four heroic puppets twitched by love, jealousy, and the gentleman's code of honour. The enigmas are created by Clare, who, in her blighted affection for Bonville, contrives to tell Lessingham, her unwanted lover, to discover and then 'kill the friend that loves him dearest'. She is echoing Ferdinand (*The Duchess of Malfi*, IV. ii. 273–4). Bonville the Bridegroom, deserting his bride Amabel to fight as second in a duel, finds he is in fact the opponent; he averts the combat by the timely discovery that the treachery has 'killed' his friendship. Clare is credible only on the basis of temporary madness; Lessingham's jealousy, while acting as foil to the generosity of Compass, leads him to slander the long-suffering Bonville. Bonville is saved by Rochfield (a young gentleman who had turned highwayman, but who had been reformed and rescued by Amabel) with the simple citation of Bonville's character and record, as a refutation of the charge. With Compass, Rochfield shares a quality almost fatal to comedy – good sense. The same good sense had refuted slander in the citizen comedy *Northward Ho!* (see page 112).

The tribunal for settling the custody of Mrs Compass's baby takes place not before the Lord Mayor in Guildhall but in the Three Tuns tavern, Blackwall, and would undoubtedly have fallen to Webster as the legal expert on the team. The merchant pleads that any man acknowledging a bastard is bound to support it; therefore, if he wishes, he may enjoy it as his own. Compass deflects the lawyer's argument briskly:

My wife's the mother and so much for the civil law, Now I come again, and, y' are gone at the common law; suppose this is my ground, I keep a sow upon it, as it might be my wife, you keep a boar, as it might be my adversary here; your boar comes foaming into my ground, jumbles with my sow and wallows in her mire, my sow cries *week*, as if she had pigs in her belly – who shall keep these pigs? he the boar or she the sow?

[IV. i. 176–81

Counsel and magistrate being instantly convinced, at the grand finale the merchant acts as 'the father to give away the bride', whilst Compass boasts, 'And I am his son, sir, and all the sons he has; and this is his grandchild and my elder brother – you'll think this strange now' (V. i. 480–82). An account of the English sea fight off Margate, where Rochfield distinguished himself, sounds topical; the likeliest date is 1624, when Webster was preparing to celebrate the Mayoralty of Sir John Gore, for plays on London cuckolds were regularly part of the sports.[12]

The date of Webster's last extant tragedy, *Appius and Virginia*, is more difficult to establish; by 1634 it was in the hands of

Christopher Beeston, now directing at the Phoenix the King and
Queen's Young Company, or Beeston's Boys (some of them were
not juvenile, but the title enabled Beeston to acquire strong powers
as their 'Governor'). *Appius and Virginia* makes sense as a play
designed for boys; Gabriele Baldini observed that it feels as if
Delacroix had taken to painting in the style of Ingres. The centre
is naturally the trial scene, where the wicked judge, Appius,
claims, through his creature, Clodius, the possession of Virginia
as his bond-slave; he alleges her to be the child of one of Clodius'
dead slaves, substituted as the daughter of the noble general Virginius by her own (dead) mother.[13] Virginius is begged by his
daughter to kill her rather than surrender her to lust; and, after
a melting farewell, which, in no derogatory sense, is rhetorical,
and emotionally simple, he does so:

> Thus I surrender her into the court (*kills her*)
> Of all the gods. And see, proud Appius, see,
> Although not justly, I have made her free.
>
> [IV. i. 343–5

Appius' cunning in the trial scene is parodied by the servile Orator,
who later prepares to greet Virginius, now advancing on Rome
at the head of the army for a military take-over. Condemned to
die by his own hand, Appius ends bravely, whereas Clodius begs
for mercy but is hailed off to the hangman. The final moral imposes
a severe standard of public rectitude:

> Better had Appius been an upright judge
> And yet an evil man, than honest man
> And yet a dissolute judge; for all disgrace
> Lights less upon the person than the place.
>
> [V. i. 157–60

The only possibility of dating lies in the description of the
mutiny by starving Roman troops commanded by Virginius and
their noble response to his appeals. (This is not part of the original
story.) It fits the summer and autumn of 1622, when Chapman
published his poem 'Pro Vere, Autumnae Lachrymae', urging the
succour of Sir Horace Vere, the 'pious and incomparable', who
was 'besieged and distressed in Mannheim'. Two years earlier
Vere, most famous and best loved commander of the day, had set
out for the Netherlands, with a body of two thousand volunteers,
to defend the cause of the Princess Elizabeth and her husband,
the Elector Palatine; the City of London on this occasion had

raised for the Protestant cause the sum of £10,000.[14] The Duke of Buckingham, who had wanted the command for his own nominee, opposed and thwarted the expedition, and after a long, heroic defence, in September 1622 Vere surrendered to the Spanish and marched out of Mannheim with the honours of war. Chapman had himself campaigned in the Low Countries; and Cyril Tourneur, who shared with Webster in publishing elegies for Prince Henry, had been there since 1613 in the service of the Veres as Lieutenant Governor of Brill. He knew the supply problems professionally.

So, under this innocently didactic play for juniors there might lurk some sharp criticism of government. Any drama involving an army *coup d'état* is potentially subversive; boys were the usual vehicle for such dangerous suggestions.[15] It has been suggested above (page 164) that Webster had used fables for this purpose earlier.

A further slight pointer to the year 1622 is that in July of that year, as the Red Bull Company was fighting for survival, Perkins and some of his fellow-actors were licensed to set up a company of boy players, under the old dignified title of Children of the Revels. Perhaps he had hoped a company of children might be attractive to Beeston, who had just switched companies at the Phoenix, for of course children could not have acted out of doors at the Red Bull; few boys had the vocal powers, their troupes played indoors. The move would again defeat Susan Baskerville's claims. If Webster were still friendly enough with Perkins to write a play for him, this might explain how it lay in the hands of the voracious Beeston, whose Boys put it on in 1639, by which date there was plenty to warrant a subversive study of a change of government in 'Rome'. Alternatively, Merchant Taylors' School would prepare a play or two when the Lord Mayor was of their company.

On the surface, *Appius and Virginia* is a clear and simple play about honest men and villains. It calls for no elaborate staging and makes no demands. Everything is cut out of the whole cloth, down to the brave death of Appius and the ignoble one of Clodius; Rome gets its new government and three cheers for everybody. Although the military are so prominent, it is devoid of fights; with all its simplicity of ethics (some would give Heywood a share in it), it would have been neither heavy enough nor noisy enough for the Red Bull. Yet its careful declamation, in a natural, simple style, would have been very suitable for boys to present before a Lord Mayor, and the one substantial part, Virginius, could have been taken by their Governor.

Webster's show of 1624, *Monuments of Honour*, followed the traditional lines of welcome for the Lord Mayor. In 1612 Dekker had written *Troia Nova Triumphans* for the last Merchant Taylor to hold the office – and John Webster the elder had sued him next year for £40, the cost of the pageant waggons. Webster took a look at this earlier show, and he kept to the traditional form – with one highly significant variation.

Webster modestly offered in his preface 'to express only with rough lines and faint shadow (as the Painter's phrase is)' the greatest care and alacrity of his company. But on the title-page he put the proud motto that he had never directly applied to his own work before, though he had several times quoted it: 'Non norunt haec monumenta mori' ('These monuments do not know how to die').

He began with two water pageants, which included, besides Oceanus and Thetis, 'seven of our most eminent navigators' encircling a fair globe. These pageants were amphibious and greeted the Lord Mayor when he landed at Paul's Chain on his return from taking the oath at Westminster. Here there was the Temple of Honour; next, a chariot with the eight English kings who had been free of the Merchant Taylors, with some single figures following on horseback;[16] next, the sea triumphs, and 'the ship called the Holy Lamb [the device of the Merchant Taylors] which brings hanging in her shrouds the Golden Fleece', its supporters the Lyon and the Camel being proper to the arms of the Company. Then followed the Monument of Charity and Learning, featuring Sir Thomas White (did the boys of Merchant Taylors' School perform here?), and lastly the Monument of Gratitude. This presented on a rock of jewels Henry, Prince of Wales, dead twelve years since. He was supported by Magistracy (tending a beehive), Liberality, with a dromedary ('showing his speed and alacrity in gratifying his followers'), Navigation, Unanimity ('showing he loved Nobility and Communalty with an entire heart'), Industry, Chastity, Justice, Obedience, Peace, Fortitude.

This 'Character of a perfect Ruler' expressed things that could not openly be said about the present government. At night the Monument was lit up from within, especially the Prince of Wales's feathers. Henry was the centre-piece of the whole show. It is

Webster's only direct political statement, and must have been made with his company's approval. Henry represented a decency in the monarchy which Webster's commentary spells out, and which had vanished in the final squalid stages of James's ignoble reign. In his dotage, James was entirely subservient to Buckingham and the new Prince of Wales; Charles's alienation was perhaps by now as familiar as James's deviousness.

After a speech by Troynovant (that is, London), comes one by Sir Philip Sidney, who was seated in the Temple of Honour with four other 'famous scholars and poets' – Chaucer, Gower, Lydgate and Sir Thomas More. These being celebrators of Honour, and the preservers both of the names of men and memories of cities to posterity, Troynovant introduces Philip Sidney:

> These beyond death a fame to monarchs give,
> And these make Cities and Societies live.
>
> [ll. 130–31

The last farewell to the Lord Mayor at the door of his lodging ends:

> Good rest, my Lord! Integrity that keeps
> The safest watch and breeds the soundest sleeps
> Make the last day of this your holding seat
> Joyful as this, or rather, more complete.
>
> [ll. 370–4

A year later, counting up the three thousand dead of St Sepulchre's parish, Webster might have heard that players were resuming at the Phoenix (they were told to close down again). The theatre he needed was there; his *White Devil* was to be revived at the Phoenix with acclaim. In a recent book, *Puritanism and Theatre*, Margot Heinemann points out that 1624 saw the climax of theatrical protest against the government's Spanish policy. The King's Men staged Middleton's *A Game at Chess* at the Globe, whilst at the Fortune Thomas Drue's *The Duchess of Suffolk* pleaded the Protestant cause of Princess Elizabeth and her husband in a story taken from Foxe's *Acts and Monuments*. As it strikingly resembles the story of the Duchess of Malfi, Webster could have acquired a new reputation as a Protestant champion if his ten-year-old play was revived with an anti-Spanish slant; whilst the age of the play would protect the players from the kind of government action that followed *A Game at Chess*. The author went into hiding, and this gave Webster the chance to compose his City pageant, usually Middleton's assignment.

The new function of Webster's tragedy for Puritans was reflected when the Rev Thomas Adams reciprocated Webster's quotation of his sermons, and took three passages from *The Duchess of Malfi*, to illuminate Original Sin, in his *Meditation on the Creed*. A fossil rhyme in Adams's prose, and the date of publication imply that Adams is the debtor, and is using Webster's published text for edification. The opponent of the theatre – who had also preached the Guildhall sermon before the election of Sir John Gore – is adopting Webster's own method.

Security is the very suburbs of hell, there is nothing but a dead wall between.... Glories like glowworms afar off shine bright; come near, they have neither heat nor light. All that the world's glory leaves behind it is but like a man that falls in snow, and there makes his print; when the sun shines forth, it melts both form and matter (*Works*, 1630, p. 1180)

[Compare *The Duchess of Malfi*, V.ii. 337–8, IV.ii, 164–5, V.v. 113–17]

Twenty years earlier, in contrasting the stone monuments of Roman wars with Harrison's ephemeral coronation carpentry, Webster had averred that print could provide for evanescent joys monuments as lasting as were humanity's enduring memory for griefs. His own share in the world's glory was entrusted to Nicholas Okes to immortalize, before the griefs of the plague year obliterated it. This contrast between immediate impression and the immortality of the printed word was learnt at school (see p. 23 above).

Webster's three stages of dramatic writing correspond to the three years when a Merchant Taylor held the office of Lord Mayor – his citizen comedies of 1605 to the Mayorality of Sir Leonard Halliday, *The White Devil* in 1612 to that of Sir John Swinnerton, and *Monuments of Honour* to that of Sir John Gore. Each could be an 'offering' from Webster.

Once again the plague had drawn a line across dramatic development. Cavalier drama did not favour the questioning that informs Webster's masterpieces, for on certain issues which deeply divided men, commitment was becoming inevitable. Webster ended with one, perhaps two political gestures. England passed from the age of Shakespeare to the age of Milton. From a casual remark of his friend Thomas Heywood, it is thought Webster was dead by 1634; he is bracketed with Fletcher, who had died in the plague of 1625. Webster's mortal exit is unmarked, but his last word remains – *Non norunt haec monumenta mori.*

A Final Perspective

It is probably more than a coincidence that Webster's preface to *The White Devil* and his friend Heywood's *Apology for Actors* appeared together in the same year. Webster models his preface on that of Jonson's *Sejanus*, decorated with sentences from Latin authors; Heywood elevates his profession with name-dropping, talking of Roscius and Pompey's theatre, all of which posterity would gladly exchange for his lost treatise on contemporary theatres, and some words on Perkins and the Red Bull.

However, the tone adopted by Webster toward his ungrateful audience differs from the gentlemanly scorn practised by Marston and Ford in their own prefaces. Webster hankers for an accepted public form: the classical, public form, with Nuntius and Messenger; but he knows that this form is not current, that it does not constitute a bond with any audience of his day. So he turns to a personal form, a form which springs out of the work itself – organic form, as it is termed nowadays. The vestigial use made of the old revenge patterns does not constitute a convention; in his plays revenge is not the resort of the thwarted against tyranny – as it had been in the days of *The Spanish Tragedy* – but the tyrannical assertion of will outside the boundaries of law. It is 'revenge' as Lope de Vega would have used the term – Spanish revenge for honour; and Spanish themes increasingly displace Italian ones on the Jacobean stage.

This interior, self-validating structure may well have evolved because of Webster's difficult position between the gentry and the citizens. Webster constantly recalls, delicately and indirectly, the struggle of such a divided self. For example, the motto from Horace on the title-page of *The Duchess of Malfi* recalls the kind of 'distinction' favoured by Hoskyns: 'if you know wiser precepts than mine, be kind and tell them to me; if not, practise mine with me'.[1] It is set out in something like a note-taker's abbreviation, and may date from Webster's days at the Middle Temple; at first sight it looks illiterate.

A more poignant memory of the Inns of Court is the pastoral note in the songs of lament: 'All the flowers of the spring / Meet to perfume our burying' or 'Call for the robin redbreast and the wren' are built in the mode of John Davies's *Astraea*, where the celebration of youth is shot through with suggestions of mortality:

> Earth now is green and heaven is blue
> Lively spring which makes all new,
> Jolly spring doth enter,
> Sweet young sunbeams do subdue
>   Angry, aged winter.
>   [*Astraea*, Hymn III

For Davies, the convention of surface beauty had to be sustained; for Webster, the spring beauty and the humble ministration of the birds are, more paradoxically, part of burial rites. The union of two incompatibles is constituted the basis of the unhappy Davies's pastoral songs, as of Webster's rites of mourning.

The unfolding of tragedy within a comic perspective, as in the masque of the madmen, brings together so many incompatibles that almost any other playwright would have had to embody the grotesque comedy in a sub-plot. This was Middleton's and Rowley's method, ten years later, when they came to write *The Changeling*, where the sub-plot of madmen is essential to the tragic sequence, but is kept separate from it. The firm structure, the clear ironies of this form are more controlled and explicit, less reverberative, than Webster's more disjunctive, more 'formless' construction. Middleton's and Rowley's composite plot replaces alternating rôles within each separate, composite character in Webster.

At the Inns of Court the Christmas Prince ruled only from supper till breakfast time; at other hours the normal discipline of the elders persisted.[2] This gives point to the exchange between the Duchess of Malfi and Antonio, when he declares that he must claim a night's lodging. 'Must? you are a Lord of Misrule,' she exclaims, to which his rejoinder is, 'Indeed my rule is only in the night.' Servant in public, 'my lord' in private, his divided selves are playfully divulged; but elsewhere the alternation is tragic, and so it may have been with Webster himself.

Long before, Mulcaster had mocked the parents who stinted

that 'Jack may be a gentleman' (see page 25). Webster himself mocked the City's social climbers, and to his friend Heywood, the actor, he 'was but Jack' at all times.[3] He defended the 'players' against the gentlemen of the Inns, giving them the more honorific title of 'actor' – and they jeered at the 'playwright-cartwright'. An 'actor' was master of an art; later Jonson was to complain that his comedy of *The New Inn* was 'never acted, but most negligently played, by some, the King's servants'.

Webster's individual form was designed for such 'actors', designed to give individuality and variety in the rôle, and to evoke variety of response from the audience.[4]

His own works have continued to provoke those extremes of enthusiasm or rejection that mark the subjective response. It has been mentioned that different theological interpretations of the one play are still forthcoming, and in 1971 two completely contradictory views of Webster, pro and con, were put forward by Ralph Berry and Christopher Ricks.[5]

If the measure of live interest is disagreement, Webster is very much alive.

 Notes

Introduction

1 See page 181. From *Monuments of Honour*. Ben Jonson had similarly placed the poets round the House of Fame in his *Masque of Queens* (2 Feb. 1609).

2 G.E. Bentley, *The Profession of Dramatist in Shakespeare's Time*, Princeton, 1971, pp. 33–4.

3 Information from Professor Reavley Gair, who is writing the history of this theatre.

4 Dekker, dedication of *If it be not Good, the Devil is in It* (1612). See J. R. Brown, preface to *The White Devil*, p. xx.

5 See Jonson, *An Expostulation with Inigo Jones*, 1631:

... Mythology, there painted on slit deal,
Or to make boards to speak! there is a task!
Painting and carpentry are the soul of masque.

6 See, e.g., Ralph Berry, *The Art of John Webster*, Oxford, 1971; Cyrus Hoy, 'Jacobean Tragedy and the Mannerist Style', *Shakespeare Survey*, 26, 1973. Ford, a more likely subject for such comparisons, was considered by Michael Neill, *Neo Stoicism and Mannerism in the Drama of Ford* (Cambridge Ph.D. thesis, 1975).

7 See Roy Strong and Stephen Orgel, *Inigo Jones, The Theatre of the Stuart Court*, 2 vols, 1973. The exhibition of Inigo Jones's work for his fourth centenary was held in 1973. Roy Strong also organized an exhibition of Elizabethan and Jacobean portraits at the Tate Gallery.

8 See G.E. Bentley, *The Jacobean and Caroline Stage*, Oxford, 1953, III, pp. 218–19.

Chapter 1
The Websters of West Smithfield

1 Dekker, *The Wonderful Year*, *Plague Pamphlets*, ed. F.P. Wilson, Oxford, 1925, p. 32.

2 Others who share this view are Chrisoganus in *Histriomastix*, by John Marston, 'Through the streets in thundering coach I ride' (ed. Wood, III, p. 275), and the *City Madam* of Massinger.

3 In 1606 one Robert Baker, another Merchant Taylor, began to build beside the Windmill, and his house was named Pickadilly Hall (a pickadil being the hem of a garment), for, unlike John Webster, he was a real tailor.

4 These were presumably lawyers and minor courtiers who did not have lodgings at the Court or with a nobleman.

5 Information from Mary Edmond. Foster, *Politics of Stability*, shows Simon Peniall holding minor offices in the parish (table 56).

6 This was the Court of Pie Powder (*pied poudré*). All strangers and travellers were allowed free movement but all fell under summary jurisdiction.

7 Rich, the follower of Thomas Cromwell, paid £1004. 4s for the rights, including the Fair. St Bartholomew's remained a Liberty.

8 The Austin Friars became the Dutch Church for reformed use. Sir Thomas Wyatt was given the Crutched Friars and made the hall into a glasshouse. The Blackfriars was used for the Revels Office, as later was the Priory of St John at Clerkenwell.

9 The Merchant Taylors were a strongly Reformed group, as was shewn under Charles I; a proof of the proselytizing nature of their foundation is suggested by their second foundation at Great Crosby, in the midst of Catholic Lancashire, and close to the Catholic stronghold of the Blundells.

10 The only criticism of Mulcaster in 1562 was of the ushers 'being northern men born, they had not taught the children to speak distinctly or to pronounce their words as they ought' (Joan Simon, *Education and Society in Tudor England*, Cambridge, 1967, p. 363). He evidently favoured his own countrymen.

11 The Probation Books which exist from this year enable the names of scholars to be recorded.

12 *Liber Famelicus* of Sir James Whitlock, Camden Society, LXX, 18.

13 In *The Boke of the Governor* (I), Sir Thomas Elyot had allowed tennis 'only if seldom used' and condemned football 'for its beastly fury and extreme violence' S. E. Lehmberg, *Sir Thomas Elyot*, 1960, p. 64). He approved of dancing.

Chapter 2
The Middle Temple: a Literary Centre

1 According to Foster, in 1595 John Borlas, son and heir to Edmond 'citizen and mercer of London', was admitted to the Middle Temple, and in 1598 Edmond Doubleday, 'son and heir of Henry, of London, merchant'. John Donne, of Lincoln's Inn, was also a citizen's son.

2   Tim Yellowhammer, in Middleton's *A Chaste Maid in Cheapside*, is at Cambridge.

3   'To head' urges the dogs to attack at the most dangerous point; Harry Hunks and Sackerson were famous bears.

4   Davies's use of classical models was copied from a general fashion. His favourite authors were the same as Webster's. Sidney (the translation of du Mornay), Montaigne and *The French Academy* were the basis of *Nosce Teipsum*. Respectful gestures towards the classics were expected, but the main influence was modern.

5   Sir John Fortescue, *De Laudibus Legum Angliae*, trans. Amos, Cambridge, 1825, pp. 183–4.

6   See Axton for a full account.

7   See Frances A. Yates, *Astraea*, 1975, for an account of the cult of Queen Elizabeth I and some continental analogues.

8   See *The Poems of Sir John Davies*, ed. Krueger and Nemser, Introduction, p. lxiv.

9   See Frances A. Yates, *A Study of Love's Labour's Lost*, Cambridge, 1936, and also Chapter 4 below.

10 The Queen, charmed by his modesty as a student, personally invited him to Court. Sir Christopher Hatton had achieved notice similarly at the Inner Temple in 1561, when he was 'Master of the Game'.

11 See the 'First Paradox' of John Donne. Benjamin Rudyard's account of these revels is summarized by Finkelpearl; it is preserved in MS. BM Egerton 1830.

12 John Hoskyns had an enormous nose, almost of Cyrano's kind.

13 Wotton's *bon mot* that an ambassador was 'an honest man sent to lie abroad for the good of his country' infuriated the King, and ruined him. Hoskyns spoke against the Scots in Parliament on 7 June 1614 and was at once sent to the Tower. His letters are in *The Life, Letters and Writings of Sir John Hoskyns*, ed. Osborn (see p. 71).

14 John Hoskyns, *Directions for Speech and Style*, is edited by Hoyt H. Hudson, Princeton Studies in English, No. 1: New Jersey, 1935. It is also in Osborn's edition of his works.

15 Compare Webster, *The White Devil*, IV, ii. 243–5.

16 See the series of articles by Richard Levin, R.A. Foakes, and T.F. Wharton in *Essays in Criticism* (No. xxii, 1972; No. xxiv, 1974; No. xxv, 1975)

17 See Finkelpearl, (*see* p. 202) pp. 86–7. I am generally endebted to him here.

18 The jolting of the coach acts like a love-machine or vibrator, and spurts ejaculations from an artificial penis so violently, that it far surpasses natural intercourse.

19 *Cupid's Whirligig* and *The Fancies Chaste and Noble* both deal with eunuchs in a *louche* manner.

Chapter 3
The Lady of St Bartholomew's: a London Legend

1 The most familiar is the frontispiece to the *Poems* of Michael Drayton, 1619.

2 Lawrence Stone, *The Family, Sex and Marriage in England*, 1977, pp. 126–7. The last sentence refers to the work of Sir John Neale on the composition of the House of Commons.

3 The family, mercers in the early Tudor period, had risen to wealth through the law; especially the first Baron Rich, the Lord Chancellor who succeeded, and indicted, Sir Thomas More. Penelope's husband, the 3rd Baron, was the son of Catherine Knyvett, later Countess of Suffolk (see below, p. 63, p. 67).

4 See Stone, p. 115.

5 See Falls, *Mountjoy: Elizabethan General*, 1954, p. 64. Mrs Wiseman, born Huddleston, had a house at Northend, Great Waltham; Penelope was therefore probably at Wanstead, Blount's house, or Leighs, the country house of Lord Rich.

6 Gilly Meyrick was Essex's steward, and a prime mover in the conspiracy. Henry Cuffe was supposed to have acquired a strong influence over Essex. The dominating servant was to be a theme in Webster's *The White Devil* (see below, p. 128).

7 See below, p. 67, for the marriage of her daughter, the notorious Frances Howard, to Penelope's young nephew, 3rd Earl of Essex.

8 The final judgment, preserved at Somerset House, is cited by Ringler, *The Poems of Sir Philip Sidney*, p. 445.

9 Two MS. versions exist, one in the Bodleian (Birch MS. 4149), another with the Stow papers in the British Library. Laud tried to curry favour with the King by writing a refutation of Blount, whilst still remaining in his service!

10 See Frances A. Yates, *A Study of Love's Labour's Lost*, Cambridge, 1936, Appendix III, from CSP Dom. 1603–10, p. 183.

11 Falls, p. 234, from Robert Johnston, *Historia Rerum Britannicarum*.

12 *The Poems of Sir Philip Sidney*, p. 446. From HMC XII, report, Appendix i (Cowper), 1888, I. p. 63.

13 See *John Gerard*, trans. P. Caraman, 1951, pp. 34–6. If her attendants were anxious to gain a convert, they may have competed with each other in these last ministrations to a feverish patient. Moreover, Penelope had a fortune worth securing; Blount left her about £1,500 a year (Falls, p. 235).

14 See p. 34, p. 56. The playwright Arthur Wilson (see Heinemann, p. 224) testifies that Penelope's mother was a good friend to players, even to the end of her very long life. He was servant to the 3rd Earl of Essex.

Chapter 4
Antonio Perez, the Spanish Spy: a London Legend

1 Ungerer is the chief source of information in this chapter, and references to the letters cited from his edition are given in the text.

2 In order to draw Don John's confidences, Pérez wrote criticisms of the King, which were shewn to the King himself before dispatch.

3 The actual killer, a soldier named Insausti, was in turn to be assassinated in a military camp in Sicily.

4 Imprisonment in darkness – the severest form of 'close imprisonment' – was to be inflicted on John Hoskyns by King James I (see p. 38).

5 Lope de Vega's play, *The Star of Seville*, is based on their story.

6 Essex married the daughter of Francis Walsingham, head of Elizabeth's Intelligence service. Walsingham was now dead. The Cecils headed the peace party in the government, Essex the war party.

7 On the rumoured death of his wife, Pérez wrote a passionate epitaph, which even after the rumour proved false he kept in circulation.

8 This witticism of Pérez derives from Seneca (*De Clementia*, I. 24. 1.) and it was to be used by Webster (cf. *The White Devil*, I. ii. 209–11).

9 Robert Vernon, the younger brother of Elizabeth Vernon, Countess of Southampton, later took part in the Essex Revolt (see pp. 59 ff.).

10 These were left to his faithful cousin Gil de Mesa, and ultimately retrieved and destroyed by Philip IV.

Chapter 5
The Plays of London Life

1 This view, found in E.K. Chambers and most subsequent writers on the stage, is summarized in Andrew Gurr, *The Shakespearean Stage 1576–1642*, Cambridge, 1970, Chapter 2. For a reassessment, see Margot Heinemann, *Puritanism and Theatre*, Cambridge, 1980.

2 See Thomas Heywood's assertion in his *Apology for Actors* that he had a share in 200 plays; about twenty are extant.

3 For Mulcaster's Boys see above, pp. 21 ff. The second theatre at St Paul's has recently been studied by W.R. Gair; see his edition of *Antonio's Revenge*, Manchester, 1978, pp. 27 ff., and an article in *Elizabethan Theatre VI*, ed. G.R. Hibbard, Macmillan of Canada, 1978.

4 See Millar McLure, *The Paul's Cross Sermons*, 1958; for a more detailed account of the players' problems at this time, see my *The Rise of the Common Player* (*A History of Elizabethan Drama*, vol. 3).

5 Information from Mary Edmond.

6 Cf. *Malone Society Collections*, I, vol. 2, p. 172. This however was part of a campaign; the Recorder of London, who voiced this protest, had a son at the Middle Temple who was a boon companion of Richard Martin.

7 From the Induction to *The Malcontent* (1604). See p. 115. It was a taunt from Essex that 'Every fool must have a *favour*', i.e. a love token from the Queen, which caused Charles Blount to challenge him to a duel (see above, p. 55).

8 Robert Milles, 'Abraham's Suite to Sodom' in John Chandos, *In God's Name*, 1611, pp. 153–4. Milles came from Lincolnshire; this Bartholomew Tide sermon, preached at Paul's Cross, drew satiric comment, and in publishing it Milles complains of its being 'injuriously handled by prophane Philistines'.

9 The story is told in C. J. Sisson, *Lost Plays of Shakespeare's Age*, Cambridge, 1936. It is also commented on by Mary Edmond in 'In Search of John Webster' (*Times Literary Supplement*, 24 Dec. 1976).

10 This sermon is also reprinted by Chandos. Adams denounced the 'upholding' of theatres in sermons at Paul's Cross and St Gregory-under-Paul's. Compare Tourneur, *The Revenger's Tragedy*, I. iii. 50–52; II. i. 218–19. But cf. p. 182.

11 The lawyers had discussed such matters earlier (see p. 32). Thomas Cromwell, first Earl of Essex, patron of the first Baron Rich, was shewn as the grandson of a Putney blacksmith who rose to be a London merchant.

12 See *Henslowe's Diary*, ed. R. A. Foakes and P. Rickert, Cambridge, 1961, pp. 201–2, 218–19.

13 *Sir Thomas Wyatt* occupies only 47 pages in Bowers's edition of Dekker's plays, and contains 1475 lines.

14 *The Chronicle of Queen Jane*, ed. J. G. Nichols, 1850, Camden Society XLVIII, gives a contemporary account. The playwrights were relying on Foxe's *Acts and Monuments*, and John Stow's *Survey of London*, 1598, but much of the material has the feel of popular ballads.

15 Act I gives the plot, and the proclamation of Queen Jane; Act II, the betrayal of her father; Act III, the Spanish marriage (Wyatt decides to rebel, Jane's father is executed); Act IV, the rebellion; Act V, the trial and execution of Jane and Dudley. The question of bequeathing the Crown by Will was still a live issue, since Henry VIII's will was held to bar the Scottish claim. This was disputed by Plowden (see above, p. 32).

16 Compare his words (V. ii. 163–7) with Ferdinand's and Bosola's over the dead Duchess of Malfi (IV. ii. 353–4).

17 Prodigals are particularly numerous *c.* 1604, including young Flowerdale in *The London Prodigal*, Matheo in *The Honest Whore*, Frank in *The Wise Woman of Hogsdon*, and in 1605, Frank Quicksilver in *Eastward Ho!* (The first of these plays is anonymous, the second by Dekker, the third by Heywood.)

18 John Day, *The Isle of Gulls*. 'Sundry people' were committed to Bridewell as a result of this play, since it satirized the Scots. This line perhaps describes the Scottish climate.

19 Cf. 'Now 'tis full sea abed over the world. . . .' *The Revenger's Tragedy*, II. ii. 135 ff.; cf. also the discovery of the devil-figure by the old Earl and the encounter with a poisoned skull by the old Duke in *The Revenger's Tragedy*.

20 In 1604, *The Phoenix* (Middleton), *Measure for Measure*, *The Honest Whore* (Dekker), *Law Tricks* (Day), *The London Prodigal* (anon); in 1605, *The Fawn* (Marston); in 1606, *The Fleire* (Sharpham).

21 A parenthesis is a 'joiner' (*Northward Ho!*, V. i. 299); this indicates his trade as a pimp. *The Old Joiner of Aldgate* (a lost play) uses the same pun.

22 The whores in Dekker's *The Honest Whore* are shewn in Bridewell, though the action is supposed to be in Milan – as the bawd in Marston's *The Malcontent* is supposed to be in Genoa. The Italian scene heightens the tragic aspects of the main plot, but the low life is unmistakeably London's. See Hunter, pp. 103–32.

23 The Earl of Southampton was Treasurer of the Virginia Company, which was launched by a City knight, Sir Thomas Smith.

24 The merchant and his chaste wife; the City whore; the young rake; the trio of suitors; Welsh humour replacing Dutch, and the old poet replacing the old Earl.

25 Young rakes are married to whores in *Measure for Measure* and *The Honest Whore*, both 1604, also in two plays of Middleton, *A Mad World, my Masters*, 1606, and *A Chaste Maid in Cheapside*, 1611.

26 *All Fools* includes, like *Northward Ho!*, a wife passed off as a sister, and the eventual triumph of the old men over the young. Ware is on the road to Hitchin, where Chapman took refuge from his creditors. Characters at the Fair which the old men visit are described in terms suggestive of Chaucer's 'churls'.

27 See Michael Scott, *The Plays of John Marston*, 1978, for a comparison with Genet's *The Balcony*.

28 Marston had carefully overseen the printing of the play (see Hunter's edition), and evidently retained some rights in his script, as Webster was later to do. Players usually claimed exclusive rights, because once a play was in print anyone could use it. Really popular plays were not printed if the players could prevent it. The jest about a play being 'lost' is repeated in the preface to Sharpham's *The Fleire*.

29 The vexed question of whether Webster contributed only the Induction to *The Malcontent*, or whether he wrote some of the extra material in the body of the play, is discussed in Hunter's edition.

Chapter 6
The White Devil

1 Richard Tarlton's 'No painted words but perfect deeds / Shall my invention show' (*Tarlton's Tragical Treatises*, 1578).

2 As he dwelt in Shoe Lane, Holborn, John Florio lived near Webster; his son-in-law was a surgeon at St Bartholomew's Hospital. This Italian Protestant had been born to refugee parents in London in 1557. He was language tutor to Queen Anne. For a full account of all the sources, see Boklund.

3 Orsini's letters to his wife describing this visit are printed in Leslie Hotson, *The First Night of Twelfth Night*, 1954, pp. 226–35. Webster changes the prince's name from Virginio to Giovanni.

4 See pp. 97–8 for Thomas Adams' sermon. Webster quotes another of his sermons, *The Gallant's Burden*, in *The Duchess of Malfi*, I. i. 49–52; III. ii. 328; V. ii. 337. See Brown's edition.

5 Full tables are given in F.P. Wilson, *The Plague in Shakespeare's London*, Oxford, 1927; also in Chambers, IV, pp. 346–51.

6 See Mary Edmond, *Review of English Studies*, No. 98, 1974, pp. 129–36.

7 The story that Leicester killed his first wife, Amy Robsart, seems to be used to taunt Brachiano (V. iii. 157–8). Leicester's agent was one Dr Julio, which is the name of the conjurer who shows Brachiano the death of his wife and Camillo.

8 I owe this information to Mary Edmond. The painters of the neighbourhood sent many of their sons to St Paul's, and the Choristers' Theatre there was particularly given to using paintings in plays. Reavley Gair has investigated this connection. Peake, the celebrated painter, was a vestryman with John Webster the elder. This confirms the view that Webster's view of painting would be based on traditional styles, rather than on Italian baroque.

9 Inga-Stina Ewbank developed the application of perspective art to Webster in 'Webster's Realism', *John Webster*, ed. Brian Morris, 'Mermaid Critical Commentaries', 1970; others have expanded her work.

10 His murderers, as they kill him, say no woman at the pesthouse could have done it 'quaintlier' (V. iii. 176–8), echoing his praise of the 'quaint' death of Camillo.

11 See pp. 43 and 114. Cf. Nicholas Brooke, *Horrid Laughter*, 1979, Chapter 4.

12 Cf. the attack of Davies upon Martin (p. 36).

13 III. ii. 51–216–17, 243. For her reply, cf. *Macbeth, II*. ii. 545: 'Tis the eye of childhood / That fears a painted devil.'

14 Bernard Beckerman in *Teaching Shakespeare*, ed. Walter Edens *et al.*, Princeton, 1977; J.O. Neville, 'Ben Jonson' (Cambridge Ph.D. thesis, 1979). Note that Webster uses the preface to *Sejanus* as model for his preface to *The White Devil*.

15 Baker-Smith and Gunby both contribute to *John Webster*, ed. Morris (see note 9).

16 See Chapter 7 for more successful use of fable; cf. also p. 179.

17 Charles Crawford began this study: Dent developed it. Lists of borrowings are given in the 'Revels Plays' edition of the two tragedies. Chapman's sources were first studied by F. L. Schoell, *Études sur l'humanisme continentale en Angleterre*, Paris, 1926. The best corrective is H. J. Oliver, *Rice Institute Studies* LX, 2, Spring 1974 (Houston), pp. 131–40.

18 'Alcestides objecting that Euripides had only in three days composed three verses, whereas he himself had written three hundred: "Thou tell'st truth" quoth he "but there's the difference – thine shall only be read for three days whereas mine shall continue three ages."'

19 Frances A. Yates, *The Art of Memory*, 1966, brought forward the rhetorical practice of building 'memory theatres'.

20 Peter Thomason in *John Webster* (see note 9) deals with this problem; see also Brown in his edition of *The White Devil*, pp. xlv–xlix: 'Each scene starts on a new note, with little or no preparation in earlier scenes.'

Chapter 7
The Duchess of Malfi

1 Addressed to Robert Carr, Earl of Somerset. Plays with contrasting double moods had been seen ever since the two parts of *Tamburlaine*; Marston, Dekker and Chapman himself had written such double plays – as Shakespeare did in *Henry IV*.

2 William Heminges, 'Elegy on Randolph's Finger'. Randolph, a minor playwright, had been at Westminster School with Heminges. I think that the allusion may suggest that Webster himself was dead, and his brother now head of the family; but the tragic jests about the Styx in *The Duchess of Malfi*, and the severed hand, might have caused an association.

3 Ben Jonson prefixed a list of actors to *Every Man out of his Humour* in his Folio of 1616, but did not indicate their rôles.

4 Boklund deals with the different accounts deriving from Bandello.

5 Plays of this period acted by the King's Men included *The Tempest*, *King Henry VIII*, *The Two Noble Kinsmen*, the very spectacular *The Second Maiden's Tragedy*, Fletcher's *Valentinian*, a lost *Twins' Tragedy*.

6 T. S. Eliot, *The Waste Land*, ed. Valerie Eliot, 1971, pp. 106–7. Eliot has slightly changed his quotation from III. iii. 61–2; and Webster has slightly changed it from *Arcadia*; see pp. 49–50.

7 Allen Tate, *The Swimmers and Other Selected Poems*, Oxford, 1970, p. 75.

8 E.g. Susan to Sir Charles Mountford in Heywood's *A Woman Killed with Kindness*, Evadne to Melantius in Beaumont and Fletcher's *A Maid's Tragedy*, the Colonel's sister to the Colonel in Middleton and Rowley's *A Fair Quarrel*, Penthea to Orgilus in Ford's *The Broken Heart*.

9 This line is modelled on William Alexander, *Julius Caesar*; cf. also *A Monumental Column*, ll. 132–3; 'We ought not think that his great triumphs need / Our wither'd laurel.'

10 In *The History of Morindos* the deceived King of Bohemia placed the body of his wife's scullion lover in a coffin and tied to it the live body of his queen, closing up the coffin.

11 *The Lords' Masque*, by Thomas Campion, for the marriage of the Princess Elizabeth, had an antimasque led by Mania with a troop of Frantics.

12 Compare her earlier words: 'With such pity men preserve alive / Pheasants and quails, when they are not fat enough to be eaten' (III. v. 110–13) and the fable she tells about preparing fish to be eaten. Her threat to starve herself to death recalls the death by self starvation of the penitent Mistress Frankford in *A Woman Killed with Kindness* and anticipates that of Penthea in *The Broken Heart*.

13 James Calderwood, 'Styles of Ceremony in *The Duchess of Malfi*', *Essays in Criticism* XII, reprinted in Hunter, *John Webster*, 'Penguin Critical Anthologies', 1969.

14 The improvized marriage ritual of the Duchess might serve as model for Giovanni and Annabella; Ferdinand has a horrible image of using his sister's heart as a sponge (II. v. .15–16) which is actually seen in the later play as Giovanni enters with Annabella's heart upon his dagger. On the other hand, 'nuptial twins' was a term applied to a married pair who were of the same age.

15 Cf. Antonio's stoic maxim, 'Through in our miseries Fortune hath a part / Yet in our nobler suff'rings she hath none; / Contempt of pain, that we may call our own' (V. iii. 56–8), a great improvement on William Alexander, 'For in our actions Fortune hath a part / But in our sufferings all things are our own'.

16 Campion, *The Lords' Masque*, and Beaumont, *The Masque of the Inner Temple and Gray's Inn*. Webster might have been associated with *The Masque of the Middle Temple and Lincoln's Inn*, by Chapman, as organized by Richard Martin.

17 See Frances A. Yates, *Shakespeare's Last Plays*, 1975, and various works by Glynne Wickham.

18 The 'Rainbow Portrait' of Queen Elizabeth, now at Hatfield, shows her in a robe covered with ears, eyes and mouths, signifying Fame. Chapman also depicts a number of such robes in his part of *Hero and Leander*.

19 Webster took material from this masque for his dedicatory letter to Lord Berkeley.

20 'Integrity of life' is denied to Beaumont's and Fletcher's heroes; Philaster, Arbaces, Amintor all have to play rôles that do not fit them. But the crisis of identity for the Duchess is insoluble; Amintor kills himself but the other two are 'adjusted'.

Chapter 8
The Citizen at Drury Lane

1 For the story of Robert Carr and Frances Howard, see page 67. When Sir Thomas Overbury opposed their marriage, he was sent to the Tower, where he died in great agony on 15 Sept. 1613 – ten days before Frances's marriage to the Earl of Essex was annulled. On 26 Dec. their marriage took place; but news of the murder soon began to leak out and eventually in May 1616 both the Countess, who pleaded guilty, and the Earl were sentenced to death; the King commuted this to imprisonment.

2 See Dekker, *Satiromastix*, l. 2. The character of Webster is also on the earlier model – e.g., the epigrammatic satire on Sir John Davies written by John Marston; see p. 41.

3 J. Cocke – there is no such name at the time on the books of Lincoln's Inn – accused the nameless 'rayler' (i.e., Webster) of correcting three 'Characters' that he had himself given to the new Overbury collection – tinker, an almanac-maker and an apparitour. Notice Fitzjeffrey's 'horsey' similes in his attack on Webster: Achilles' bull-headed horse, Bucephalus, and the centaur.

4 See John Orrell, 'Inigo Jones at the Cockpit', *Shakespeare Survey*, XXX, 1977, where the drawings from Worcester College, Oxford, are supplemented by pictures of cockpits.

5 As one of the Queen's Men, Beeston would meet Inigo Jones, who was working on various building plans for the Queen. They had also worked together for Henry, Prince of Wales. Beeston had been apprenticed to Augustine Philips, of Shakespeare's company, with whom he had acted in 1598 in Jonson's *Every Man Out of his Humour*. In 1602 he transferred to Worcester's, later Queen Anne's, Men and succeeded Greene as leader in 1612.

6 See C.J. Sisson, 'The Red Bull and the Importunate Widow', *Shakespeare Survey*, VII, 1954. Susan's first husband had been Robert Brown, leader of the troupe at the Boar's Head; her second was his successor, Thomas Greene; and her third, James Baskerville, who turned out to be a bigamist and fled, whilst Susan continued to press her claims in good times and bad.

7 Shirley's edition, Introduction, p. xvii. See also D.C. Gunby, *Modern Language Review*, XLIII, 1968, pp. 545–58, who interprets it as 'a thesis play' about overruling Providence.

8 The quotations from *The Devil is an Ass* fix the upward date for Webster's play, and *A Fair Quarrel* the lower limit, which places it early in 1617 – i.e., at opening of the Cockpit, or Phoenix, Theatre.

9 Two years after he had invited them to the Phoenix, Beeston ejected Prince Charles's Men, including Rowley, and imported Lady Elizabeth's Men. After a spell at the old Curtain in Shoreditch, Prince Charles's Men went back to the Red Bull.

10 See C. J. Sisson, *Lost Plays of Shakespeare's Age*, Cambridge, 1936, pp. 80–124, and Mary Edmond, *Times Literary Supplement*, 24 Dec. 1976; cf. page 97.

11 Later he played the Fat Bishop in the great scandalous success of the age, Middleton's *Game at Chess*, 1624.

12 The upward date is fixed by a reference to the execution of Gratten Flood in Newgate on 18 Jan. 1624; the downward date from the imitation of this play in Massinger's *Parliament of Love*, licensed for the Cockpit company in Nov. 1624; see *The Works of Philip Massinger*, ed. P. Edwards and C. Gibson, Oxford, 1976, II, 2, p. 104, where Massinger's debt to this play is worked out.

13 This is Webster's third study of a bastardy case, *The Devil's Law Case* and *A Cure for a Cuckold* both turning on such an issue.

14 Sir Horace Vere is the likeliest original for Webster's 'Character of a Noble Commander in the Wars'. Lucas suggests 1625 as a date, but no plays could have been composed in the plague year, nor was the City as involved then as in 1622. An additional case for giving the play to boys may lie with two newly discovered plays of this period, written for boys, which turned up at Warwick, and which I have not yet seen.

15 Heywood makes this point in his *Apology for Actors*. A judicial scandal was reflected in Massinger's *A New Way to Pay Old Debts*, given at the Phoenix, which was rather liable to put on risky plays – e.g., Ben Jonson's *A Tale of a Tub*.

16 Webster emphasizes that the chariot was drawn by four horses, 'for porters would have made it move totteringly and improperly'. Dekker had also discarded porters in *Troia Nova Triumphans*. In the Holy Week processions at Seville to this day the pageants are carried by men marching underneath and supporting them.

A Final Perspective

1 From Horace, *Epistles*, I, VI, 67–8. Cf. Hoskyns, *Directions for Speech and Style*, p. 42: 'As being charged you have brought very light reasons, you may answer: "If by *light* you mean clear, I am glad you do see them; if by *light* you mean of no weight I am sorry you do not feel them."'

2 See William Dugdale, *Origines Juridiciales*, 1666, p. 157.

3 *The Hierarchy of the Blessed Angels*, 1634, IV, p. 206. 'Fletcher and Webster, of that learned pack,/None of the mean'st, yet neither was but Jack.' That Heywood here uses the past tense is the first evidence of Webster's decease. Fletcher died in 1625.

4 For a beautiful example of how this response could be evoked in a masque, see the extended speech in Shirley, *Love's Cruelty* (1631).

5 See Chapter 6, note 15, for the contrary theological interpretations. The

two works appearing in 1971 were Ralph Berry, *The Art of John Webster*; and the chapter on Webster, Tourneur and Middleton in *The Sphere History of Literature in the English Language*, vol. 3; *English Drama to 1710*.

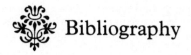 # Bibliography

Place of publication London unless otherwise stated.

Editions of Webster's Work

Collected Editions

The Collected Works were edited in 1830 by A. Dyce, in 1857 by W.C. Hazlitt (virtually a reprint of Dyce).

The Complete Works of John Webster, ed. F.L. Lucas, 4 vols, 1927, reprinted 1966. Slightly revised editions of *The White Devil* and *The Duchess of Malfi* were issued as separate volumes in 1958. All later editors owe much to Lucas. The three best plays offer few textual complications, as each exists in one authoritative early text, prefaced by the author. The canon of the plays is more difficult. Lucas left out all the early work, whilst printing other works which he deemed to be collaborative. Modern students of Middleton accept the ascription to him on the title-page of *Anything for a Quiet Life*, 1662, and there is no support for Webster's part in *The Fair Maid of the Inn*, from the first folio of Beaumont and Fletcher, 1647. Lucas was unaware of the values of Elizabethan punctuation, e.g. a full stop silently inserted after line 12 obscures the verses to Stephen Harrison.

Separate Works: Plays
Issued with prefatory matter by the author

'The White Divel or The Tragedy of Paulo Giordano Ursini, Duke of Brachiano with the Life and Death of Vittoria Corombona the famous Venetian Curtizan. Acted by the Queenes Majesties Servants. Written by John Webster. *Non inferiora secutus*. London, printed by N.O., for Thomas Archer, and are to be sold at his Shop in Pope's Head Pallace, near the Royal Exchange. 1612.' A facsimile was issued by the Scolar Press, 1970. The best modern edition is by J. R. Brown, 'The Revels Plays', 1960. There are numerous others, and the play also appears in anthologies – e.g. Russell A. Fraser and Norman Rabkin, *Drama of the English Renaissance*, 2 vols, 1976, the most comprehensive recent collection.

'The Tragedy of the Duchesse of Malfy. As it was presented privately, at the Blackfriars, and publicly at the Globe, by the King's Majesties Servants. The perfect and exact copy, with diverse things printed, that the length of the play would not bear in the Presentment. Written by John Webster. *Hora- Si quid Candidus imperti si non his utere mecum.* London. Printed by Nicholas Okes, for John Waterson, and are to be sold at the sign of the Crown, in Paules Church-yard. 1623.' A facsimile was issued by the Scolar Press, 1968. The best modern edition is again by J. R. Brown, 'The Revels Plays', 1964. Again, there are numerous other editions and frequent anthologizing.

The two tragedies were issued with Tourneur's plays in the old Mermaid series, ed. J. A. Symonds, 1888, with Ford in the Everyman Library, 1954, with *The Devil's Law Case* in *John Webster, Three Plays*, ed. D.C. Gunby, Penguin English Library, 1972; separately by Elizabeth Brennan in the new Mermaid series.

'*The Devil's Law Case or, When Women go to Law, the Devill is full of Businesse.* A new Tragecomedy. The true and perfect copy from the Original. As it was approvedly well acted by her Majesties Servants. Written by John Webster. *Non quam diu, sed quam bene.* London. Printed by A. M. for John Grismand, and are to be sold at his shop in Pauls Alley at the sign of the Gunne. 1623.' The best modern edition is by Frances A. Shirley, 'The Regents Renaissance Drama Series', 1971. Gunby and Elizabeth Brennan have also edited it, but it has been neither anthologized nor revived on the stage.

A new edition of the three plays, by Inga-Stina Ewbank and Jonathan Dollimore, is announced from Cambridge.

Plays ascribed to Webster in Whole or in Part

'*Appius and Virginia.* A Tragedy. By John Webster. London, printed for Rich. Marriott in St Dunstan's Church-yard, Fleet Street. 1654.' No prefatory matter or indication of performance. Some assume Heywood's collaboration. Reprinted by Lucas.

'*The Famous History of Sir Thomas Wyat.* With the Coronation of Queen Mary and the coming in of King Philip. As it was played by the Queen's Majesty's servants. Written by Thomas Dickers and John Webster. London, printed by E. A. for Thomas Archer and are to be sold at his shop in the Pope's Head Pallace, near the Royal Exchange. 1607.' Reprinted in Fredson Bowers, *The Dramatic Works of Thomas Decker*, I, Cambridge, 1953. This excellent edition has been completed by four volumes of commentary by Cyrus Hoy.

'*Westward Hoe.* As it hath been divers times Acted by the Children of Paules, written by Thomas Decker and John Webster. Printed at London and are to be sold by John Hodges dwelling in Paules Churchyard. 1607.' Reprinted in Bowers, II, Cambridge, 1955.

'*Northward Hoe.* Sundry times Acted by the Children of Paules. By Thomas Decker and John Webster. Imprinted at London by G. Eld. 1607.' Reprinted in Bowers, II.

'*A Cure for a Cuckold.* A Pleasant Comedy, as it hath been several times acted with great Applause. Written by John Webster and William Rowley. *Placere Cupio*. Printed by Thomas Johnson and are to be sold by Francis Kirkman at his shop at the sign of John Fletcher's Head, over against the Angel-Inne on the Backside of St Clements, without Temple Bar, 1661.' Reprinted in Lucas, III.

Another play attributed by Kirkman to Webster, but universally rejected, is *The Thracian Wonder*, 1661. Lost plays include *Caesar's Fall or The Two Shapes*, 1602, *Christmas Comes but Once a Year*, also 1602, both collaborative, entered in Henslowe's *Diary*; *The Guise*, mentioned by Webster in the dedication of *The Devil's Law Case*; *The Late Murder of the Son upon the Mother or Keep the Widow Waking*, licensed September 1624 as by Webster and Ford, actually with Dekker and Rowley also.

Additions by Webster

'*The Malcontent*. Augmented by Marston. With the Additions played by the King's Majesties Servants. Written by John Webster. 1604. At London. Printed by V.S. for William Apsley and are to be sold at his shop in Paules Church-yard.' The best modern edition is by G.K. Hunter, 'The Revels Plays', 1975, but the play appears in collected editions of Marston. It has been revived under the direction of Jonathan Miller.

Non-dramatic Works

'"*A Monumental Column*." Erected to the Living Memory of the ever-glorious Henry, late Prince of Wales. *Virgil. Ostendent Terris hunc Tantum Fata*. By John Webster. London, printed by *N.O.* for William Wolby, dwelling in Paules Church-yard at the sign of the Swan. 1613.' Printed together with elegies by Tourneur and Heywood. Reprinted by Lucas,III.

New Characters (Drawn to the Life) of Severall Persons, in Several Qualities.... 1615. A group of separate Characters added to the sixth edition of Sir Thomas Overbury's *Characters*. Ascribed to Webster by Lucas and generally accepted. Some other 'Characters' have since been suggested as his also.

'*Monuments of Honor* ... invented and written by John Webster, Merchant Taylor. *Non norunt haec monumenta mori* [Arms of the Company]. Printed at London by Nicholas Okes 1624.' Reprinted in Lucas, III.

Biography

Mary Edmond, 'In Search of John Webster', *Times Literary Supplement*, 24 Dec. 1976, supersedes all previous writers; a letter from Mark Eccles in the issue for 21 Jan. 1977 adds further matter – disposing, for instance, of the 'ghost' character, Webster the actor.

Criticism and Scholarship

Charles Lamb, *Specimens of the English Dramatic Poets*, 1808, revived interest in Webster; Rupert Brooke, *John Webster and the Elizabethan Drama*, 1916, initiated modern criticism, advanced by T.S. Eliot in a number of essays, collected in his *Selected Essays*, 1931, and also in his poetry. E.E. Stoll, *John Webster*, 1904, and Charles Crawford, *Collectanea*, 1906, are now out of date, on scholarly matters. G. Boklund, *The Sources of The White Devil*, Uppsala, 1957, and *The Duchess of Malfi, Sources, Themes, Characters*, Harvard, 1962, investigate the origins of the tragedies; R.W. Dent, *John Webster's Borrowing*, California, 1960, traces literary parallels; J.R. Brown wrote a series of articles on the printing of the plays, the results being incorporated in his editions. Material for critical debate has been well anthologized by G.K. and S.K. Hunter, *John Webster*, Penguin Critical Anthologies, Harmondsworth, 1969.

Webster's London

John Stow, *Survey of London*, 1598, is the prime source of information. Stow, a working tailor, of St Michael's Cornhill, was edited by C.L. Kingsford, 2 vols, Oxford, 1908. Useful modern works include Fran. C. Chalfont, *Ben Jonson's London*, a Jacobean place-name dictionary, Athens, Georgia, 1977; Frank Freeman Foster, *The Politics of Stability*, a portrait of the rulers of Elizabethan London, Royal Historical Society, 1975; Laurence Stone, *An Elizabethan, Sir Horatio Palavicino*, 1956; G. Brett James, *The Growth of Stuart London*, 1973.

Richard Mulcaster and the Merchant Taylors' School

R. Mulcaster, *Positions*, 1581, abridged and ed. R.L. De Molen, New York, 1971; *Elementarie*, 1582, ed. and introduced by E.T. Campagnac, Oxford, 1927. F.W.M. Draper, *Four Centuries of Merchant Taylors' School*, Oxford, 1962; C.M. Clode, *Early History of the Merchant Taylors' Company*, 1888.

The Middle Temple as a Literary Centre

The Register of Admissions to the Honourable Society of the Middle Temple, ed. H.A.C. Sturgess, 3 vols, 1949. *Middle Temple Records*, ed. C.T. Martin, 4 vols, 1904–5; J.P. Finkelpearl, *John Marston of the Middle Temple*, Harvard, 1969; *The Life, Letters and Writings of Sir John Hoskyns*, ed. Louise Osborne, Yale, 1937; *The Poems of Sir John Davies*, ed. Robert Krueger and Ruby Nemser, Oxford, 1975; Marie Axton, *The Queen's Two Bodies*, Royal Historical Society, 1977.

The Lady of St Bartholomew's

Maude S. Rawson, *Penelope Rich and her Circle*, 1911; Cyril B. Falls, *Mountjoy, Elizabethan General*, 1953, also 'Penelope Rich and the Poets', in *Essays by Divers Hands*, 3rd series, XXVIII, Royal Society of Literature of the United Kingdom, 1956; *The Poems of Sir Philip Sidney*, ed. W.A. Ringler, Oxford, 1962.

Antonio Pérez, the Spanish Spy

Gustav Ungerer, *A Spaniard in Elizabethan England; the Correspondence of Antonio Pérez's Exile*, 2 vols, 1975–6; G. Marañon, *Antonio Pérez, Span-*

ish Traitor, trans. C. D. Ley, 1954; Robert Naunton, *Fragmenta Regalia*, 1824.

The Jacobean Theatre; Stage and Audience

E. K. Chambers, *The Elizabethan Stage*, Oxford, 1924, continues to 1616; G. E. Bentley, *The Jacobean and Caroline Stage*, Oxford, 1941–68, continues the work from that date to 1642. In *The Profession of the Dramatist in Shakespeare's Time*, Princeton, 1971, Bentley distinguishes Webster from the 'fully professional' dramatists, Heywood or Shakespeare. G. K. Hunter, *Dramatic Identities and Cultural Tradition*, Liverpool, 1978, collects his studies of Marston and the Choristers' Theatres.

Current theories of the stage are best found in *Shakespeare Survey*, Cambridge 1948–, or in the biannual *Elizabethan Theatre*, Macmillan of Canada with the University of Waterloo. *The Revels History of Drama in English*, ed. Clifford Leech and T. W. Craik, III, 1576–1613, 1975, has useful accounts of staging and good illustrations and bibliography.

Among recent studies of individual theatres are William Ingram on Francis Langley, *A London Life in the Brazen Age*, Harvard, 1978; Herbert Berry, ed., *The First Public Playhouse*, Montreal (McGill), 1979, the work on the theatre at Paul's by Reavley Gair cited in Chapter 5, note 3, which is to be expanded into a book. T. J. King, *Shakespearean Staging 1599–1642*, has a chapter on the staging of *Twelfth Night* at the Middle Temple in 1602.

The 'Malone Society Collections' offer some material; the forthcoming series of documents promised to accompany 'The Revels Plays' (Manchester) will supply more.

General Social Background

Marie-Thérèse Jones-Davies, *Un peintre de la vie Londinienne: Thomas Dekker*, 2 vols, Paris, 1958, and the annotations to Fredson Bower's edition of Dekker, compiled by Cyrus Hoy, supply material relevant to Webster.

M. C. Bradbrook, *A History of Elizabethan Drama*, vol. III, *The Rise of the Common Player*, 1962, deals with the social history of the actors and their relation with their audience vol. VI, *The Living Monument*, 1976, deals with Jacobean drama.

Studies of Webster's theology by D. C. Gunby and Dominic Baker-Smith (see Chapter 6, note 15) suffice for any but the specialist in that subject, who may consult Gunby's thesis on *Anglicanism in the Plays of John Webster*, Cambridge, 1967.

Margot Heinemann, *Puritanism and Theatre, Thomas Middleton and Opposition Drama under the Early Stuarts*, Cambridge, 1980, supplies new information on the political tensions of James I's reign.

Webster's Family Tree

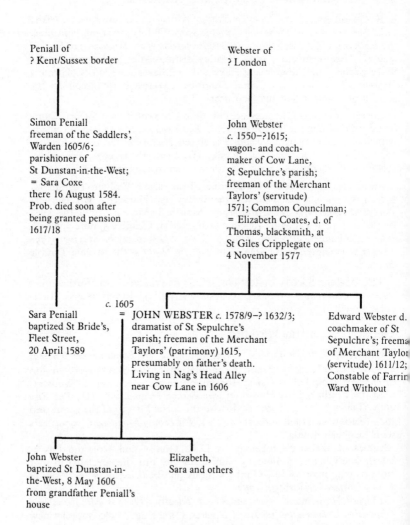

Peniall of
? Kent/Sussex border

Webster of
? London

Simon Peniall
freeman of the Saddlers',
Warden 1605/6;
parishioner of
St Dunstan-in-the-West;
= Sara Coxe
there 16 August 1584.
Prob. died soon after
being granted pension
1617/18

John Webster
c. 1550–?1615;
wagon- and coach-
maker of Cow Lane,
St Sepulchre's parish;
freeman of the Merchant
Taylors' (servitude)
1571; Common Councilman;
= Elizabeth Coates, d. of
Thomas, blacksmith, at
St Giles Cripplegate on
4 November 1577

Sara Peniall
baptized St Bride's,
Fleet Street,
20 April 1589

c. 1605
=

JOHN WEBSTER *c.* 1578/9–? 1632/3;
dramatist of St Sepulchre's
parish; freeman of the Merchant
Taylors' (patrimony) 1615,
presumably on father's death.
Living in Nag's Head Alley
near Cow Lane in 1606

Edward Webster d.
coachmaker of St
Sepulchre's; freema
of Merchant Taylor
(servitude) 1611/12;
Constable of Farrir
Ward Without

John Webster
baptized St Dunstan-in-
the-West, 8 May 1606
from grandfather Peniall's
house

Elizabeth,
Sara and others

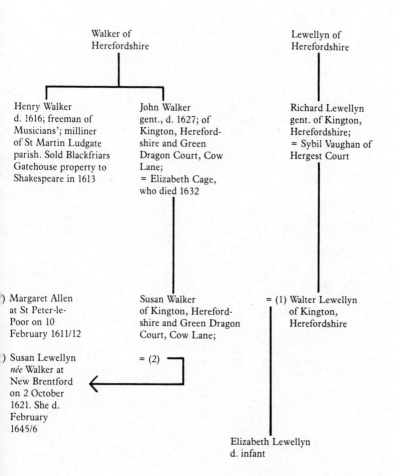

Walker of
Herefordshire

Lewellyn of
Herefordshire

Henry Walker
d. 1616; freeman of
Musicians'; milliner
of St Martin Ludgate
parish. Sold Blackfriars
Gatehouse property to
Shakespeare in 1613

John Walker
gent., d. 1627; of
Kington, Hereford-
shire and Green
Dragon Court, Cow
Lane;
= Elizabeth Cage,
who died 1632

Richard Lewellyn
gent. of Kington,
Herefordshire;
= Sybil Vaughan of
Hergest Court

) Margaret Allen
at St Peter-le-
Poor on 10
February 1611/12

) Susan Lewellyn
née Walker at
New Brentford
on 2 October
1621. She d.
February
1645/6

Susan Walker
of Kington, Hereford-
shire and Green Dragon
Court, Cow Lane;

= (2)

= (1) Walter Lewellyn
of Kington,
Herefordshire

Elizabeth Lewellyn
d. infant

Index

The main text and the notes are indexed, but not the bibliography.

When a subject is named in the text and also in a related note, the text page only is indexed: the superscript numeral leads to the note. Page numbers in the notes are given for subjects mentioned in the text but named only in the note, and for additional material introduced in the notes. The note number appears in brackets immediately after the page number.